RESPONSE TO *INJUSTICE, HIDDEN IN PLAIN SIGHT* ...

"*Injustice* draws the veil from attitudes and actions towards wildlife that have pushed Australia into an extinction crisis. Understanding how we got here is vital to recovering the natural world – a must read."

— ERICA MARTIN, CEO, HUMANE SOCIETY INTERNATIONAL AUSTRALIA

"Maria Taylor has written an excellent account of the decades of misinformation and malfeasance concerning our relationship with Australia's kangaroo populations and other native wildlife since settlement, obviously both a biological research and a moral issue. As the book shows, so far, we have failed both."

— DR GEOFF MOSLEY, SPEAKING FROM 50 YEARS WORKING WITH THE AUSTRALIAN CONSERVATION FOUNDATION (ACF), AUSTRALIAN DIRECTOR, CENTER FOR THE ADVANCEMENT OF THE STEADY STATE ECONOMY

"In the wake of the Australian colonial land grab, what place remains for the continent's unique wildlife? Taylor's exposé of the past and present Australian wildlife industries will shock and dismay, and her call for a more responsible, regenerative stewardship must be heeded."

— ASSOCIATE PROFESSOR ANDREA GAYNOR, HISTORY, THE UNIVERSITY OF WESTERN AUSTRALIA

"Everyone who cares about the future of Australia's unique wildlife should read this book."

— ONDINE SHERMAN, AUTHOR, AND CO-FOUNDER OF *VOICELESS* THE ANIMAL PROTECTION INSTITUTE

INJUSTICE

Hidden in plain sight the war on Australian nature kangaroo, koala, emu ... hunted, sold, homeless ... where lies truce, healing?

MARIA TAYLOR

An investigation and cultural history

First published 2021 by Maria Taylor

Produced by Independent Ink
independentink.com.au

Cover design by Maria Biaggini
Internal design by Independent Ink
Typeset in 11.75/16 pt Minion Pro by Post Pre-press Group, Brisbane
Cover image courtesy of Garmarroongoo Michael Huddleston

A catalogue record for this book is available from the National Library of Australia

ISBN 978-0-6450993-3-1 (paperback)
ISBN 978-0-6450993-1-7 (epub)
ISBN 978-0-6450993-2-4 (kindle)

Disclaimer

This book is dedicated to the many caring and compassionate Australians – First Australians, new Australians and international friends who have watched in sorrow, anger and empathy (and many have taken action) for Australia's unique wildlife – disrespected and decimated since settlement by economic and political forces. Some of the champions for the voiceless have stories that inform these pages, both looking back and looking forward. All are thanked. Through the decades, and now more than ever, the hope is to stand in the way of the destroyers of the wonders of our natural world: the native animals, plants, ecosystems and the planet's life support systems. Australia's story is everyone's story in the modern world.

I am indebted to the archives of the Australian Wildlife Protection Council (AWPC) which yielded a 50-year documentary history of the fight for Australia's wildlife, and exposed institutions and traditions mobilised on the side of a colonial makeover of nature. The documentary record exists also thanks to journalists and news services who penetrated conventions of silence and, across the decades, recorded what was happening in Australia far from its cities.

"In Australia power belonged neither to visionaries nor to women, but to ruthless and tough men. Throughout its history its people had been taught to equate material success with happiness, and material achievement with public virtue."

— MANNING CLARK, *A SHORT HISTORY OF AUSTRALIA*

"If such a simple outcome as retrieving the kangaroo from being a wrongfully accused enemy in its own country, treated as vermin in such a despicably cruel manner with no place to hide, cannot be achieved by such a prosperous, educated and secure civilisation as Australia, then what hope for the planet?"

— DAVID NICHOLLS, FORMER KANGAROO SHOOTER

WHAT THE WORLD SAW JANUARY 2020

Their bodies lie piled up by the side of the road, barely visible through the ochre haze: dozens, maybe hundreds of kangaroos that tried to outrun the flames and perished, in their droves, in the attempt.

. . .

Australia is burning ... The scale of the devastation – entire towns wiped out, thousands sheltering on the beach to await military evacuation by sea – is hard to overestimate.

But to the rest of the world looking on in horror, among the most ghastly images are those showing the toll on Australia's native wildlife. A kangaroo, backlit by flames. A dead joey, charred and still clinging to the fence that it ran up against. Battered koalas, battling serious burns – these are the faces put forward in appeals ...

The power of these images speaks to the hold of Australian wildlife on our collective imagination. If you know nothing else about Australia ... you know Skippy the Bush Kangaroo. Same with a koala, platypus, dingo, echidna, kookaburra, wombat, possum, emu, saltwater croc – take your pick.

. . .

[Australia's] fauna is instantly recognisable, symbolic of a wild and ancient continent truly unlike any other on Earth. But one of the many ways in which Australia is special is that if you do go there, you'll actually see these species.

EXCERPTED FROM ELLE HUNT'S 'THE WORLD LOVES KANGAROOS AND KOALAS. NOW WE ARE WATCHING THEM DIE IN DROVES': COURTESY OF *GUARDIAN NEWS* AND *MEDIA LTD* 2020 (COPYRIGHT)

AUTHOR'S NOTE

Writing about wildlife and focusing in particular on the fate of macropods, I was faced with the open question of capitalising animal names, or not, for a general audience and staying consistent. In the end I settled on a hybrid model with capitals and lower case that readers will find in the following pages.

For the extended family of kangaroo species to distinguish them by their common names, I settled for this system: Eastern Grey kangaroo, Red kangaroo, Western Grey kangaroo, Wallaroo, Euro, Brush-tailed Rock-wallaby, also distantly-related Potoroo and Bettong (rat-kangaroos). I used the same logic for other sub-species that had distinguishing common names – such as Southern Hairy-nosed wombat, similarly for some birds with double-barrelled names. Apologies in advance for remaining inconsistencies and also to those other central characters of this book – emu, koala, dingo and all native species – who did not receive the capitalisation treatment.

CONTENTS

FOREWORD, THE JOURNEY

It was time to write this buried history, and its contemporary outcomes. A wildlife tragedy had been unfolding before my eyes while working as a regional journalist for the last decade. I had written bits and pieces of the local story, and had felt sadness, anger, and the knowledge of being manipulated by a public narrative, but I didn't yet know the scope of what I would find.

When a young friend, a well-educated person, said in all sincerity that he thought kangaroos in Australia were farmed, while a steady stream of news items crossed my desk about state-sanctioned violence against some remaining native animals – normalised by silence and conformity – the hour was clearly late. It was past time to look squarely at a mostly hidden story: what happened between the new nation of Australia and the indigenous wildlife of the land? And what terrible legacy has continued to this day?

Colonial Australia's war against animals, plants and ecosystems started in parallel with the dispossession of the Indigenous people after 1788. The bid to radically makeover an ancient continent and everything that already existed there when the First Fleet arrived – without troubling to understand it first – is a history that became buried, while it seeded a dominant Australian culture.

The long dispossession of the native fauna has left a modern legacy of hatred and bloodshed, especially in rural areas. Baffling to many newer immigrants, compassionate Australians and foreign visitors is the demonization accepted casually and targeted at the national emblem: the flying kangaroo. Skippy to many overseas fans. Tracing how the animal that holds up one side of the national coat of arms came to receive such disrespect and lethal treatment ultimately structured the chapters and form of this book.

It became clear that the murderous fate of the kangaroo is framed by the beliefs, values, economic priorities and human behaviour that helped shape the new nation. Lethal attacks in the name of property rights, commerce and wildlife management are also aimed at other common terrestrial Australian wildlife, particularly wombats and dingos, but also wallabies, possums, eagles and other birds, including emus – the animal that holds up the other side of the national coat of arms.

The kangaroo's fate reflects them all, and is also the standout case, which I learned during a decade of watching the annual mass killing – called 'kangaroo management' – of the national emblem in the nation's capital – an expensive government program cloaked in claims of science and demanding conformity of thinking to an extraordinary degree.

Nationally, the kangaroo continues to endure an industrial-scale hunt for its skin and meat, one that emerged first in colonial times. Australia is globally unique in hunting down its national emblem as either a 'pest' or a commodity. The annual hunt is now the world's largest on-land wildlife slaughter, shrouded in silence or indifference within its own country.

I learned how the attached mantle of wildlife 'management' is mostly about maintaining the right to profit from a style of farming and grazing first established in 1788. Private property rights and laws upholding them dispossessed both Indigenous peoples and every native animal under the then British empire.

The stories I learned and have shared in the following chapters unpack some history and its contemporary consequences for wildlife. The question for me became: how exactly did we arrive at this frame of disrespect – even hatred – that is allied to a culture of lethal management?

What happened to the abundant wildlife and lush ecosystems encountered by the first settlers? How was it that Australia's globally-unique marsupial and macropod animals, and many of the continent's unique birds, and its apex predator the dingo, came to be deliberately exterminated, rather than respected and studied?

With their homes long ago or recently taken as someone's private property, where they exist under sufferance, our animal brethren are recognised only by some people as sentient beings with family, and as essential parts of the country's ecosystems. Australian First Nations knew this. But in our dominant modern culture, the blinkers stay on until a native species is pushed to the brink of extinction – like that other Australian icon, the koala – to then qualify for sympathy and 'saving'.

In researching and writing this book I wanted to make sense of how the values of the past have hung on. The historical threads are linked to Australia's world-leading rates of mammalian extinctions and are now pinned to reports of accelerated global mass extinctions of wildlife. Biodiversity at all levels is in crisis in Australia. In November of 2019, 248 scientists signed an open letter to the Australian Prime Minister in which they said that Australia is facing an extinction crisis, that the decline of diversity and numbers have risen to an alarming rate: "In the last decade alone three of our native species have been wiped out. Another 17 animals could go extinct in the next 20 years."[1] There was no reported reaction from the government.

The stories in the following pages proceed through the voices and experiences of some of the many champions for Australian native animals. I met some in person and others through historical books and archives. Many of those speaking for our voiceless fellow species have been marginalised, disregarded, and even attacked in a mainstream culture that demands conformity in 'managing' and changing the nature of Australia. But I also learned that activists and sympathetic biologists have scored significant victories against the commercial wildlife trade – in the case of kangaroos, taking their message to the United States, Britain, Europe and Russia.

Is there hope for a more compassionate future? I wondered how to bridge the cultural gap between the powerful mainstream belief in lethal management and the exploitation of Australia's unique animals, and the values of those Australians who pick up the pieces, shelter and save the survivors. I spoke about these issues with former kangaroo shooters who have nightmares from what they have seen and done, as well as with regenerative farmers, conservationists and Indigenous people.

There is a different way to live within ancient Australia, with its plants and animals and landforms. In the final chapter, titled Sharing, I talk with landholders including farmers who are regenerating the land and showing how we might share with the native wildlife.

I meet forward-looking people including Terri Irwin, better known for Australia Zoo and popular conservation documentaries. From the 1990s on, Terri and her late husband Steve Irwin did much to rehabilitate Australian wildlife in the minds of the public. Together Steve and Terri started doing things differently on a production property in central Queensland, welcoming all native wildlife while retaining a good income there. I learned from Terri and other landholders how biodiversity has thrived, how drought has been mitigated and about the options of adding wildlife tourism to the income and educational stream, catering to enthusiastic visitors wielding a camera or paintbrush – a globally winning formula for sustaining rural economies.

At the conclusion of this investigative journey, I know there are rewarding ways to conserve Australia's natural assets, to live peacefully with the wildlife, and to leave behind as history the tradition to change and destroy.

DATELINE 2018–19: THE LEGACY

As I sit down to write on a wintery morning in June, the local community electronic noticeboard is again buzzing with opinions related to kangaroos on road verges, and the inconvenience this poses to motorists who might hit them if they cross and thereby occasion a notable auto repair bill. Cull every kangaroo in Australia, says the woman who started the conversation, before calming down and advocating culling the roadside shrubbery instead.

I look outside at a couple of Red-necked wallabies mowing the lawn. In the later afternoon the local mob of Eastern Grey kangaroos emerge across our rocky and treed ridgetop, more or fewer depending on the season. Over the years we've been a nursery, sheltering the same extended family of mothers and joeys. We supplement feed in tougher times. In recent years we've come to know a few of the big males who stop by.

The alpha male is shy, and at the same time instinctively guards the rest. We're getting to recognise each other as individuals, with pet names and distinctive behaviours. We worry that if they stray too far searching for food, they might get shot or run over. Their home ranges are now covered in houses guarded by fences and dogs.

The birds, possums and lizards enjoy a handout too. A growing family of shy and cute Swamp wallabies, part of the formal family of kangaroos and seemingly marooned in hobby block land, also started enjoying some sweet potato in the recent drought. Like the Red-necked wallabies, they are partial to sampling the rose bushes and other exotic flora. The handouts might continue to distract them, I hope.

There are a lot of kangaroos on road verges in Australia now, and a lot in rural residential acreage like mine, and in towns and villages and Melbourne suburbs. Same story for birds and brushtail possums. Everywhere, former wildlife habitat is being transformed to new suburbs, shopping malls, roads, industrial parks, and new cropping enterprises.

In Queanbeyan, the nearest regional town, residents not so long ago lost a lengthy battle to save bushland behind the city from a new four-lane highway spearheaded by a developer-friendly local council, whose planning vision, as elsewhere, revolves around accommodating auto traffic. Wildlife corridors are going under asphalt and concrete. A resident told me that the fairly tame kangaroo mob she knew is gone, that wombats are being found run-over, sometimes by bulldozers, and that she just found a totally lost joey.

With drought searing the eastern part of the continent, kangaroo numbers are again blamed – straight-faced by politicians and some graziers – for the woes of the pastoral industry, as if climatic boom and bust hasn't been the history of the country. The mythology of (bad) hyper-abundance clings to the animals as they try to survive amongst humans. The ongoing debate in my neighbourhood reflects understanding and compassion, but also a mindset that sees only competition and economic loss rather than the possibility of sharing with native fauna, even 200 years after colonisation.

Inland, any traveller can see the back-to-back pastoral and cropping properties that have, since colonial times, labelled as 'pests' to be killed without question the kangaroos and other macropod native grazers, birds of prey, and the Australian native dog the dingo – a conviction that has been passed down through the generations to become tradition.

The situation I survey today is the legacy of Australia's colonial settlement history. In the following pages I learn how and why, with farming allotments that came to cover the land, the native animals were hunted and removed as thoroughly as the native vegetation. Sheep, in ever greater numbers after 1788, were imported along with many other European animals and plants to make the countryside more like 'home.' The goal from the beginning was a continent-scale back paddock to the mother country.

The well-being of the imported fauna and flora, as staples of the British colonial economy, were the focus of an imperial biological science that morphed into today's conservation science.

From the pastoral industry and its political supporters, the cry against competition for grass moved through an era of bounties, that decimated Australian native grazers big and small, to today's kangaroo skin and meat industry that cranked into high gear from the mid-20th century. That industry became another of today's 'must-have' export industries in the view of successive governments – the kangaroo now badged a 'renewable natural resource,' 'harvested' like a wild plant crop, only it's more bloody.

Destruction of common mammal and bird species that bother agriculturalists hasn't stopped at grazing kangaroos, wombats and emus, but has extended to flying foxes, possums, wedge-tailed eagles, cockatoos, parrots and dingos. The persistent economic narrative – that this is about jobs and exports – matches the rhetoric around logging native forests and removing any obstacle in the way of ever-expanding human projects.

The mainstream media has noted that continuing habitat loss particularly affects tree-dwelling now-threatened species like gliders and the beloved koala. Koalas, I learn from the historical record, were hunted just as mercilessly in the late 19th and early 20th centuries as kangaroos are today, with similar justifications. The koala populations never recovered to earlier times.

In 2020, the NSW government was presented with an internal inquiry reporting that the iconic koala may be extinct in the state by 2050 if its gum tree habitat continues to be logged, or removed to house an increasing human population. The 2019–20 bushfires along the east coast proved particularly devastating for the remaining koalas, (with a population of anywhere from 15,000 to 36,000 animals before the fires). One third of remaining habitat burned.[1]

WORLD-CLASS EXTINCTION RATES

As a result of this history, there is the broader context of Australia's world-class record of biodiversity destruction and mammalian extinctions in a little over 200 years.

Since colonial settlement, about 54 species of Australia's unique animals have become extinct according to federal government surveys, including 34 land mammals – or more than one in 10 on a growing list. A further 21 percent of Australian endemic land mammal species were assessed as threatened by 2015, with a rate of loss of one to two extinctions per decade. In contrast, only one native land mammal in continental North America has met a similar fate since that continent was colonised.[2] Some 60 Australian plant species have been lost during the same timeframe.[3,4]

The world-beating statistics were presented to national politicians in 2018. A federal government document on conserving threatened species was judged by scientists and reporters as unserious, totally deficient and doomed to fail. It did not address any of the real and ongoing drivers destroying native animals and plants – starting with habitat loss and including wildlife management policies.[5]

Perhaps jolted by the sheer number of declining Australian species, the federal government senate in 2018 paid attention by launching an enquiry into what it described as an "extinction crisis" of native species. *The Guardian* news site, which led some of the reporting on this crisis, quoted scientists describing the situation confronting Australia's threatened species as a "national disgrace,"[6] saying the systems and laws that are supposed to protect them are "broken." The federal government's most recent State of the Environment report[7] confirmed biodiversity loss had further increased since 2011.

The senate had at its disposal data showing that some 1,800 Australian plant and animal species and ecological communities (ecological communities include woodlands, forests and wetlands) are now at risk of extinction due to human activities. The numbers are increasing, and may be an underestimate of the true picture.[8]

Yet as this book was going to press, the federal Australian government was manoeuvring to cement state powers over native species with few overarching national safeguards – the states being the very entities that since settlement have brought Australia's fauna and flora to its present-day desperate state.

As if to underscore that point, the endangered status of Australia's remaining koala population in the state of NSW was once again in the news, thanks to a perfect storm of habitat loss due to development, catastrophic 2019–20 bushfires linked to climate change and, looking ahead, the state's resumption of logging in unburned forest habitats.[9]

Globally, the record is hardly better. Since 1970, in just 50 years, humankind has wiped out 60 percent of remaining mammal, bird, fish and reptile populations that represent 4000 species. This is an almost unimaginable revelation that, according to ecological scientists, rivals climate change in its impact on life as we know it.

A 2018 scientific report brought together under the aegis of the World Wildlife Fund documents that human populations, their habitat destruction for agriculture and development, their aquatic pollution and freshwater extraction, and their ability to eat their way through the world's animal species on land and sea, are "destroying the web of life, billions of years in the making, upon which human society ultimately depends for clean air, water and everything else.

"This is far more than just being about losing the wonders of nature, desperately sad though that is," Mike Barrett, executive director of science and conservation at WWF, told *The Guardian* newspaper. "This is actually now jeopardising the future of people. Nature is not a 'nice to have' – it is our life-support system."[10]

In May 2019, a United Nations summary report contained equally apocalyptic and widely reported findings about the global loss of biodiversity, summarised as one million species now threatened with extinction. It also said countries should learn more from Indigenous management of natural systems, most of which have shown better conservation of species[11].

At about the same time, a report was published by the *New York Times,* assembling the evidence that insects are crashing as well. Not hedging, the report is called 'The Insect Apocalypse is here', citing climate change, habitat destruction and man-made chemicals as the main culprits.[12] A scientific paper on the same subject jolted the world soon after.

Professor Johan Rockström, a global sustainability expert at the Potsdam Institute for Climate Impact Research in Germany, warns in the WWF report: "Only by addressing both ecosystems and climate do we stand a chance of safeguarding a stable planet for humanity's future on Earth."

The statistics, domestically and globally, offer a compelling reason to safeguard the species we have left and to treasure the common species that can live with us.

CARRYING ON REGARDLESS AS NSW DECLARES OPEN SEASON

Instead, several state governments, including NSW where I live, increased their efforts to encourage additional species towards the endangered or extinct roll call, still arguing as governments have since colonial times that there is a never-ending supply, not to worry.

By mid-2018, regulations were rolling out of Sydney to cut "red tape". This was code to enable clearing of more native vegetation on private land – basically at landholders' whims. Native forest logging was ramped up. Both moves would threaten remaining koala, glider, possum, wombat, bird, reptile and amphibian populations. Not forgetting the insects.

The long-demonised kangaroo would soon face more guns as some kind of political band-aid for the severe drought that had settled on the state. Something was about to happen, with no sector of the community – barring farmers – having been consulted.

On the 8 August 2018, the NSW Coalition government of Liberal and National Party politicians took their cue from colonial land management methods and declared a de facto open season on the kangaroos. On properties of almost any size larger than basic suburban, a phone call or email would get a landholder and shooter consent to kill 50, 100, 250 or more kangaroos on their land, depending on property size and offering repeat permits – a new non-commercial 'cull'. NSW also has an ongoing commercial 'harvest' for meat and skins that involves all but a few areas of the state, and relies on private landholder access.

In 2018, a new unit was set up in the NSW National Parks and Wildlife Service (NPWS) expressly to administer the killing of kangaroo species non-commercially. The parks service had long been in charge of handing out the licenses for the commercial kill. Someone had a sense of irony: the new unit was called the Biodiversity Reform Team.

A month later, more than a million licenses had been handed out to kill kangaroos commercially and otherwise. The number of licenses had almost doubled after the 8 August 'reforms' got into gear. I heard the man from NSW National Parks concede that unfortunately this reforming government had no resources for monitoring or vetting, no way to check exactly what was being shot and specifically why, or by whom, or whether the shooter could accomplish a killing headshot. Or what happened to dependent joeys. No one was asking or checking.

National Parks, the guardians of the state's wildlife in public perception, was just keen to respond to "lots of calls" from landholder groups and the NSW Farmers association, and make harming kangaroos as painless as possible for landholders to "get the grass back," the same National Parks and Wildlife Service spokesperson told a landholder gathering I attended.

Getting the grass back included a registry through the Department of Primary Industries (agriculture), then headed by the National Party MP Niall Blair, for city recreational shooters to come out to the drought-stricken countryside and help out. 'Farmer assist', they called it. Local Land Services, a front desk operation managed by the department, would be matching shooters with landholders.

A valid firearms license was the only requirement. The department thoughtfully provided "best practice" advice for shooting adults, for bashing pouch joeys to death, and for dressing wild meat. Too bad about the neighbours (bullets can travel three kilometres or more) or anyone who cares about the fate of Australian wildlife – they weren't asked. If neighbours were lucky, they might simply be advised it was happening next door to them.[13]

This 'help the farmers' initiative started in the run-up to a tight state election and would continue as the same politicians were voted back into office in March 2019. Primary Industries had set up a website to recruit the recreational shooters, so it was hardly a secret operation. But when I asked what competence such shooters would need, the department's media office quickly passed the buck, saying that it wasn't their program, to ask National Parks. After the election, Primary Industries continued the offensive by posting on its Facebook page the same call for volunteers, aimed at recreational hunters.

The comment stream from would-be hunters provided a reality check: people pointed out the requirement by landholders for insurance, the reluctance of many landholders to let such volunteers on the property, and people mostly never heard back after registering. The suspicion was voiced that the whole program was window-dressing, set up for the benefit of relevant politicians to woo their on-farm voters.

I heard the man from National Parks at a presentation about managing kangaroos, organised by a chapter of Landcare in my district. The audience of graziers and hobby farm owners were faced with a change from fairly benign climate conditions to one of Australia's predictable dry periods, the length of the dry made more uncertain now by climate change. Who knew whether these landholders would grasp the opportunity to kill every kangaroo on the place. But in case they wanted to, commercial kangaroo industry representatives were present to help out, seeking more access to properties.

I asked why anyone thought there was a need for open season shooting in addition to the large commercial hunt quota which was never filled. The answer was that the market for meat and skins is depressed – a welcome admission for some activists who have worked long on international campaigns (explored later in this book), and for citizens who love their country's wildlife. Just as in neighbouring Queensland, NSW politicians, to help the farmers, had decided that not enough animals were being killed commercially.

I soon found out that not only bullets, but hundreds of kilometres of interlocking exclusion fencing covering multiple properties, are being aimed at keeping remaining native animals off habitat and wildlife corridors, now the commercial property of someone who might be excited by the profits of the current sheep or cattle market or just be hurting from the drought.

I saw some vast land-holdings with the fencing in south-east Queensland that are now owned by overseas pension funds. Queensland taxpayers have paid much of the fencing bill. Exclusion cluster fencing was being promoted to NSW graziers as well by 2018. The attached public rhetoric never varies and is seldom questioned, even as to logic.

Despite 3–7 years of drought in Queensland and parts of NSW, kangaroo numbers, according to a 7 August 2019 story in *The Land* newspaper, a bastion of traditional farmer thinking, are "out of control" in many parts of NSW including the southern Riverina. Farmers called on the NSW state government to fund kangaroo exclusion fencing. The story came with the image of a grazier with one hand on a two-metre-high ringlock and barbed wire fence. She was from the NSW Farmers' Deniliquin branch and was quoted as saying that "farmers need to preserve every blade of grass and cropping country where possible".[14]

WHAT HAPPENS WHEN THE PUBLIC IS ENCOURAGED TO KILL THE WILDLIFE

A late addition to the Landcare panel on kangaroo management I attended was a long-time local wildlife rescuer and research associate with the Sydney University of Technology Centre for Compassionate Conservation. He showed the assembled land-holders cringe-making pictures of some of the mis-shot kangaroos that had come into care. Jaws blown off, stomach shots, leg shots, a recent image of a little doe kangaroo with a bullet lodged at the base of her tail. Local wildlife rescuers regularly find bewildered dependent joeys that still rely on mother for milk. One had tried to climb back into the pouch of a stomach-shot mother.

Some months later, I got a call from this wildlife rescuer and his partner. They had been called to help a couple in our neighbourhood capture for euthanasia a large male Eastern Grey kangaroo that had its lower jaw shot off. He had survived for four days on and off the couple's verandah (the kangaroo always disappearing when the rescuers approached until the last time). The kind neighbours were understandably distraught.

Several months after that incident came news that in another rural residential community, unknown perpetrators on two occasions had tied kangaroos to the back of their vehicles and dragged them to death. Here were outcomes of dog-whistling 'kill as you choose' by government authorities. Taking up the baton, church-going property-owners organized a neighbourhood killing event a few kilometres from me. These were snapshots from a small cross section of just one local district, and far from the worst – although many neighbours took a more compassionate approach. As I had learned, compassion is not always possible to admit in rural Australia.

At the Landcare forum, non-lethal methods like sheep guardian dogs were given a nod. I thought about the fact that in Australia's mostly privatized landscape, whether it is shooting, high fences, turning off water points, or installing Maremma dogs, getting the kangaroos off one property – thereby disrupting a more natural, more dispersed grazing regime – simply meant the neighbours got a higher density of animals. Some people then identified a problem of having 'too many' kangaroos.

Australia has no ecological conservation plans for marsupials not yet labelled as threatened with extinction. There is some legal designation of 'protected native species' but that has not stopped extensive killing of herbivores and other native species. A national kangaroo plan that includes the word conservation exists. But from the start it was targeted at counting and then 'harvesting' kangaroos for the skin and meat trade.

With no overarching national protection or regional conservation strategies, every landholder can make his own plan to rid the property of native animals – always with government approval unless the animal is already heading for extinction. The politicians who support lethal wildlife management inhabit all major political parties in Australia.

Farmer lobby groups tend to be right at the top of state politicians' visitor numbers. The next example of their influence soon arrived.

TURN THE NATIONAL EMBLEM INTO PET FOOD FOR DOGS AND CATS

The commercial export trade for skins and meat of the remaining large kangaroos started in the 1950s and the state of Victoria was well represented in the intervening decades. But in the early 1980s it was stopped when regional extinctions occurred. Kangaroos in Victoria had been slowly recovering since then. Meanwhile the state remained a favoured conduit for the illegal trade in skins and meat.

In March 2019, a five-year-long trial in Victoria to revive the commercial killing and use of kangaroo parts came to a close. The program was strongly supported by farmers who were culling kangaroos on their own initiative anyway, and by pet food manufacturers and the macropod skin trade. The arguments in favour were the usual: profit and rural jobs, turning a pest to farmers into a commercial resource. The public was not asked.

At the end of the five-year trial, the body count of kangaroos was hovering around the one million mark. In the case of Red kangaroos, the kill rate under the trial was said to have increased by up to 700 percent (not counting the abandoned joeys) from previous statistics. Greys and the Wallaroos were also more heavily hunted than previously.[15]

The trial ended with a troubled assessment from the Victorian Department of Environment, confirming that creating a financial incentive to kill leads to abuses. The department doubted it could control the impacts of an industry that needs a sustained body count, while Australian conditions guarantee wildlife population boom and bust.

The department showed that during the trial there was deliberate overshooting of allowed numbers, false claims of damage by graziers to allow more shooting, and animal cruelty as inevitable.[16]

Yet on 29 March 2019, a Victorian Labor government, badged as progressive, handed a victory to the Victorian Farmers Federation and the pet food and kangaroo skin merchants – brushing aside evidence of community opposition and departmental misgivings. The promise was a permanent trade with harvest zones and quotas, just like the rest of the country.[17]

The farmers spoke of "out of control" macropod numbers, the politicians said 'nothing to see here', pledging "sustainable" management. The rhetoric aimed at the public has not varied since the beginning of the 20th century when it was used to normalise the commercial slaughter of koalas.

Damage control permits for other species were also on the rise. After 2015, not counting the dead in duck hunting season, 397,549 birds were killed in Victoria with state government blessing – almost half of which were from a range of parrot species.[18]

South Australia, which is home to the country's largest kangaroo meat processor, would soon follow Victoria to ramp up kangaroo 'harvesting'. A familiar argument in support of the industry came along, badged as science: kangaroos were overabundant, were hurting other native flora and fauna, and would starve unless first killed and Australians got over their aversion to eating the national emblem.

Then, back in Victoria, a totally different wildlife story erupted. The Greens party in federal parliament and various news organisations loudly denounced a headline-grabbing event. Politicians and/or media normally ignore Australia's domestic commercial and farmer wildlife killing – it's not happening in the narrative. But here they were handed an irresistible headline: Chinese high-rollers being enticed to Melbourne's Crown Casino with promises of sex workers, money laundering opportunities, and the possibility to shoot game including the marsupial wombat on a private country estate. Foreigners killing native wildlife![19]

Once some reporters became interested in wombats, they probed a little further and found that in fact the cute ground-dwelling wombats (and other native species) are routinely killed to please rural landholders, with the number of wombats officially slaughtered doubling since 2009. As one reporter calculated, three wombat-killing permits are handed out each week in Victoria. Worse, a lot of local council areas have no permit requirements at all, guaranteeing a lot more carnage.

A related opinion piece compared[20] Victoria's general attitude to wildlife – from hosting, despite decades of community opposition, the months-long duck-hunting season – to marsupial slaughter. The piece also reminded readers that given a chance, ecotourism would be lot more popular and profitable than appealing to the odd high-roller hunting safari.

"The wombat-hunting scandal spread abroad, and coverage included links to previous Aussie wombat stories, including the tale of Tonka the wombat from Townsville, who specialised in tummy-rubs and cuddles," wrote Jo Wilkinson. "When he died in 2016 the response was overwhelming. For some, Tonka had been the highlight of their Australian trip." The article about Tonka reported that crocodiles, koalas and kangaroos were the biggest drawcard for the 60,000 people who visited this sanctuary each year.[21]

QUESTIONS FROM THE BUSH

Many Australians do support wildlife privately, with no official support. In my rural residential neighbourhood there are high numbers of kangaroos and wallabies. We are surrounded by grazing blocks where people have been shooting all the while. The kangaroos are not flying in from the sky or having biologically impossible birth rates just here.

Over time, and as more subdivision has covered their home ranges, they have found sanctuary where they could be relatively unmolested, where people are willing to share and many appreciate living with the wildlife. But the densities are not natural and far from universal.

I formed some questions in my 30 years of living 'in the bush' – sharing space, some understanding, and a little food with my fellow creatures here. I thought it odd that there has been almost no research since settlement on the ecological role and benefits of Australia's pouched mammals that evolved with the landscape over millions of years.

Aboriginal people understood the role of the native animals in keeping the country healthy. Over the centuries they understood co-dependence, a web of life on this ancient continent. But the British and those who followed were more interested in applying knowledge for the great makeover to a European pastoral vision. I also had to question on what basis kangaroos are routinely charged with infesting the country in 'plague proportions' (so apparently anything done to them doesn't matter).

Kangaroos and wallabies have survived 200 years of colonial recreational hunting and settler 'pest management' that has led to the extinction or critical endangerment of smaller kangaroo species. The remaining large kangaroos: Red, Eastern and Western Grey kangaroos, and Wallaroos (also known as Euros) continue to be subjected to the world's largest land-based commercial wildlife hunt for skins and meat, largely an export trade – a fact few Australians appreciate and that no research effort examines for genetic or ultimate population impact.

The mythology of 'too many' kangaroos is the glib justification from farmers, government and media. As I probed further, it was evident that the answers lay not with counting arguments but, as so often with environmental issues, with first unpacking the values that underlie the policies, myths and beliefs that can be held with total conviction and have nothing to do with ecological understanding.

In this landscape of belief, kangaroos become more virtual than real: appearing in staggering millions in counts and quotas on government computers, forever hopping into sunsets on tourist brochures, and adorning airplane tails. But across Australia, unlike in my neighbourhood, a modern traveller is unlikely to see a living kangaroo outside of some reserved land. The killing of abundant wildlife had become the unremarkable norm of what Australians do.

For the past decade in my capacity as a journalist, I have learned from a distinguished company of 20th century whistleblowers and citizen activists who, often at great personal cost, have unmasked the cruelty and mass slaughter, the demonisation, injustice and yes, big lies and fake facts, clouding the existence of the remaining large species of kangaroos and other remaining common wildlife. Their David and Goliath battle against entrenched interests and traditional values inform some of the stories ahead.

The documentary archives I examined took me early on to Broken Hill in the NSW west, part of the great semi-arid heart of Australia. Attempts in that country by settlers to run sheep led to severe conflict with the nature of Australia and its native animals.

But some Australians with a deeper vision saw there the opportunity for peaceful co-existence and economic well-being, hand in hand.

RED KANGAROO, THE HOUR IS LATE, BUT ...

"Big Reds are like the bull elephants of Africa. They are what tourists want to see. You feel embarrassed because there is none left to show them ... the big kangaroos have been shot out ... nobody is looking after the Big Reds."

— TOURISM BUSH SAFARI OPERATORS EARLY 2000s AS TOLD TO
LES HUTCHINSON IN 'KANGAROOS: FROM ICON TO ASSET'

"Bloody pests," mutters Johnson. He is accompanied by an American journalist and they are driving in a Land Cruiser rattling with meat hooks.

"Soon enough the hunt begins. Johnson spots a kangaroo, bent forward swinging its head side to side snipping the dry grass. He closes in at 150 yards and switches on a spotlight mounted on the windshield.

"It is a red kangaroo, an 80-pound buck with a ponderous tail. Light freezes the creature ... His head pops up, he sits tall and dazed, uncertain of the meaning of this sudden attention. He lifts his paws and tucks them under his chin as if in prayer. A 'fools' prayers, because it is already too late."

— FROM *BOING, BOING BOING ... BANG* A REPORT TO AMERICA FROM
OUTBACK BROKEN HILL, BY LAURA BLUMENFELD, *WASHINGTON POST*, 1994

THE HUNTED FUGITIVE ELSEWHERE KNOWN AS SKIPPY

"If you are unfortunate enough to go 'bush walking' for 20 kilometres in any direction in the sheep-degraded landscapes around Broken Hill, you'll see the terrified, scattered, sole survivors of the nightly slaughter. Young kangaroos left alone, wandering in full daylight, with no family for company and affection, no mob mates or mentors, no older experienced kangaroos to stand watch against dog pack attacks or lead them to better areas during drought time.

"When a kangaroo family heads to a waterhole to drink each night, as it needs to, the shooters will be waiting there in ambush with their spotlight, high-power rifles and vicious dogs. Is that any way you'd like to live?"

Now retired science teacher Les Hutchinson wrote these observations in October 2002 when he was working in the iconic mining town in north-west NSW.

Hutchinson, like many others, saw disappointed tourists leave Australia, never having had the wildlife experience of viewing mobs of free-living big kangaroos in the outback. As he told a national wildlife conservation organisation, "these beautiful animals need wide open spaces and need to move in family groups and neighbourly mobs, and even to mass in large mobs during migrations and bad seasons".

But, he wrote: "The kangaroos' entire territory, one that they arguably should be left with, the semi-desert, has been taken over by sheep graziers, making the kangaroos trespassers on their own land, where not even one of them is welcome ... and every blade of grass or leaf of foliage is begrudged them (and) a campaign of blame and vilification is waged against them."

He saw unmotivated school students in Broken Hill boast that they don't need to study – that they could always get a job as a roo shooter. At nights he observed as many as 120 kangaroo-killing one-ton trucks return to Broken Hill kangaroo processing plants. The meat would fetch a meagre $1.50 a kilo.

Working in Broken Hill and looking around, he was convinced wildlife ecotourism could be a durable and sustainable economic bulwark, but, he wrote, "our ecotourism status is currently that of a nationwide boneyard of skeletons of our largest kangaroos".

In 2002, veterinarian and kangaroo defender John Auty and zoologist David Croft came to Broken Hill for a community roundtable, leading a discussion on the benefits of ecotourism for the region. An article penned by Les Hutchinson appeared in the town paper the *Barrier Daily Truth*. (The venerable *Daily Truth* has recorded a century of worker–boss relations in this tough mining town. Broken Hill also has the dubious distinction of being the model for journalist Kenneth Cooke's 1970s Australian rural-gothic horror story *Wake in Fright* – a drunken weekend crowned by a savage kangaroo hunt.)

John Auty wrote and spoke often in those days from his first-hand experience as a government veterinarian, in charge of animal welfare for the Commonwealth, who had worked for years in semi-arid, stock-raising country.

LIFE AND PROSPERITY BACK TO THE DEAD HEART

Auty formed the view that there was no future for the post-colonial pastoral industries in the semi-desert, echoing conclusions from earlier Australian biological scientists. He also pointed out the wealth of taxpayer subsidies that keep pastoralists going in marginal lands: infrastructure, control of unwanted native and feral animals, including the substantial cost of baiting and dingo fencing, disease management, drought relief, tax relief, fuel subsidies ...

He noted that the West Kimberley sheep industry, for which pastoralists had been poisoning wallabies with arsenic in the 1960s–70s, was no more. Further south, the WA government was poisoning water sources to rid the pastoralists of a million feral goats.

Auty's vision for the centre of Australia, what he called Reanimating the Dead Heart, was this: two million hectares of the semi-arid and arid lands of Australia eventually returned to the public domain as one great continuous national park, probably managed by local Aboriginal groups. Destocking and managed tourism going hand in hand. There would then be no need for solutions to the 'kangaroo problem'. This could either happen by present attrition, with "desertification", the loss of many more species of flora and fauna or in a planned way.

The *Barrier Truth* article added Croft's ideas for inland tourism, featuring the Red kangaroo – a future akin to whale watching on the eastern coast. Perhaps it was not too late.

"These animals are worth far more to Australians alive than dead," said Croft. He had studied the great national parks of the arid lands of southern Africa as a model and learned that tourism brought in a lot more income to the regions than struggling stock operations. The unique kangaroo mobs would rival the appeal of springbok or wildebeest herds. The unique behavioural traits of the kangaroo from boxing to pouch young had already made the kangaroo, Skippy, a world-wide top tourist 'must see'.

"Rather than harvesting these kangaroos for minimal returns," said Croft, "those with the imagination to go beyond the 19th century view of wildlife exploitation will profit by encouraging wildlife tourism on their properties in the form of farm holidays." He had no doubt it could be done. He had spent 20 years at the University of NSW Fowler's Gap Arid Zone Research Station. Work there showed that conservative sheep stocking to retain chenopod shrubs (valuable drought fodder) meant the Red kangaroo and sheep – who do not eat the same plants normally – can co-exist even in dry times.[1]

In the event, post-colonial views of Australian native grazers prevailed in Broken Hill as elsewhere. Kangaroos were 'pests' to be removed from sheep enterprises. The economically attractive ecotourism proposals languished and expired.

I saw the national value frame from that same year (2002) reflected in archived correspondence between a citizen who wrote about the benefits of inland ecotourism and concerns about the fate of the Red kangaroo and the Australian Tourism Commission. The commission is a statutory body established to promote Australia as a tourism destination. It did not think Red kangaroos were worth talking about as a tourist attraction. It was on board with the graziers and the official land management view of the large macropods.

The "facts" the Tourism Commission passed on about the status quo of kangaroo "harvesting" included: that kangaroos have "thrived" in Australia since settlement. The commission's words here are in quotation marks because words matter in persuading citizens how to think about things. The commission told the enquiring citizen that aerial surveys before 2002 estimated large kangaroo populations at 25 million or maybe it was upward of 40 million? Anyway, kangaroos are the most numerous land mammals on earth, said the commission's note.

In this view, the unique animal that holds up one side of the national emblem "do immense damage to pastoral properties" – ruining crops and fences and competing with livestock for food and water; "harvesting" turns a long-time pest into an economic resource; harvesting is strictly regulated to prevent cruelty and flexible quotas respond to seasonal conditions.

The fact sheet referred the citizen to the Director, federal National Parks and Wildlife Service; the public relations director of Environment Australia, and the then communications manager of CSIRO Wildlife and Ecology.

THEY ALL AGREE

The official stamp of approval animates this story of wildlife treatment in Australia and how Australia treats Skippy. Media reports have used the words of politicians, government officials and applied ecologists for decades to justify what is happening, and to counter any animal welfare or population sustainability concerns. 'Must-have' economic and export arguments are cited without need of defence.

A typical example is a 1997 *Australian Financial Review* story about a consumer campaign at the time, led by the International Fund for Animal Welfare. (Consumer campaigns to stop kangaroo meat and skins sold overseas continue to the present day. More on that later). The *Fin Review*'s story quoted the then premier of NSW Bob Carr. He accuses independent NSW Member of the Legislative Assembly, Richard Jones, who was lending his weight to the wildlife cause, of "sabotaging the State's efforts to open a new export market in Europe".[2]

I spent some time on this journey with the documentary record, looking for those with professional expertise whose eyes and ears were not closed to the tragedy befalling Australia's wildlife and the increasingly bad outlook for the Red kangaroo in particular. It appeared mainstream warnings have been suppressed, not understood or forgotten.

Thus, no one would have called the 1960s chief of the CSIRO Division of Wildlife Research, Harry Frith, a bleeding heart for kangaroos. On the contrary, in a report from 1968, his stated views of kangaroos as a "resource" and as a "game meat" source fit with the hard-nosed, rationalist thinking of the time, and since, about Australia's national symbol and its place in the national export economy.

But Frith was a thorough biologist and did appreciate Australia's unique biodiversity. Elsewhere in these pages I record his comments about the destruction for colonial dairy farms of the unique east coast rainforest ecosystems and the abundant wildlife that once lived there.

His 1968 scientific commentary and critique of the over-shooting of the Red kangaroo, published in a newsletter by the Australian Conservation Foundation, describes an unabated pattern of killing on behalf of western sheep graziers and a growing game meat and skins 'harvest', while disregarding the Red's basic biology that determines the breeding stock holding up the population's future.[3]

Dry seasons and drought (becoming more frequent with climate change) play a big role in reproductive capability. Red females outside of captive conditions may not be sexually mature until five years of age in bad years, with an average in good seasons of two-and-a-half years. Many pouch young do not survive even a mild drought. Frith's research showed 83 percent of joeys failing to leave the pouch under those conditions. Red kangaroos have the added ability to cease breeding in poor season until rain falls (also observed in Greys).

Frith reported statistics from the mid-1960s such as the following: in central Australia, on one station, 14,000 Red kangaroos were shot each year; in central NSW, on one property with 6,000 sheep, 7,000 kangaroos were shot each year – and in WA, 13,000 Wallaroos/Euros were poisoned in a year. He concluded that the large numbers of kangaroos on their home territories would have been competing with the stock at the time.

But he also concluded that there was no control over the commercial 'harvesting' rate that ensued and the numbers of kangaroos declined precipitously within a year or so of such numbers being killed. Aerial counts over hundreds of square miles recorded population drops of 70 percent and more.

Already 50 years ago, Frith noted other evidence that the hunt was unsustainable to the population. Smaller average size and immature animals were recorded at the chillers. The magnificent big Reds were being systematically shot out – bigger skins, more meat at pennies a pound.

In 2001 it was again noted, at a NSW government-convened conference, that the average age of a shot Red kangaroo was only two years of age, below sexual maturity for females, when in normal life these resilient macropods could make it to 20 or more years. I was also learning about the 'mystery' disease epidemics hammering the survivors in the decades since the 1960s.

THE RED KANGAROOS WILL BE GONE AND THE GREYS SOON AFTER

On 27 May 1998, Pat O'Brien, then president of a wildlife conservation group in central Queensland and kangaroo campaigner for the Australian Wildlife Protection Council, wrote to the Director of the Australian Conservation Foundation.

He wrote of the pressure from well-funded industry groups and bureaucrats to exploit Australia's wildlife for profit. He noted Queensland nature was already reeling from mega-dams, vegetation removal, mines, chemical plants, "dead coral by the bucketful". Now the state was being offered proposals for extending export trade of Australia's wildlife, alive or dead.

"In Central Queensland there have been proposals to farm and harvest native water rats for skins, bandicoots for meat and fur, capture of native birds for export as talking cage birds, game hunting in National Parks and other horrible proposals ... we believe a strong illegal market already exists in Queensland, supplying the Victorian native pet market ...

"The worst issue is the large kangaroos. I sit on the Queensland Macropod Management Advisory Committee and regularly communicate with conservation representatives on the NSW Macropod Committee. Both committees are structured to facilitate the industry which is totally out of control ... In recent meetings that I have had with shooter groups, they are saying that unless there are dramatic management changes, our red roos will be gone in 10 years and the greys soon after."[4]

When I spoke with Mick McIntyre, director of *Kangaroo,* a recent documentary about Australia's 'love/hate' relationship with its national emblem, I asked him what footage his drones had picked up of Red kangaroos in western NSW. Across the vast semi-arid outback of western NSW, he said they filmed very few kangaroos, and the only large ones were seen in a national park.

At the end of 2019, the Queensland government – which has handed out numerous kangaroo destruction permits to graziers in recent years, and used taxpayer money to help graziers build miles of deadly fencing traps for a renewed wool industry – halted the 2020 commercial kangaroo hunt. Numbers of Grey kangaroos and Wallaroos/Euros had fallen below critical population markers. Reds were not mentioned.

The national broadcaster, the ABC, as well as rural newspapers, thereupon solicited the opinions of rural commercial operators who thought it was a waste to stop the hunt and let this free 'product' starve to death. Starvation was not documented. Decades after the alarm was raised for the fate of the Big Reds, there were no voices in these reports for the welfare of the other species of large kangaroos, or for non-lethal directions to share the land and Australia's unique wildlife heritage.[5]

DATELINE 1788: PRIVATE PROPERTY TAKEOVER

"Property rights necessarily generate violent and oftentimes lethal processes of dispossession … if property rights produce freedom and prosperity, they do so very selectively."

— ANDREASSON S, 'STAND AND DELIVER: PRIVATE PROPERTY AND THE POLITICS OF GLOBAL DISPOSSESSION', *POLITICAL STUDIES*, VOL 54, 2006

"In all the new worlds to which they migrated during the nineteenth century, the British faced conflict … raising the condition of struggle to an ecological law [as] civilisation and nature were considered to be deeply antithetical. The social Darwinist Thomas Huxley cited Tasmania as an example … a shipload of English colonists there put an end to the wilderness; they cleared away the native vegetation, extirpated or drove out the indigenous populations of animals and people and took measures to defend themselves against the recovery or re-immigration of either. In their place they introduced English grain and fruit trees, English dogs, sheep, cattle and horses. English men settled amidst an English garden."

— LINES W J, *TAMING THE GREAT SOUTH LAND, A HISTORY OF THE CONQUEST OF NATURE IN AUSTRALIA*

"Australia was being run as an industrialised export business."

— HORNE D, *MONEY MADE US*

Homestead. Gerard Krefft manuscript and pictorial collection, ca. 1856–1895, PXD9 image 28, courtesy of Dixson Library, State Library of New South Wales.

BUILDING A NEW NATION FOR AN EXPORT ECONOMY

From the perspective of Australian wildlife, with the settlers that came in waves after 1788 the original life-sustaining habitat was rapidly 'owned': cleared, silted over and eaten out by hard-hooved exotic animals, often overstocked, or it was ploughed up and planted.

The destruction of native ecosystems and therefore wildlife's ability to survive continues as normal business practice by many who own production property. The culture is supported by state government politicians who legislate to remove yet more remnant native vegetation and native wildlife, even, as I saw in 2018, removing modest protection policies.

In this story, as in politics and policy always, beliefs and values are key. The colonisers believed that the labour of industrious Christians allied with private property rights transformed their conquests from barbarism and waste into civilisation. "Defiance of this new order equalled rebellion against the creator of the universe," wrote William Lines in his confronting history of the deliberate destruction of the First Australians.[1] The United States by this time had already coined a term for the steady takeover of land and dispossession of people and native animals: 'Manifest Destiny'.

The land management mindset the English colonists brought to Australia did not need to understand how everything had worked before, the long-evolved ecosystems, or what we now call 'environmental services' offered by native plants and animals. Plus, in the 17th century Descartes and the so-called mechanists had planted the commonly-held idea that animals were soulless mechanical units to be manipulated by humans, so no one had to worry about their pain and suffering.

I was reminded by the words of some Aboriginal people about just how culturally bound these ideas are, and how opposite to the traditional thinking of the First Australians. For instance, South

Australian Antikarinya elder Bill Lennon, whose family now oper-
ates a cattle station on the edge of the Great Victoria Desert, defends
the dingo against the pest management ethos and prejudice that
came with the white man.

He told a reporter for *Australian Geographic* that growing up in
that arid region "those old dingoes didn't bother us. We live together;
my grandmother and grandfather each had a dingo … They are one
of our totems. When an Aboriginal man goes through the law he
might become a perentie man, an emu man, a kangaroo man or a
dog man. Those dingoes watch over the dog men and make them
spiritually strong. They do their job – they are part of our Dreaming."[2]

The introduced ideas and beliefs about private property that
underpin settler dispossession of humans and every other native
entity, stem from British Isles political economists led by John
Locke and Adam Smith. They provided a blueprint for the takeover
of new lands and the removal of what was there before. In the US,
regardless of the British crown being pushed out, Locke's ideas
were seminal to the establishment of the American republic after
the 1776 revolution. Just as followed in Australia, the ideas drove
American policy and practice of homesteading on former Native
American land –justifing the settlers' activities.

The destruction of wildlife in North America followed the
familiar colonial pattern. It simply took place earlier than in
Australia, where some larger-population targets like the big kangaroos remain today. In the US, some 60 million beaver were killed
after European settlement. Similar millions of buffalo still roamed
the Great Plains in 1840 but were almost exterminated in 40 years
of frantic hunting, and the billions-strong Passenger pigeon was
actually exterminated by 1914. Bears, wolves, mountain lions and
birds of prey have been extensively hunted both for sport and to
accommodate farmers/ranchers.

Drilling into the values that Europeans, in Australia led by immigrants from the British Isles, brought with their invasions, the start is to remember what 'new world' colonisation was about at the baseline.

Australian colonisation followed the model of 'Europe versus the rest of the world' that started with the merchant explorers of the 16th century. The rest of the world was seen as the storehouse and back paddock of Europe. Exports to the mother countries were the reason for new colonies to exist and be supported by investment from 'home'. Colonialism in its various guises, either direct invasions or trade collaboration with previous invader elites, was well established around the globe by the time the First Fleet sailed into Botany Bay.

The Australian guiding economic narrative today remains a nation that exports food, fibre and minerals, with native species as possibly inconvenient intrusions on the hoped-for prosperity. These ideas were only strengthened in the 1980s as neo-liberalism became the dominant ideology in English-speaking Western countries, downplaying the role of governments and regulation in the public interest while elevating 'the market'. At the same time globalisation was elected the driver of market forces. These economic beliefs have cemented the Australian status quo. It is based on the idea that exporting each country's 'natural advantages' is the path to national prosperity (downplaying the prospect that multinational corporations might be prospering more and that domestic industry is dismantled).

As a result, the people who own a lot of Australian land and exploit natural resources (which include grass and water as well as mineralised rock) wield disproportionate influence on national affairs. Their activities and interests have long been framed as indispensable and unarguable.

The fabled bedrock of the nation's wealth – money 'off the sheep's back' – was no mere lucky gamble in a new colony that was established first to house convicts. Despite what generations of new Australians were taught, it appears the convicts were soon shipped out to mind the sheep owned by absentee English gentry – as were poor people and later a growing surplus industrial middle class.

PRE-EMINENCE OF SHEEP FARMERS, PRIVATE PROPERTY, IN EXPORT NATION

Fleshing out the sheep saga, social historian of Australia's national identity, Donald Horne (author of the well-known *The Lucky Country*), unpacks the pre-eminence of the sheep farmer, squatter, pastoralist, livestock primary producer in the Australian mythology of nation building.

Following two centuries of European countries heavily exploiting or plundering the Americas, Africa and Asia for everything from spices, to fur animals, to gold, to whales and seals, to human beings for slave labour, the industrial revolution happened.

Europe's textile and carpet factories mechanised and needed wool. "Flocks of sheep moved into virgin pastures in Australia, New Zealand, South Africa, North America and Argentina. European settlers would survey a new region, clear its vegetation, arrange plants in straight rows, build houses, set up labour lines and turn the region into an engine for producing exports." And the growth of railways meant cropping could expand across previously remote landscapes; refrigeration meant grass could be converted to exportable beef and mutton as well as butter for English breakfast tables.[3]

Investment (for instance in railways and other infrastructure) and bulk labour were the two elements supplied by the mother country. While slaves provided bulk labour in some colonies, in others, including parts of North America and then Australia, convicts got the job – followed by assisted immigration, "the world's greatest planned movement of people".[4]

The waves of Australian settlement that followed, and the dispossession of everything native, came as new immigrants raced to get a patch of country to raise sheep and shear their coats for export. Some established huge estates, others took up smaller 'runs'. Many came with no agricultural experience, let alone appreciation of Australian conditions, but they were armoured with firm and religious beliefs that anything they did with European methods and blueprints was an improvement over what they found on the ground. This was a surge every bit as frantic and destructive as the gold rush that came next.

The land rush after 1788 was guided by very deliberate application of the predominant English idea for establishing colonies: putting in place English laws of private property and the concept of land improvement to establish ownership. A private property-based settlement strategy allowed newcomers to treat both the humans and wildlife they found already inhabiting the continent with no respect. It also justified and normalised massacres on both fronts.

Indeed, as I delved into the history of wildlife and Australian culture, the private property value structure kept presenting itself as a key to the beliefs and activities of present-day Australians and policies regarding wildlife. Not coincidentally, Australians' traditional life goals of home ownership on a plot of land enclosed by a fence, plus the national obsession with real estate and acceptance of migration as a central economic growth driver, come from these colonial beginnings.

From these beginnings, agricultural enterprises continue to have economic power and political influence considerably beyond their numbers and modern-day contributions to the national economy. The private property frame they inhabit could not be further from the understandings of living on this ancient continent held by the First Australians. I felt I needed to understand that better before going on.

Fraser Island Butchulla man Hayden Richards and his dingo friend.

THE DREAMING OF MUTUAL RESPONSIBILITY

Following the recent horrific bushfires in eastern Australia, the need to learn from Aboriginal knowledge again rose in public discussions. Mostly that talk revolved around how Aboriginal people kept the country open with cool patch burning. But there is much more than how and when to burn to learn from Indigenous knowledge of Australian ecology and 'country'.

The natural world is central to the Dreaming – the Aboriginal cosmic sense of time and eternal law governing human relations with the land. The Dreaming stories and the songlines, also known as dreaming tracks, have been explained to new Australians as the original tracks of ancestors that sang the country into being, and are the timeless guides to the geography and ecologies of the continent. Kinship networks allowed shared knowledge throughout Australia. Young Aboriginal people were brought up with this knowledge and ritual to become people of physical courage, resilience, pride and extensive ecological knowledge.[5]

I came across a presentation from the late Australian anthropologist Deborah Rose who explained more, in accessible language, about how Aboriginal groups saw themselves and the plants and animals in the landscape. Much more than just patch burning techniques, this view of living in Australia, gained over centuries, offers a key to what we call 'sustainability', both practically and spiritually, on this continent of unique plants, animals and ecosystems.

Everything is interconnected and must be viewed reciprocally – an understanding that connects past, present and change. It's a vision that Western environmentalists might understand as the 'web of life' that also includes humans – not as dominators but as parallel nations, a little akin to St Francis' compassionate theology – brother wolf, sister bird – woven in.

From Rose I got a clearer glimpse of how Aboriginal people view what we call their totem animals within the broad context of their kinship with animals and plants and their whole environment.

Rose reported from a small community in the Northern Territory, where she stayed for two years to learn about the people's understanding and relationship to the dingo. That relationship was at the forefront after the NT government dropped aerial baits of 1080 poison on the community and its surroundings to the outrage of the people there, morally and in terms of rights.[6]

DINGO RESPECT WOVEN INTO COUNTRY

The dingo, since colonial times, and still today, is one of modern Australia's most persecuted native animals. Australia's apex predator has little to no government protection. Instead, as a designated 'wild dog', the dingo is the target of National Parks and other state authorities' shooting – and 1080 baiting, which causes an excruciating, lingering death.

The dingo's movements in original habitat across the continent are restricted by miles of fencing – including a 5,614 kilometre fence from Queensland to South Australia, one of the longest man-made structures in the world – built to shield sheep graziers from the free-living Aboriginal companion. The state-spanning fence, built in the 1880s, enjoys ongoing patrols and maintenance paid for by the taxpayer.

In Aboriginal culture, the dingo is venerated and respected. "Right across Australia dingos are important Dreaming person-ages – their tracks and stories are major connecting links, and they figure in major songs and ceremonies," wrote Deborah Rose. "My dingo teachers explained that there was a time when dingos and humans were all one species. We have now gone in separate directions – one dog direction and one human direction – but we are something like siblings, being descended from ancestral dingos …"

Rose wrote of mutual obligations with the natural world:

"The Aboriginal term country denotes a spatial unit – large enough to support a group of people, small enough to be intimately known in every detail and home to the living things whose lives come and go in that place. One of the foundational moral principles of life in country is that a country and its living things take care of their own: that is to say the connections between people, other living things and their country … is to take care and to be cared for.

"I have used the term 'eco-place' to get at the fact that country is not just a homeland for humans, but is a homeland for all the living things that are there and I want to emphasise that care moves through country and into and out of species … In contemporary ecological terms we would say that country is a self-organising system … but humans are not the only organisers. Not only is organisation shared, but humans get organised by others as well."

TOTEMS AND MUTUAL RESPECT

Rose wrote that there has been a long history of academic study of totemism in Australia, but only recently (writing in 2004) did researchers start looking at the practical relationships and what they entailed in restraints, taboos and protection of refuges that care for the well-being of the totemic species. There were past and present bonds between ancestors both human and animal or plant and the present-day humans. An emu might have been an ancestor. Translating a lot of this to post-colonial thinking, what comes to the fore is respect and understanding the connections and reciprocal obligations and responsibility of each creature's role.

Aboriginal stories can have non-human narrators and teachers, but in this sibling way it can be human knowledge too. Dingo stories speak to having one's interest folded into another's, having connection. Modern dog owners might understand that concept.

Rose points out that central Australia has experienced among the highest rates of mammalian extinction in the world since settlement. Indigenous people have found their country diminished in "sociality, sentience and connectivity." One starts to understand what many First Australians must feel at the modern Australian persecution of the dingo and other native species and the European ways of thinking about land ownership, property rights and domination of other species.

Totems are still a mystery to many post-colonial Australians, wrote Rose. "It's about relationships. Totemism can be seen as a mode of kinship which brings a human group and a species or other element of the natural world into relationship."[7]

Kangaroos are a respected totem animal for some groups that believe the health of country is maintained through their tracks, as I learned from some south-east Australian Indigenous people. They told me the industrial-scale killing of kangaroos by white

Australia destroys the songlines and Dreaming tracks they helped create and keep energised.

I found more plain English enlightenment in M.R. O'Connor's recent book *Wayfinding*. O'Connor's goal was to explain a skill that modern societies find very amazing – the abilities of Indigenous peoples worldwide to make their way across landscapes without the benefit of map-making and GPS. To understand navigation, she first had to understand cultures. She talked with north and central-west Australian elders as they travelled together across country and sat around campfires.[8]

Describing a relationship between humans and their totem animals, she wrote:

> "In Wardaman tradition the white cockatoo is the bird that keeps an eye on other important birds like the wedge-tail eagles and diver ducks. The latter are supposed to ensure that people are following traditional rules leading up the wet-season sacred ceremonies. Together, the birds are guardians of the law, making sure secrets aren't divulged to the wrong people, that taboos aren't broken, that certain borders aren't crossed."[9]

A key to understanding these totemic traditions encoded into Aboriginal law and passed on through Dreaming stories, is understanding the requirement to leave the land as found – expressed through a patchwork of totem responsibilities upheld by neighbouring clans that supported conservation of the land and of the breeding populations of all the species thereon. The First Australians knew that ecosystems, the web of life, underpinned survival of humans. The biodiversity and abundance of animal populations encountered by the European settlers attest to that.

Intimately related to Indigenous navigation skills across songlines created and maintained with totem animals, were First Australian trade routes. Acknowledging trade routes conflicts with convenient traditional ideas about Aboriginal culture. Writes O'Connor:

> "European colonisers were convinced that Aboriginal people wandered the land in a struggle for survival and a constant search for food and water ... But today it is irrefutable that Aboriginal trade routes could easily compete with civilization's greatest examples such as the Inca and Incense roads." Aboriginal oral history may also be the world's oldest living example of transmission between generations.[10]

However, the colonisers did avail themselves of the landscape expertise of the Indigenous people in their explorations for new pastures – sometimes persuading them to help with the aid of neck chains and also infamously demanding their navigating skills as the native police forces of the frontier wars.

TRADE ROUTES AND VILLAGES

Knowledge of transcontinental trade routes, and the skills it took to maintain them, complement recent works showing that some First Nations had housing and villages, maintained water sources, and employed deliberate landscaping and agriculture – for example wild yam fields tended by women, storage granaries, fish weirs, and the patch burning techniques to manage 'game' and more.[11]

Knowing that history is written by the victors, author and academic Bruce Pascoe was amazed to find plenty of descriptions of housing and agricultural activity that had been downplayed and ignored for a century and more. In his 2014 book *Dark Emu*, Pascoe quotes surveyor Thomas Mitchell who extensively documented what he saw in the first decades of the 1800s as he criss-crossed the southern states looking for more places to settle with roads and estates. He and other explorers noted wood or stone houses, some with thatched conical roofs, some in the north like longhouses for 40–50 people, familiar from islands to Australia's north.

Pascoe recounts that explorer Charles Sturt, looking for pastoral land north of Adelaide in the 1840s, was saved from expiring from heat and thirst by Aboriginal people in what is now called Sturt's Stony Desert near Cooper's Creek. Sturt documented in his travel journals how some First Australians lived in inland villages, and how hospitable they were to strangers who might as well have dropped out of the sky – a hospitality soon to be repaid by a land grab.[12]

Notable and touching is an anecdote from Sturt's journal from that first encounter with a large group of Aboriginal people, recounted by Pascoe.

"Several of them brought us large troughs of water, and when we had taken a little, held them up for our horses to drink; an instance of nerve that is very remarkable, for I am quite sure that no white man (having never seen or heard of a horse before …) would deliberately have walked up to what must have appeared to them most formidable brutes, and, placing the troughs they carried against their breasts, they allowed the horses to drink, with their noses almost touching them. They likewise offered us some roasted duck and some cake. When we walked over to their camp they pointed to a large new hut and told us we could sleep there." In a desert with scarce wood they also gave Sturt and his men some wood to make a fire. The encounter with the horses is arresting and, as Pascoe notes wryly: "new house, roast duck and cake: Sturt was doing it tough amongst the savages!"[13]

Explorers estimated large healthy populations judging by the size of the villages. Many were to be obliterated in the south within decades after the first wave of white settlers imported smallpox along with the sheep. The smallpox killed tens of thousands of people wherever contact eventuated, followed in later decades by the ravages of syphilis, leprosy and influenza epidemics.

'Natives crossing Murray in bark canoe' (top) and 'Native houses or graves' Hamilton Station Murrumbidgee. (bottom). Gerard Krefft manuscript and pictorial collection, ca. 1856–1895, PXD9, courtesy of Dixson Library, State Library of New South Wales.

The Colonised. Samual Thomas Gill, courtesy of Dixson Library, State Library of New South Wales.

The early soldiers and settlers destroyed the houses after the smallpox plague, or to lay more definite claim to land they were taking, and the sheep and cattle compacted the soil and killed the sustaining wild yam pastures. Later waves of settlers often observed little of the First Australians except for dispossessed, frightened or angry people who sometimes fought back. They were framed by the British as heathens and savages, sheltering in the bush, or being 'saved' and pressed into serving the new lords of the land. In far northern Australia, traditional societies continued for far longer than in the quickly-settled south – well into the 20th century.

FATAL CULTURAL DIVIDE

White settlers viewed the First Nations ethos of reciprocal communal sharing as criminal behaviour (in the vein of 'I'm entitled to take your land but I'm not sharing my cattle or crops'). The whites' cultural refusal to share outside of their understanding of economic relationships and property became reflected in the laws they imposed.

In his 1966 exploration of the fatal impact on Pacific Ocean societies following first contact by Captain Cook, popular historian Alan Moorehead wrote of what came next as Europeans, with their animals, plants and other imports, tore down the bush and rearranged the land. "The aborigines fell back steadily before this invasion ... when their own tribal laws collapsed the aborigines found they could not understand the new English laws, by which they were governed, particularly the law of property. When they found that they owned nothing, that they had virtually no rights of any kind, that they were aliens in their own country, they were bewildered and resentful."[14] This is putting the impact of the clash of cultures mildly.

Those who did not immediately fall to the imported European diseases and engaged in armed defence of their land and people, or who were simply hungry after their traditional lands and food sources were occupied, were branded as 'criminals' and hunted by colonial police and settlers. There is mounting evidence of systematic and brutal massacres.[15]

Colonial observer (and one-time Fleet Street reporter) Daisy Bates was a product of her Victorian British upbringing and believed that the First Nations would gradually disappear under the imposition of European civilisation. Nevertheless, in her later years she became a prominent whistleblower, exposing the cruelty of the dispossession of the Indigenous people.

Bates eventually lived with and helped survivors. She testified that they were treated as trespassers on their own land as sources of food disappeared. She wrote they were treated as criminals and sent away to unfamiliar places.[16]

The hospitality and help extended to early explorers and settlers was part of tribal cultures – extended beyond kinship sharing obligations as a matter of custom between groups, if individuals strayed far from their own area, even if no one knew why they were there or where they came from. Such generous, unquestioning behaviour towards strangers doing strange things is described from Western Australia's Kimberley region as late as the 1930s regarding help given to ethnographic expeditions.[17]

What noted anthropologist W.E.H. 'Bill' Stanner described as the incompatibility of the market and the Dreaming continues its severe consequences for surviving First Australians. The land dispossession moved on from outright massacres and forced labour to the Stolen Generations of children as authorities tried other ways to wipe out the Indigenous cultures. And, as in colonial societies elsewhere, 20th century Australia delivered alcohol and passive welfare to remote ghettos of defeated people, with catastrophic results. Despite some progress, land rights, embedded racism and lack of legal equality/autonomy remain matters of despair for many.[18]

The full legacy of Aboriginal dispossession is beyond the scope of this book, but Australians can learn from contemporary writers and reporters in this field. As I was heading into book production, an ABC News network piece by reporter Stan Grant crossed my screen. It simply and powerfully brings the story, with a personal narrative, into today's frame of Black Lives Matter.[19]

PRIVATE PROPERTY AND IMPROVEMENTS EQUALLED OWNERSHIP

The philosophy behind the strategy of dividing up a continent with back-to-back private property blocks, with 'improvement' mandated, helps explain the colonists' ideas about *terra nullius* and about their rights versus the Indigenous people, animals and ecosystems: if it wasn't 'improved' in terms the British understood, it wasn't owned. It was described as empty 'wasteland' and up for grabs.

'Improvement' was narrowly constructed in terms of European agriculture, science, political theory and even religion, with its ideas of God's design for human beings. Naming every river, mountain and other landscape feature to honour English officials and explorers also signalled possession over what the colonists preferred to think was uninhabited land despite early-on seeing otherwise. The land itself and its features, like some rivers running inland, could not have been more alien to people used to the British Isles. They considered it their duty to improve the nature of Australia.

Oft-quoted explorer and surveyor Thomas Mitchell is a good example of this thinking. While documenting what he saw and experienced of Aboriginal settlements, land management, and abundant native animals and plants in healthy ecosystems, he nevertheless viewed this mainly with calculations of how the grasslands could be put to use for introducing stock and enriching the colonists, and how the whole could efficiently be turned into English-style villages, farms, inns and roads.[20]

WHAT WERE THEY THINKING?

The particular ideas of private property that have shaped modern Australia, from red-brick suburbia to outback cattle station, are not that old, although the notion that individuals can own land goes back to before Greek and Roman times. The specific ideas that shaped British colonial settlement stem from Enlightenment philosophers of the 18th century and earlier ideas about human and animal nature.

In a recent book about private property as an organising principle for Western governments and colonial settlement since the Industrial revolution, journalist Andro Linklater supplied the context for a good deal of what has happened.[21]

He unpacked how Puritan theology and 18th century liberal philosophy together provided a moral justification for dispossession and land takeovers. The former proposed that private property was innate to human existence; the latter that land possession improved by human labour rendered an inalienable right. The key elements were to individualise land ownership in a commercial and trading context – the opposite of most then-existing relationships between land, wildlife and people. As Linklater wrote: "This involved the acquisition of territory, its survey and sale as private property and the power of [the state] to supervise the whole thing."[22]

The idea that a person's labour upon a piece of land bestowed an ownership right was put in practice by agrarian cultivation, ploughing and sowing or pasturing animals. The land ownership was delineated by enclosure, i.e. fencing. This was juxtaposed with the claim that Indigenous people merely harvested the fruits of the land as hunter gatherers, an idea that clings on in popular descriptions about the time.

The philosophy of Englishman John Locke and his contemporaries, including the US founding fathers and colonial administrators elsewhere, deliberately interwove the Christian, Protestant views of virtue and worth. God meant for the land to belong to the industrious and rational – people with a work ethic as defined by fixed toil and commerce, not 'idle' people who might go walkabout. God did not recommend retaining any native ecological association of plants and animals that got in the way of improvements and commerce.

Referring to the Book of Genesis in the Bible, the colonial theorists claimed God commanded Man to labour, subdue, till and sow. 'Be fruitful and multiply and replenish the earth and subdue it' is frequently quoted. From there it was just a short leap to saying God authorised dominion and that meant appropriation of the land in order to subdue, and build replicas of English farms and towns in the service of civilized commerce.[23]

Contemporary histories record such ideas as key to how people thought at the time of settlement. So, we have eminent Australian historian Manning Clarke describing how Lachlan Macquarie, who governed NSW between 1810 and 1822, set about civilising the Aborigines. He aimed to "teach them habits of industry and decency so that they might abandon the indolence and squalor of their own way of life and join the working classes in both settlements".[24]

Goldfields yard NSW or Victoria 1871–76 with Aboriginal servant, emu, brolga and poultry. Personal photograph, Holtermann collection, ON 4 Box 37 No 3, courtesy of Mitchell Library, State Library of New South Wales

Earlier in his chronology, Clarke, using terms like "barbarism" to describe what the settlers thought they found on the ground, noted the British hopes that the Aboriginal people would come into the fold of the labouring classes along with the convicts and servants. "The European hoped that the Aborigine would perceive the benefits of civilization, abandon the life of the savage, and become a labourer on the bottom rung of the ladder of European society."[25]

In stark contrast Manning Clarke reports Captain James Cook's observation some 80 years earlier of Aboriginal relationships with the land and its flora and fauna. After travelling up the east coast of Australia, Cook reported of the First Australians,

> "They may appear to some to be the most wretched people upon the earth: but in reality they are far more happier than we Europeans; being wholly unacquainted not only with the superfluous but necessary Conveniences so much sought after in Europe ... The Earth and the sea of their own accord furnishes them with all things necessary for life; they covet not Magnificent Houses ... they live in a warm and fine Climate and enjoy a very wholesome Air; so they have very little need of Clothing ... In short they seem'd to set not value upon anything we gave them nor would they ever part with anything of their own."[26]

– concluding that the First Australians he met were wholly satisfied with how they worked with the land to provide for their needs.

But to the Europeans that Cook was scouting for, the natural environment and its biota were viewed as inert 'commodities' put there by God to be manipulated for human progress. Civilisation and nature were viewed to be in opposition, both from religious interpretations and from colonial experience elsewhere. Dispossession and long-term ecological collapse have been the outcomes, as Europeans, armed with these ideas and with their farming methods, fanned across the globe.

In a recent book calling for a new perspective on land management and farming in Australia, Charles Massy identified this commodification of nature, what he called the post-Enlightenment, 'Mechanical Mind'.[27] A sheep farmer in southern NSW himself, Massy is one of a cohort of regenerative farmers bent on restoring and working with Australia's unique environments. (I get to more of their work in the Sharing chapter.)

He describes the colonial mindset in his own family that was repeated across the countryside. Everywhere, trees were considered merely as obstacles to more grass for sheep, and needed to be removed. A good day for his grandfather was to start the day ringbarking big old trees, proceed to burning already ringbarked trees, and in the evening shoot native birds. Degraded fertile landscapes, treeless production land, silted watercourses, and destroyed wildlife habitat would become the inheritance of later graziers, in stark contrast to the park-like scenes that greeted the first settlers and explorers.

The semi-arid home of the Red kangaroo was the next frontier. It did not go well. Consider, as Donald Horne did, what happened in short order to the Western Division of NSW ("an area somewhat larger than Great Britain"), or later to the Victorian and South Australian mallee. These were more fragile landscapes with little and uncertain rainfall that from the beginning did not promise a European farming Eden, but were nevertheless stubbornly divided up into private farming allotments for the dream of pastoral profit.

What the settlers found were ecosystems in delicate balance. In western NSW, saltbush, mulga, mallee and native grasses provided ground cover to protect the soil from drying out until the next rains came (at which point the native grazing animals had evolved to enjoy a banquet).

"Into this frugal but workable balance, busy [immigrant] humans, spreading along the Darling in the 1870s, introduced a river life of paddle-steamers and river ports serviced by camel trains, joined in the 1880s by railways to Bourke from Sydney and to Broken Hill from Adelaide. The future promised continuing expansion: to the myth that rain followed the flocks had been added the myth that flocks followed the flocks, or, as a government commission put it in 1883, 'judicious stocking undoubtedly increases the capacity of the country to carry sheep.'[28]

The large holdings to run sheep extended up to a million hectares. It took barely another decade for disaster to strike. The way sheep graze, tearing up roots, and the power of the axe to destroy the vegetation, collided with the drought of the 1890s, turning the area into a dustbowl of dead sheep. In 1891, 15 million sheep were counted. By 1903 the area supported four million, arguably still too many.

"When it rained ... with the ground cover torn out, rainwater evaporated. A new natural order developed in the west – a natural division of the soil into fine particles that blew off as dust and large particles that piled up as dunes of sand. When all the topsoil was blown away, there was left only claypans."[29]

A century later in 2018, dust storms and daily red dust coming from the west again coated inland and coastal communities, following renewed government-sanctioned rounds of tree clearing in eastern states. Meanwhile, in another well-trodden colonial response, kangaroos were being widely shot by the grazing community and scapegoated for the lack of grass on paddocks that were often over-stocked for conditions. Drought, now lengthened and more frequent due to climate change, is a repeated cycle.

Recently, Bruce Pascoe declared in an urgent essay that the colonial ethos has never left Australia and conspires to continue wrecking the country's environment and Indigenous communities. The First Australians, he writes, had the ability "to live as

350 neighbouring nations without land war, not without rancour, for that is the human condition, but without a lust for land and power, without religious war, without slaves, without poverty, but with a profound sense of responsibility for the health of Mother Earth".[30]

I find this history and message has not reached the popular news in Australia. The mainstream media and the public still question little said by Australia's major landholders, their farmer lobby groups, and the politicians who are their ideological partners, when it comes to land and wildlife management.

Some of the strong voices in this book belong to journalists and researchers who published in the last 50 years, but it was a journey in itself to access their work. There are some present-day academic voices starting to question the sacred cow of traditional values that have shielded Australian pastoralism and agriculture for 200 years. But they are still drowned out by mainstream narratives of export-driven farming.[31]

'FREE MEN' UNDER PATRIARCHAL MODEL MANAGE A NEW CONTINENT

There are other driving beliefs that have shaped Australia and its political economy. By the time of 19th century colonial expansions, Judeo-Christian thinking had long proposed that humans – at least Christians – are exceptional and outside the natural world, and that they were sent here to dominate it. Such beliefs have brought unexamined consequences: from climate change denial that humans are responsible or can be affected, to assumed 'rights' to destroy or enslave other species, to progress myths about the normality of taming and destroying nature for ever-expanding growth, extraction and consumption. Cultural myths like ever-forward 'progress' have embedded colonial values and aspirations.[32]

In a seminal paper of environmental history, Lynn White Jr.

argued that Western feelings of exceptionalism are a fundamental religious myth. "What people do about their ecology depends on what they think about themselves in relation to the things around them. Human ecology is deeply conditioned by beliefs about our nature and destiny – that is by religion."[33]

A managerial stance towards the natural world also comes with believing in 'dominion' rather than 'stewardship'. There are widely-accepted cultural assumptions in Western societies on this score. It is not surprising that wildlife management is an arena that has been guided by ideas that humans have to manage other species that either offer economic gain or conflict with it. A frequent go-to solution is killing. In Australia this has not changed since the first colonial days, and is part of the Christian patriarchal attitudes that were imported.

Sheep grazier Charles Massy saw this as part of the culture he inherited: "[The religious view] then blended with classical and pastoral attitudes towards nature as something that can be ploughed and cultivated, used as a commodity and manipulated as a resource, tamed and subdued for human benefit – particularly by males ... with females viewed as passive and receptive."[34]

Under the British, laws and development favoured those who dealt in money, and engaged in commercialism and trade with the old country. Culturally and economically the new world settlement push was about 'free men' (convicts therefore excepted until they were freed and granted land) favouring independence, individualism and masculine prerogatives. A Christian version of God-sanctioned patriarchy was the accepted way to rule the women, the land, indigenous inhabitants and the natural environment.

Freedom and individualism were also heavily welded to the use of a gun. A recent bit of historical research from the United States sheds interesting light on the colonial roots of that country's toxic, free-for-all gun culture, suggesting that settler desire to take ever more land from the original inhabitants is at least one reason behind the Second Amendment to the Constitution.

A frequent argument is that the Second Amendment was intended to ensure free citizens in the new American colony could bear arms as an insurance policy against government oppression. Researcher Roxanne Dunbar-Ortiz found that there was more to it. "What colonists considered oppressive was any restriction put on them in regard to obtaining land," she writes.[35]

The idealised Anglo settler-farmers she found "had long formed militias for the purpose of raiding and razing Indigenous communities and seizing their land and resources and the Native communities fought back". She found early colonial instructions that every settler home had to have a functioning firearm to ward off the fightback from the Indigenous people. The Second Amendment ratified in 1791 enshrined these rights as the right of people to keep and bear arms. In the US these 'rights' were deemed even more important in a slave-owning society.

BLUEPRINT FOR EXPANDED COLONISATION

After the early convict era, the American colonisation blueprint was used in Britain to drive outward migration of a growing industrial-revolution working class that might have caused trouble for the capital-owning class in the motherland. Around 1830, one-time youthful con man turned aspiring politician Edward Gibbon Wakefield founded the National Colonization Society with the help of influential thinkers including the economist John Stuart Mill and philosopher Jeremy Bentham.

The Society's founding ideas were to send off surplus working-class people to the colonies while also solving the problem of poor people: send them as servants or convicts. Wakefield's challenge was to discover the best way to put so-called wasteland to use to further the interests of British investors, while supplying an immigrant work force. Australia got a boost for the imperial resource extraction economy focused on the wool industry, soon joined by mining, supplemented by 'harvesting' nature's bounty in the form of killing land and sea mammalian wildlife and birds.

Land speculation was then as now a winner, writes William Lines in his 1990s history.

> "In 1835, John Morphett, one of several wealthy individuals attracted by the huge profits likely from colonial land speculation wrote: 'The purchase of land in new colonies, experience has shown to be one of the most profitable modes of employing capital which commercial enterprise or speculation has ever discovered.'"[36]

Secure title would become the key after a period of free-for-all land grabs without legal basis – in Australia the so-called squatters. Mapping and legal terms like 'parishes' and 'Torrance Title' stem from that time. The notion of 'improvement' also relied on prevailing beliefs in scientific measurement, linear arrangements and what was considered rational and logical. Engineering feats were necessary to re-arrange strange Australian nature for commerce. The rectangular domestic block was the rational outcome of land surveys placing straight lines on maps. Establishing orderly villages and towns based on a grid system was considered central to civilisation.

In this way, the colonial American blueprint for carving up the landscape into back-to-back private holdings with unbridled private rights was imported to tame Australia for commerce and development. That was a crucial frame for this story. It meant leaving little public habitat where wildlife could roam freely.

Introduced stock and crops covered most of the country by the 20th century. Importantly for the enduring relationship with wildlife, the legal framework imposed few rules governing the private disposition of land and all it entailed. Legislation on all aspects of public and economic life sprang from the private property nexus.

The fate of now homeless wildlife, individually and as populations, would be subject to the ideas and activities of each private property owner: legally and by default, with lack of monitoring or enforcement of regulations that crept in over the decades.

Private property, concluded William Lines in *Taming the Great South Land*, "subverted the environment, destroyed the material basis of an Aboriginal culture inextricably bound to topography, flora and fauna, and delivered the land into the hands of the pastoral pioneer" and his introduced animals, plant species and pathogens.[37]

Political scientist Stefan Andreasson agreed, looking globally: "At the root of the problem of violent exploitation and dispossession stands the problem of private property as conceived by [English philosopher and the father of classical liberal thought, John] Locke, and subsequently expounded upon by a vast array of liberal scholars" as a prerequisite of freedom and economic betterment.[38]

Unlike in the United States or Canada, in Australia no formal attempt was made to buy the land from or recognise ownership of the original inhabitants. As long as Australian Indigenous people were cast as nomadic hunter gatherers who did not cultivate and 'improve' in this private property worldview, English law decided they had no innate claim on the land. That was the state of things until native title legal reforms, starting with the High Court Mabo decision of 1992 recognising Indigenous title to land.

MANY PRIVATE RIGHTS, PUBLIC INTEREST MARGINAL

A legal review of this history shows that the concept of private property we have inherited confers a bundle of rights and privileges to the property owner that allows him to control others, both human and non-human, and most resources of the land, barring mineral rights.[39]

The property-owner's actions have consequences (that can affect both neighbours and the wider society), but an owner's rights are asymmetrically stronger than those of a nearby neighbour or compared to those who don't enjoy private property rights, which certainly includes all non-human animals. Individuals with property rights "revel in a zone of unchecked discretionary action that others, whether private citizens or government officials, may not invade".[40]

Here's a clue to why monitoring and government regulation of land-holder actions in the greater public interest are so fraught, and why protest against dominant cultural ideas – say of disposing of inconvenient wildlife, vegetation or habitat – has offered such a steep challenge.

Such sweeping property rights embedded in law assisted the new nation's self-image: Australia as a resource export quarry run by enterprising businessmen. For farmers, the soil and water and vegetation are the raw materials that belong to the business.

This worldview was extended to wildlife as an exportable raw resource viewed as belonging to a landholder or holder of a commercial license to kill (despite thin latter-day environmental laws calling wildlife protected native species belonging to everyone). The dominant cultural view soon became that free-living species, not yet driven to a state of 'endangered,' need an economic justification for their continuing existence – making it puzzling that Australia has hardly picked up on the economic potential of terrestrial ecotourism. Conversely, economic development or human convenience has long been considered a normal reason to eliminate them.

SETTLERS FRAMED AS VICTIMS IN A SAVAGE COUNTRY

Myths and stories are integral to nation-building, and few founding narratives have been as attractive as the theme of hardy pioneering by European settlers beset by cruel nature and natives. Such a myth required minimising the brutal imperial and economic invasion of Australia. Rearranging popular history is colonial tradition, and not confined to Australia. The emerging stories highlighted persistence and justified conflict.

The favoured stories pit pastoralists, explorers and developers against forces that needed to be tamed and subdued, and, in the view of some, exterminated. Breaking the great silence about what went before and how settlement was actually accomplished has only recently become a theme for more historical research: delving back into early printed documents, finding evidence both of shocking massacres and some early moral resistance to that approach.[41]

The settler-as-victim narrative – with punishment for whistleblowers going against the cultural mainstream – drives historian Mark McKenna's shattering account of the destruction of the Yaburara people of the Pilbara coast. This was during the development of the West Australian pearling industry (after sheep succumbed to drought). The Yaburara people were pressed into indentured servitude or outright slavery (called blackbirding) to dive for pearls. They were beaten and murdered individually when not conforming to their servant roles, or for not harvesting enough pearls, and chained by the neck for taking foodstuff as their land and game were overrun.

And then, in a not-unusual revenge plot for the murder of a policeman and two other whites, a 'hunt' for the Indigenous culprits was accompanied by a massacre of possibly 150 people in 1892, and the longer-term total destruction of their culture.[42]

"By the early twentieth century, the Flying Foam Massacre was increasingly remembered as an example of a handful of exposed settlers who had no alternative but to resort to violence in order to assert their possession of the land," writes McKenna. Indigenous people were given a lesson they would not soon forget, while violence and intimidation were seen as "essential components of the white man's civilising influence".

The settlers saw themselves as victims, and the wealthy pastoralists and pearlers who made their fortune while profiting from silencing the natives became pillars of Perth society.[43] Similar violence and intimidation have been essential tools in the colonial relationship with wildlife too.

In Perth in 1886, Anglican missionary Thomas Gribble published *Dark Deeds in a Sunny Land*, documenting many examples of settler brutality including the Flying Foam Massacre. Gribble was run out of town, disowned by the church hierarchy, the government and the conservative press (who painted the settlers, the pearlers and their patrons as the victims), and ended up penniless after losing a libel case. His courage, and that of many others, was said to have influenced the British government to make some concessions and not cede responsibility for Aboriginal affairs to that colonial society.[44]

Wildlife defenders, like Thomas Gribble in 1886, are painted as the community's hostile fringe minority. There are many who think differently amongst rural communities and on farms, who are true conservationists and love native animals and flora, but they frequently self-censor. Many say, and have told me, that they fear to speak out against neighbouring wildlife shooting or tree removal, or to assert their different ideas. Here lies the companion issue of enforced cultural conformity.

For example, Queensland pastoral landholders who retain native vegetation testified to a news reporter in 2018 that they are vilified by their neighbours for not conforming and cutting down enough native trees to match others around them. "Within the 30 years that we have not cleared, they went from saying 'You don't understand' to 'You have to do it' to 'You don't want to clear? What's wrong with you?'" said one woman whose family has long run cattle on a property in central Queensland with good results, and who now claims her neighbours hate them.

Another woman landholder (the gender bias here is not unusual in my research), told the reporter that her defence of the value of trees had led to neighbours stealing stock and shooting her dogs. "There is still a huge cultural thing about the male conquering everything," she said – remaining linked, it seems, to the colonial imperatives to clear and kill.[45]

Closer to the city, a still-not-unusual story of some people's demands for a conforming view of the countryside was told to me by writer and former publishing professional Peter Hylands, who for 40 years with his artist/photographer wife Andrea owned a historic house on an old goldfields subdivision block within the boundaries of what became a Victorian state park. They were eventually driven out.

Arriving in Australia as 20-year-olds, the Hylands did not come equipped with traditional ideas about the natural environment. Across the years they appreciated their wildlife, planted trees, and saw a rich biodiversity return to their block. But they say they were tormented by people who liked access to the nearby public land for unregulated activities and who did not like conservationists – 'outsiders' with different ideas. The local police and council provided no help.

"It does not take a lot of bad people to make life a misery, particularly when the goal posts shift endlessly and governments and police justify or just make excuses," Peter told me.

To this day, the themes of valiant country battlers versus 'them', the unenlightened city conservationists, flavour much of the media reporting on the grievances of farmers and business. The colonial land takeover way of thinking has endured and has narrowed to a battle front with what remains of the country's wildlife. A popular frame still amplified by media in 2020 pleads the case of the embattled rural landholders, mainstays of 'our' agricultural export economy, up against intolerable challenges to economic well-being from the weather and from native grazers that in their view compete for the grass or native predators that might threaten sheep.

In Australia in 2019–20, the dingo, the kangaroo and the emu were facing an escalated application of shooting, poisoning and cluster fencing, particularly in the eastern states. The traditional rhetoric continued against 'them,' those 'pests.' Extended drought has been the backdrop, doing its own deadly work across cattle and sheep properties in Queensland and NSW. I visited central Queensland and got this picture first-hand, detailed in a later chapter. The carnage in Queensland set the model for the again-escalating war on wildlife in NSW.

'THE ENVIRONMENT' STARTS BEYOND THE PROPERTY LINE

As a result of these beginnings and property rights, an enduring belief in Australia and other post-colonial cultures is that 'the environment' starts somewhere beyond the property boundary, and that no one should be able to tell a landholder how to manage the flora and fauna on his/her land (apart from certain neighbours apparently). Often overlooked is the sheer extent of back-to-back and fenced-off private property harbouring much of the nation's remaining biodiversity and wildlife.

Twentieth century environmental laws were gradually established to represent the broader public interest in protecting the environment – land, water and habitat. But in Australia, environmental laws are weak and fragmented between the states and the federal government, with most of the power to do good or harm resting with the states, and the federal government's main levers being some control over exports, water and endangered species protection. Even these legal gains have come under increasing attack from conservative governments and their ideological supporters – rural landholders, industry groups, and think tanks pushing libertarian, small government blueprints.

Land clearing has re-emerged as a crucible for this tension between embedded ideas of private property and the greater public interest, and governments' uneasy sway over both. Land clearing also delivers wildlife habitat destruction and destroys a major sink for greenhouse gases to combat global warming and climate change.[46]

Libertarian, property-rights radicals have made headlines in Australia in recent years (as in the US). Australian examples include a NSW sheep grazier, Peter Spencer, whose 2010 stunt of spending 52 days suspended on a 15-metre-high platform was protesting his inability to do whatever he wanted on his property due to regulations protecting native vegetation and prohibiting certain land clearing activities.

In 2014, farmer Ian Turnbull fatally shot environmental compliance officer Glendon Turner in the course of a running dispute with the NSW government's Office of Environment and Heritage over the Turnbull family's land clearing, deemed illegal, in the north of the state. While the aged Turnbull was incarcerated and then died of natural causes, his property rights point of view won out with the state government.

In 2017, Glendon Turner's widow and family were again in the news to protest, in their husband and fathers' memory, actions by the NSW government to join Queensland and 'reform' previous state protections against clearing native vegetation on private property.

Heeding expanding corporate cropping enterprises that need big stretches of level, treeless land, in 2016 and 2017 the Liberal–National Party Coalition in NSW overturned protections and rules against land clearing gained through the *Native Vegetation Act 2003*, a Labor Party legacy. With much of the state cleared long ago, the new laws promised further native vegetation fragmentation with biodiversity 'offsets,' somewhere, in a sea of fenced, 'improved' production land on the most nutritious habitat. The same had happened in Queensland a decade earlier. Topsoil blowing away and dust storms were only the most visible impacts.

Until a change of state government from the Liberal–National Party to Labor in 2015 eventually slowed it, Queensland alone rocketed Australia to the top tier of countries clearing vegetation globally, with a related climb in greenhouse gas emissions domestically – while cancelling out any benefit from the federal government's tree planting program as a remedy for climate change.*[47]

In NSW, tree-clearing also rose 800 percent within a couple of years of changed regulation 'reforms' from 2016.[48] The government narrative pushing the NSW tree-clearing changes did not shy away from propaganda and disinformation. Said Western Sydney University economist Neil Perry in a piece for *The Conversation*:

"The [NSW] government's argument for taking this approach is that the current system 'doesn't deliver'. This is simply not true … A 2009 review of the Native Vegetation Act (NVA) stated that from 2006–2008 the legislation led directly to the conservation or rehabilitation of 250,000 hectares.[49]

"If the aim is to conserve biodiversity and deliver ecologically sustainable development, the NVA certainly has delivered. Of course, the NVA may not be delivering maximum short-term economic gains for some farmers and large agribusiness firms, but that is another matter."[50]

---

* In one year, 2015–16, 400,000 hectares of bushland was cleared in Queensland, tripling the rate since 2010. The federal government's 20 million trees program, at a cost to taxpayers of $50 million, was supposed to replace 20 million trees by 2020 to redress some of the damage from past land clearing. But Queensland researchers reported that "just one year of increased land clearing in Queensland has already removed many more trees than will be painstakingly planted during the entire program."

The government deregulation 'reforms' (politicians always call their changes 'reforms') rely on the good intentions and ecological and landscape knowledge of individual landholders and corporations. The 'reformed' legislation put in place do-it-yourself assessments of economic and environmental values of a property and whether actions remove necessary habitat or endanger vulnerable species. Here were all the hallmarks of colonial private-property thinking, dropping newer values of public interest in retaining vegetation and habitat that had made some gains.

One farmer told a reporter from *The Sydney Morning Herald:* "The thing that won't work is self-assessment ... Ecosystems and agriculture management are complex. I haven't seen anyone put those together without technical assistance." In the same report, Tamworth beef grazier Brian Tomalin went to the heart of the matter when he noted that the rejection by many farmers of the native vegetation rules "was a philosophical objection to the government telling them what to do" on their private property, an approach that extended to other areas of environmental law, including water. But "there's nothing unique about farming that you don't have to abide by community standards," Tomalin added.

In NSW, Freedom of Information material obtained in 2018 by conservation groups and environmental lawyers show a Liberal Party state leadership in a tight pre-electoral framework pandering to their coalition colleagues in the National Party that represents the traditional rural vote.

Having handed the National Party the reins of land, water, forest and wildlife management/removal, the internal horse-trading further led to a tick-a-box approach by the Liberal environment minister on native vegetation laws. This had immediate consequences of further endangering dwindling koala populations in NSW among other ill effects.[51]

In August 2018, rule changes engineered by the same National

Party politicians unleashed an open killing season on kangaroos on private land, big and small in NSW, aided by recreational shooters, as I described earlier. If further evidence was needed, here was a bloody reminder of the party's cynical appeal to the most traditional rural voters in the lead-up to a state election.

Easing 'red tape' for farmers, translated as no monitoring or oversight, was the catchcry for this lethal program, as it has been for the reversal on vegetation clearance, the very public interest responsibility that environment officer Glendon Turner died defending.

MOVING BACKWARDS WITH THE NATIONAL PARTY

The political voice that has long claimed to represent primary producers, rural business, and regional voters is the National Party of Australia. The party has wielded unrepresentative influence on the management of natural features in Australian states for a very long time.

Founded in 1920 as the Australian Country Party, the positive goal was the equitable distribution between city and country of tax income and infrastructure. The party also branded itself as the upholder of traditional land management and family values – although a series of recent hypocritical sex scandals has tarnished the latter claim. The Country Party, morphing into the National Party, found political influence by becoming the coalition partner of the dominant Tory party that opposes the Labor Party, the mostly centre-to-right-wing Liberal Party.

These days the Nationals draw less than seven percent of the country-wide vote by themselves, although they can attract twice that in NSW and Queensland state politics in coalition. Despite this unrepresentative vote, they wield great power over the natural environment as part of their coalition with the Liberal Party that hands them the natural resource portfolios.

The Nationals claim to uphold traditional values, the pre-eminence of the agricultural sector, and private property rights. That translates to a rhetoric of not caring, really, about the public interest in nature conservation or environmental protections – or the risks of greenhouse gas emissions and global warming. Those are 'greenie' values that country people reject, according to this narrative. (Where it suits them to care, the Nationals do come out against coal mining or gas fracking on farmland.)

The culture wars of this 'us and them' narrative declared against environmentally-minded citizens and scientists helped immobilise the country on climate change action since the 1990s. The winner has been the status quo: developers of fossil fuels and the boosters of traditional export agriculture.[52]

I found a sterling example of how traditional ideas endure and become embedded in politics and culture, with the case of Joh Bjelke-Petersen. Private land clearing, fencing and development were alive and well in Queensland in 1968 when Bjelke-Petersen became premier. Then the leader of the state Country Party (before it became the National Party), he took the reins for 19 years as premier.

His tenure built on Australia's tradition as a quarry for multi-national corporations aided by extensive infrastructure development by government. The historical continuity from colonial thinking was very apparent on his watch – which only ended because of controversies about widespread police corruption.

Bjelke-Petersen, raised in rural poverty, made his fortune by clearing land. He was one of the first contractors to push over the brigalow vegetation with large bulldozers for more grazing area.[53] The classic confluence of Christian beliefs about a man's place on earth (one biographer claimed Bjelke-Petersen believed he was appointed by God to save Australia from socialism) with ideas about progress, improvement, and the right to get rich were transparent during his tenure.[54]

The premier's longevity was aided by a tradition in Queensland to gerrymander electoral boundaries in favour of country voters represented by conservative politicians. Not coincidentally then, winning country marginal seats in Queensland is a dominant theme for federal politicians of both major parties, chaining them to support for traditional resource development, whether agriculture or mining.

The culture is not confined to Queensland or exclusively to the National Party. Beliefs and values stemming from two centuries of private property rights thinking set the legal and public administration frameworks that dictate what happens to the natural environment in almost every state decision. Short-term profit for property owners and commercial interests regularly trump the public interest across the land. Whether the issue is city sprawl development or tearing down a healthy and rare box gum woodland reserve (and its native animal inhabitants) for two coal mines, as happened in NSW in the 2000s, the system favours development. The coal mines went ahead, even while the economics of one mine made no sense in the marketplace.[55]

Joh Bjelke-Petersen embodied the post-colonial power of tradition. Continent-wide habitat loss suffered by all species, high extinction rates, and deliberate extermination, as I was learning, have been a hallmark of Australian agriculture and development since 1788. Underlying it all is the blanketing of Australia with private property rights. Today's citizens have been left with an artificial distribution of remaining native species, and more myths than good science and solutions about how to co-exist.

MYTHS AND MIGHT OF AN INDUSTRIALISED EXPORT BUSINESS

When I was growing up in the Snowy Mountains, the daughter of post-war immigrants, a favoured teen reading genre was about the life and times of young ladies who grew up in the bush, went to boarding school, and came home in the holidays to 'the station,' featuring lovely old colonial houses surrounded by European gardens and orchards. There would be the faithful horse for a wild gallop across open paddocks, a bit of mustering, or more sedate summer rides along the river, and picnics with country neighbours. White neighbours, of course. Stories often accompanied by a mystery to solve, or romance to consider. This sounded like an enviable lifestyle to me, and probably was. A generation of post-war girls may have grown up horse-crazy as a result. But this idyllic picture is framed by a whole set of cultural assumptions and aspirations.

Back in 1976, social analyst Donald Horne drew a persuasive history of the elite role of the farmer and grazier in the Australian national self-image, building on the initial land rush and 'improvements' for the export wool industry. The families that successfully made a go of this, for longer or shorter time, were elevated to high status in the cultural landscape, and what they did was seen as unmitigated good. Sitting on extensive land added commensurate credibility and influence.

Horne describes how from the mid-1900s on, to facilitate exports, the 'primary producer' (as farmers and graziers came to be called) enjoyed "proper development" with the aid of public works, subsidies, bounties, tax concessions, slogans, commodity pools and marketing schemes. "Exports seemed so important that to raise questions of economic rationality could seem seditious. And there tended to be no distinction between subsidizing exports and subsidizing farmers."[56] Since that time, 'primary producer' has come to include multi-national and corporate agribusinesses that have exercised a new round of extreme pressure on Australia's soil, water flora, and fauna.

Exploiting soil, water, forest and wildlife, and later geological wealth, enjoyed further government support with research and education, government pest control, cheap land and credit, immi-grant labour, public works and government sponsored marketing and protections. "Australia was being run as an industrialised export business," concluded Horne.

Over time, the elite, hereditary landholder became mainly a cultural idea and aspiration, but one with enduring influence on the national discourse and culture – significantly on how to think and conform in regard to the natural world. That entrepreneurs with city fortunes still feel the need to add the profile of country squire attests to this attraction, or possibly to the tax benefits attached to farm production.

Against this background and stoked by the political clout of the National Party, federal and state Australian governments still consider it their job in the 21st century to internationally promote the private, industrial-scale kangaroo killing business. Similarly, politicians and bureaucracies have favoured export cotton growers over the needs of native fish, other wildlife, and river communities.

In January 2019, a drought year, a natural catastrophe mesmer-ised the nation. It capped decades of misjudgement of a natural ecosystem and vital waterway in the world's second-driest conti-nent. Australians were handed chapter and verse on the impacts of harnessing Australia's most important inland waterways to short-term export success.

EXPORT THE LIFE-GIVING WATER

Images of crying fishermen holding asphyxiated Murray cod lit up television screens. It was reported that a major arterial of the Murray–Darling Basin, the iconic Darling River, was so low on water and so loaded with algae that increased summer heat was causing it to lose its oxygen supply. More than a million fish washed up dead. There would be several more mass fish kills in following weeks. Some Murray cod had managed until then to live for 70–80 years, surviving earlier droughts.[57]

As with their federal counterparts, responsibility for water and inland rivers was handed to the state National Party by their bigger coalition partners once in power. In the National's hands, water was moved to the departments of Primary Industries and Agriculture at state and federal levels. In NSW, every natural resource was run by the portfolio of Primary Industries, whose brief is to continue supporting rural export industries.

In the over-extended Darling catchments, irrigated cotton growers with vast fields and massive storages were supported by sympathetic bureaucrats and politicians who granted them very generous, legal, water extraction deals. The government denied dealing in favouritism.

Several big cotton irrigators were able to purchase water licenses that allow a business to take 300 percent of their legal allocation in one year regardless of river flow. Illegal pumping and theft of taxpayer-purchased water, bought back for the environment, were other strategies of some big cropping operations. The Australian public were alerted to this in July 2017 with a major ABC *Four Corners* investigation *(Pumped)*. The program uncovered bureaucratic corruption linked to favoured treatment of some irrigators in NSW.

RIVER FLOW EXPORTED AS COTTON WITH WILDLIFE IMPACTS

"Water diversions have disrupted the natural balance of wetlands that support massive ecosystems," wrote Fran Sheldon, professor at the Australian Rivers Institute, Griffith University, in the wake of the fish kill report. "Unless we allow flows to resume, we're in danger of seeing one of the worst environmental catastrophes in Australia." She added that state and federal governments had been warned since the 1990s about mismanagement of the river and its wetlands flow system. She compared the Australian reckless or ignorant diversions for corporate agriculture to the drying out of the Aral Sea in central Asia.

What ecosystems? The Darling River is a so-called 'dryland river' which naturally has periods of low flows complemented by periodic high flows. Most of its water is held within a vast network of wetlands and floodplain channels. Both are semi-arid. More worryingly, explained Sheldon, both have had more the 50 percent of their average inflows extracted for irrigation.

She reported that the river's low and medium flow events have disappeared into artificial water storages for irrigation – some likened to the size of Sydney Harbour – drying the wetlands and the floodplains at the end of the tributaries that would normally sustain the natural environment, its native plants and animals, and also river communities.[58]

All the main tributaries of the Darling River have floodplain wetland complexes in their lower reaches (such as the Gwydir Wetlands, Macquarie Marshes, and Narran Lakes). When the rivers flow they absorb the water from upstream, before releasing water downstream to the next wetland complex, the wetlands acting like a series of tipping buckets. Regular river flows are essential for these sponge-like wetlands.

The wildlife along the river, ranging from river mussels to fish, birds to marsupials, cannot cope with the artificially changed conditions – particularly a dry river, minus its deep pools and channels that allowed those old Murray cod to survive previous droughts.

Extended drying out of the wetlands threatens the death of bird breeding colonies and habitat for other native animals and wetland plants. I had the privilege to visit and document the Gwydir Wetlands and the Macquarie Marshes in the 1990s for a documentary film. The wetlands are a haven for waterbird family life – ibis, heron, spoonbill, ducks and waders in great numbers. Sights and sounds few get to witness in a lifetime. (An unexpectedly wet year following the most recent drought brought some life back to the wetlands).

Charges of mismanagement, corruption, and not heeding repeated warnings have been levelled at the NSW and federal governments, their National Party ministers for water, and the federal agency charged with administering water in the system, the Murray–Darling Basin Commission. The Commission oversaw a political balancing act meant to craft a fair deal between the needs of environment, community and commercial sectors. The political horse trading, spurred by angry irrigators, sowed the seeds of the most recent disaster on the river.

In this saga too, 'the environment' is always framed as an outside entity, something beyond the farm or town fence, something whose needs can be negotiated and whittled and stolen away, rather than the basis on which the whole enterprise rests. The crash was inevitable.

A tilt to a water market made things worse – it took away the frame of a non-negotiable asset underpinning local survival. Thus, the Menindee Lakes outside Broken Hill, fed by the Darling and offering significant fish breeding grounds as well as town water, were deliberately "decommissioned" or allowed to dry out as "inefficient" and prone to evaporation. The water was sold elsewhere.

"The new on-farm dams that have been built upstream in northern NSW and southern Queensland by cotton growers in the home country of the former and current [federal] water ministers Barnaby Joyce and David Littleproud, are much, much bigger and deeper," wrote regional author Helen Vivian with some irony a year before the fish kills, reviewing the river's problems including water market fraud under National Party management. Taxpayers would foot the bill for a new mega pipeline from the Murray River to Broken Hill to compensate for Menindee water loss.[59]

A quote used by Vivian from *The Australian* newspaper, not a big friend of environmentalists, had then federal Water Minister Barnaby Joyce indicating that letting the Menindee Lakes dry out by starving them of water "was a much better alternative than having to withdraw water entitlements from large cotton producers like Chinese-owned Cubbie Station, the biggest user of water in Australia".[60]

Cubbie Station, because of its size and provenance, is almost a national byword for big cotton. In 2019 it was still a joint venture of an Australian property management company and Chinese textile industry investors. It is said to be the biggest farm in the southern hemisphere, amalgamating twelve floodplain properties for a total of 51 licences. Its Queensland storages stretch for more than 28 kilometres along the Culgoa River that feeds the Barwon. The present ownership bought it in 2012, despite the previous owners going into receivership after spending more than $300 million and enduring a five-year dry spell. Both major political parties supported the sale.[61]

Ninety percent of the cotton grown in Australia is exported South Australian federal senator Rex Patrick told the parliament in February 2019. Cotton, he said, is just a recent example of mining the country for exports, this time on a very unsuitable river system, even if the dry climate is suitable. He reminded the parliament that export activity is actually under the control of the federal government and does not need agreement between states and territories. He called for a ban on cotton exports in a couple of years, noting: "About 20 percent of the basin water goes to cotton. It's like exporting 20 percent of the Murray–Darling to China and India. It's not in the national interest: it goes to food security and the environment."[62]

He suggested that cotton growing where appropriate could be directed to a domestic market, with the aim of value adding with processing. Such ideas turned out to be a red flag to a bull. The reported response was typical of both the language and the thinking that has long driven the untouchability of export commodities, whether cotton or kangaroos. The chief executive of Cotton Australia, Adam Kay, called Patrick's proposal "a reckless attack on rural communities and hardworking Australian farmers. If cotton was to be banned in Australia, farmers would use their water to grow the next most profitable crop," he said.[63]

FINAL LOSS OF COUNTRY, CULTURE

The dying river reports got worse as the weeks passed. It was like reading reports from a war zone – a war against the environment and everything that had previously lived within it. By mid-January 2019, there had been three major fish death events. One report zoomed in on the Namoi and Barwon Rivers around Walgett in north-central NSW. These feeder rivers of the Darling – the Narran, the Namoi and the Barwon – were dry or reduced to a series of green, stagnant weir pools. The fish they supported were dead and gone, as certainly as those in the lower Darling. Nearby Ramsar-listed Narran Lakes and wetlands were empty, with breeding grounds of native birds and fish dried-out.

The town itself had run out of river water and was on life support bore/ground water. Images of big river red gums showed them leaning off banks with their roots exposed, figuratively gasping.

The local Indigenous elders talked to a couple of reporters. They lamented the drying of the rivers and the ruin of what the waterways have supported ecologically and culturally. This has never happened before, they said. They named the culprits: greed and water diversion, tree clearing, drought, and climate change. Reporter Lorena Allam and photographer Carly Earl documented their story for *Guardian Australia*, with the ambient temperature hitting 49 degrees celsius.[64]

In Lightning Ridge, Rhonda Ashby teaches Gamilaraay language at the school. She was born and raised in Walgett on the banks of the Barwon. She said she has no words for the sadness she feels:

"I remember those rivers being crystal clear. As kids we used to dive for mussels and throw them back up the bank to cook and eat.

"The river has a responsibility not just to us, but to plants and animals. It has a right to connect up to other waters. It's the bloodline of this country. It's like us: if our blood stops flowing, we get sick. The water, if that flow stops, we all become sick."

Brenda McBride is a senior Gamilaraay-Yuwalaraay woman who cares for an area of birthing trees near the Narran River, where reporter Lorena Allam says her own grandmother was born. The babies were immediately introduced to the river. But there is no river now. The water, McBride knew, is held in massive dams upstream by irrigators, miners and pastoralists, including the huge Cubbie Station.

"Where is our water?" continued McBride. "For our totems – you're the turtle, I'm the *dhinawan*, the emu. That's a part of you, gone. Everyone's pulling the water out, so it's just not coming here. With land clearing we get dust storms every week. It just breaks your heart."

"This to me is the ultimate destruction of our culture," Gamilaraay elder Virginia Robinson told the reporters, sitting with the Dhariwaa Elders group in Walgett. "All people think about now is there's no water. Aboriginal people were very close to nature and that's all unbalanced now. There's no nature to go back to. We've got no water, no special places to go, no animals to hunt. Our totem animals are dead, their bones are everywhere."

DARLING BASIN DREAMS

Two British educators also supplied context: "The Darling River Basin had been occupied by Aborigines for 30,000 years before the new white colonists pushed their way over the mountains and into the outback. For the clans that inhabited the Basin, the Darling was mapped out in stories and songs that described the rivers and the countryside. For the Europeans, the geography of the Basin was a perplexing jigsaw puzzle that took over fifty years to complete … [But they coveted] a promised land of lush pastures, rich soils and park-like woodlands."[65]

CARING, MEET
THE MACROPODS

"I reflected on my experience with the joey: the way it held its arms out to me to be picked up just like a human baby would; the way it looked up at me seeking love and reassurance; the way it nestled into my body and went to sleep ..."

— CHRIS 'BROLGA' BARNES RECOUNTING HIS INTRODUCTION TO
RESCUING BABY KANGAROOS IN 2013 BOOK *KANGAROO DUNDEE*

Photo: Maria Taylor

The other day I was again stopped in my tracks as I observed an adult Grey kangaroo effortlessly clearing a 4-foot (1.2-metre) fence in my neighbourhood. Wildlife rescuer Dr Rosemary Austen told me that a large male apparently cleared a 6.6-foot (2-metre) fence at their animal recovery centre. The approach might be side-on, not unlike a human competitive high-jumper.

Of the pouched mammals called marsupials, six large kangaroo species and seven species of wallaby are closely related and share the genus name *Macropus*, derived from ancient Greek for 'long foot'. That includes the Red kangaroo, the Eastern and Western Greys and the Wallaroo/Euro that are the target of the commercial hunt. (The Antilopine kangaroo and the Bernard's Wallaroo in the northern tropics are not commercially hunted).

The outstanding evolutionary success of *Macropus* in a change-able and often harsh environment over millions of years has been attributed to three traits: they ferment grass in the foregut before the contents are released for further digestion and thus hold food for longer and recycle components of metabolism; they hop; and they have an economical pattern of reproduction.[1]

While a similar foregut digestion pattern characterises sheep, cattle, and camels, kangaroos are able to utilise much poorer vege-tation with low nitrogen content and Wallaroos/Euros can survive without drinking much water because of their unique metabolic processes. Kangaroos also have a lower metabolic rate than same-sized introduced mammals, meaning their energy requirements are less.[2]

There is an oft-misunderstood comparison between sheep and kangaroos and their impact on grazing land. Research has shown kangaroos use less feed to maintain energy individually and in aggregate than the same number of wool sheep, let alone meat sheep or goats. Under normal circumstances, sheep and kangaroos have been shown to prefer different plants, and unlike sheep – or unless confined by modern circumstances – kangaroos know when to stop eating, move on, and protect their resource.

A UNIQUE AUSTRALIAN

The distinctive athleticism, speed and energy efficiency shown by the large kangaroos is on display with movement across the countryside – movement that has awed those who appreciate the unique, from tourists to advertising agencies.

The advantage of hopping as a means of locomotion was discovered in 1973 by Australian biologists Terence Dawson and Richard Taylor. Dawson has studied kangaroos for 50 years through the University of NSW and its Arid Zone Research Station at Fowler's Gap. He poured this knowledge into the seminal book *Kangaroos*, which tells the reader most of what they might want to know about kangaroo physiology, social relations, and unique adaptive features to the Australian environment.

Here I learned that the earliest ancestors of kangaroos are likely to have branched off from a small tree-dwelling possum-like marsupial sometime after 55 million years ago when the known fossil record for marsupials starts. How and when hopping evolved is still uncertain, but the advantages are better described. Hopping, writes Dawson, is an extension of the gallop to achieve higher speeds. One might imagine a highly energetic possum doing this on the ground to avoid predators.[3]

The fossil evidence indicates the macropod ancestors of today's species appeared somewhere between 12 and 28 million years ago. The kangaroo types we see today have their origins at least a million years ago, says zoologist David Croft.[4]

Kangaroos attain optimal energy use at higher speeds. At 22 kilometres per hour, hopping provides substantial benefits, using about 25 percent less energy than that measured for a dog running at the same speed. At 40 kilometres per hour, the gap could widen further to 50 percent energy use compared to a four-footed mammal. "This energy efficiency, together with structural specialisations, allows kangaroos to go even faster. If given time to get moving they can out-speed quadrupedal predators such as dingos."[5]

In a country where the weather has long been boom and bust, economy of movement allows kangaroo mobs to travel rapidly for relatively large distances, like 25 kilometres, to the next ephemeral rainfall and better food. This is particularly an adaptive advantage for arid range species including the Red kangaroo, but it is also a reason they have been demonised as descending in 'plague proportions.'

"Kangaroos are really special mammals," says Dawson. "Work over the past half century has turned the notion that they belong to an inefficient, primitive group of mammals totally on its head." Together with American and Canadian scientists, he identified another handy adaptive feature: the use by the kangaroos of their tail as a "fifth leg" for forward momentum while grazing, which they do much of the time.[6]

As with much previous work, this discovery also relied on study of the heavily hunted Red kangaroo – the largest of the remaining kangaroo species. Published in 2014, the finding was that when grazing, these large macropods move both hind feet forward as a pair while the tail is more than a resting point. It releases movement energy just like a leg would. The researchers established that the muscles in the tail as well as in the hind legs are highly aerobic, with a lot of mitochondria – the power houses in cells that provide energy.

Zoologist David Croft, who across decades straddled the divide between academic and advocate, and also conducted research through the University of NSW and its Arid Zone Research Station at Fowler's Gap, thinks we would do well to emulate the kangaroo and call ourselves 'a kangaroo' with pride in this country.

He wrote that, "if we did, we would be celebrating diversity, the successful occupation of most of Australia's terrestrial ecosystems, resilience to our climatic extremes, athleticism, careful conservation of energy and water needs, and individualism in a rich social life". Croft also encouraged Australians to learn from the Aboriginal peoples that we are part of the land, and with the kangaroo, re-establish our relationship to it.[7]

ROLE OF NATIVE GRAZERS: VITAL FOR ECOSYSTEMS

If you go looking for studies on the ecological roles of native grazers, as I have, you will come up short, because there is hardly any literature. This lack is allied with the wildlife management focus and funding aimed at studies to benefit commercial interests, particularly for the pastoral industry since colonial times.

Macropod biologist Dan Ramp, who co-founded the Centre for Compassionate Conservation at the University of Technology Sydney, has given some thought to the ecological value of macropods and common species of marsupials in general. He provided independent information to the administrative appeals tribunals in Canberra, Australian Capital Territory, and to officials in that jurisdiction, where kangaroos are killed annually on city reserves and on pastoral leases administered by the ACT – to little avail. Instead, the ACT doubled down, with a novel ecological argument for its killing program. More on that in a later chapter.

Ramp starts from a basic point – healthy ecosystem function is intertwined with the species that evolved with that ecosystem. For native grasses and grassy woodlands, that includes native herbivores. He highlights the importance of remaining native herbivores (common kangaroos, wallabies, wombats) as key species in grassland ecosystems. They have a role in maintaining environments beneficial to other species, like grassland insects and reptiles. Mostly overlooked is their key role in keeping ecosystems functioning when other rarer or endangered grassland/woodland animals drop out.

"Native herbivores, such as kangaroos and wombats, play a vital role in ecosystems," he notes. "They can play key roles in conferring short-term resistance to reductions in ecosystem functions, as rare and uncommon species are lost from the system. We now have entered earth's sixth mass extinction event, this time human driven. The setting aside of protected areas may not be sufficient to prevent loss of biodiversity."[8]

Kangaroos can be regenerators of native grasses in a number of ways. Their movements and activities across the ground can disperse and bury grass and other seeds. As nutrient recyclers, their urine and faeces are well-matched natural fertilisers. Their role in grassland regeneration, with seed dispersal after drought and fire, evolved with the continental ecosystems. Unlike intro-duced livestock, kangaroos do not disturb or pull up root systems, and therefore grasslands regenerate quickly. Kangaroos are also soft-footed, and don't compact the soil or cause erosion, both of which impacts damage native plant ecosystems.

Historical records show that kangaroos were plentiful in the grasslands and woodland ecosystems the settlers found. Kangaroo home ranges tend to be areas that offer shelter near some food source.[9] Europeans in the longer term did not improve habitat beyond a short-term flush of grass after clearing. Dams and stock water points were established, but natural water courses were being silted up and the riparian zone eroded by introduced stock.

A lot of argument and mythology in Australia claims that kanga-roos breed in 'uncontrollable' and intolerable numbers, requiring lethal management. The public is left with the impression that the kangaroo species, where the female may have one joey a year and infant mortality is high, somehow matches pigs, goats, dogs and cats, some of which produce litters of up to 10 every year.

There is research showing that kangaroo populations are naturally stable over time. Dan Ramp was part of a team that conducted a seminal study at Yan Yean reserve in Victoria at the end of the 1990s. That study, in a confined area where the researcher had access to historical data, took place in a temperate grassland ecosystem with Eastern Grey kangaroos minus natural predators or road-kill possibility. The kangaroo population reached equilibrium and stayed stably self-regulating over a 50-year period.[10]

Anecdotal stories I learned from Canberra suburban householders told how they lived with neighbourhood kangaroo mobs for 20–30 years, called them friends, and observed stable numbers overall – until recently, when the government came to kill them.

WHAT THREATENS NATIVE GRASSLANDS?
START WITH INVASIVE WEEDS

In July 2013 I reported on biodiversity in the Queanbeyan Nature Reserve bordering Canberra. By this time, kangaroos in the ACT were suddenly being painted in government press releases as a threat to various endangered species, including the Grassland Earless Dragon. In the Queanbeyan reserve, where no culling took place, three of Australia's most endangered species were recovering or maintaining their populations following a drought that hit the area five years earlier.

One was the Earless Dragon whose population count had dropped from 50 to nil during the drought. But by 2013 the little lizards were recolonising the reserve. The other two endangered species there were the Golden Sun moth and the daisy-like Button Wrinklewort.

The NSW government ecologist based in Queanbeyan said that habitat conditions – dryness, for example – were the operative influences on the presence of these species. The scientific view here was that sympathetic grazing by unregulated native grazers or modest stock numbers was a natural sequence, keeping the country open with varied grass heights. In turn, these created shelter for other species. The patchwork pattern retained soil moisture and encouraged insects – food for the dragon, for example.

Grassland grazed by unconfined kangaroos retained tall tussocks, which disappeared with heavy stock grazing. In similar fashion, a 2012 national recovery plan for the Button Wrinklewort lauded kangaroo grazing for keeping the landscape open for this native plant. Domestic stock will eat this plant but kangaroos don't. The Golden Sun moths were also doing well in a grazed, diverse plant community.

Weeds, according to the ecologist and to recovery plans, are far more of a threat to endangered grassland species than native grazers. Other threats are habitat fragmentation, agricultural practices, urban expansion, changed fire regimes, and predation by domestic and feral animals.[11]

Photo: Maria Taylor

"Kangaroos have a social life not unlike humans, with strong mother and joey ties, companions, relatives and the like. When continually shot, kangaroos fret for loved ones, [and are] forced to live their own lives in a state of spasmodic terror. Kangaroos can be and are horribly wounded, in pouch joeys are bludgeoned to death. The out of pouch joeys, all alone for the first time in their short lives, panic-stricken after witnessing the brutal death of their mothers, are left to die from starvation or hypothermia (or foxes). The survivors live in a state of constant fear with proper social order in constant disarray and upheaval," wrote former kangaroo shooter David Nicholls.[12]

There are a lot of kangaroos now in my neighbourhood on the fringes of Canberra, the national capital that kills the national emblem. The countryside is rural residential – a mix of hobby block farming, people who feed horses, and people who live in remnant bushland that escaped or has regrown from the clearing for sheep grazing 75 to 100 years ago. The grazing activity led to widespread land degradation on relatively poor soils.

In a nearby new subdivision I have seen 20 kangaroos on newly-laid turf in front of a house. Across the street another 20. More on other blocks. All land that used to be their home range. They have nowhere else to go while big landholders continue to shoot on adjoining properties. In addition, sometimes deadly fences, dogs, and motor vehicles are the main predators.

There have been times when discussing the research findings for this book that I was asked why people should care about the fate of animals that are regularly described as units of production or 'pests.' Good question, so I decided, in addition to sharing the unique qualities of kangaroos just described, to visit some caring experts in my region to pose that question and find out more.

Not far from where I live, Rosemary Austen and her partner Steve Garlick rescue or take in the injured victims of car, fence and malignant humans at their Possumwood Wildlife recovery and research property. More caring work is carried out by dedicated volunteer wildlife rescuers operating through an organisation called Wildcare in our area. At Possumwood, Dr Austen, a general medical practitioner and also credentialed microbiologist and zoologist, performs first responder emergency care. Then begins the challenging phase of long-term recovery care, which is not the easiest with wild animals.

At any one time, Possumwood has had 40–50 animals in residence, including kangaroos, wallabies, wombats, birds, and other road and fence casualties. Most recently: bushfire victims. They once helped an eagle recover. Across 15 years, several thousand animals have been helped and released.

Rosemary's partner Steve Garlick is a professor of economics and more recently has turned to research in animal behaviour and ethics. In the early 2000s he was a founder of the Animal Justice Party that now affords a political platform to animal issues in state and federal elections. Together they have written papers on the emotional lives of Australian native animals and their on-ground experience of post-traumatic stress disorder in these animals, as well as on trans-species learning.[13]

Their rescue work has demonstrated the close link between emotional stability and family and group structure for social animals like kangaroos. Indeed, Steve and Rosemary have seen that the will to live, exhibited by rescued joeys, depends on these social links. (Contrary to a common Australian myth that joeys, orphaned by human activity, are tough little nuggets that bound off into the sunset to live happily ever after.) Exhibiting symptoms of post-traumatic stress, as do humans – including inability to settle or relate, heightened anxiety and hypervigilance – rescued animals, and that includes domestic captives like pigs, need a de-stressing therapy routine and the opportunity of re-bonding with others, not always of the same species.[14]

Kangaroos, wombats, birds, little possums, and gliders that need emergency surgery end up in the clinic of another local legend – veterinarian Howard Ralph, a big man with hands to match, who performs the most intricate, seemingly miraculous repair work on small bodies. He's known as the vet who can or will fix a broken kangaroo leg where others can't or won't. I talked to both of them – at an earlier time for articles, and more recently to learn what they have learned from working so closely with animals that are commonly lumped together as undifferentiated units in populations needing management.

RARE RECOGNITION FOR SAVING WILDLIFE

At an Australia Day ceremony in 2016, where she was honoured as Bungendore Citizen of the year, Rosemary Austen told the audience that many regional residents have been terrific in their concern for wildlife, bringing hundreds of injured creatures to Possumwood, often in conjunction with Wildcare or the Native Animal Rescue Group.

She highlighted the health benefits of getting involved and volunteering somewhere. She praised fellow honourees the Bungendore Show workers, and admitted that she has allowed herself the time and pleasure to enter (and win) some flower arranging competitions at the annual show in early February.

Later, I sit down with Rosemary at a Bungendore café. A small woman with short-cut greying hair and an unflappable, sweet manner, Rosemary is everyone's favourite auntie, fronting an immense amount of professional training and physical stamina that she dedicates, along with Steve, to rescuing and releasing native animals. Most days she first puts in a full shift seeing human patients. At times she has ended her day by driving for two hours to a less populated release site to check on her kangaroo patients. There were many return journeys taking the animals there singly or in pairs in the first place.

Returning along a lonely country road at 1am, she said it's not unusual to pick up another patient hit and left there by a human behind the wheel. Like the wombat with the spinal injury who could not roll over. Rosemary stopped and checked her pouch, at which point "the dear little thing opened her eyes and looked at me in terror".

Nevertheless, a rescue had to be affected knowing that the wombat would either die of hypothermia or a fox would rip her open. So Rosemary rolled the big animal into a blanket, picked her up, and took her home for assessment and care or euthanasia. It wasn't easy work. She says ruefully that after 20 years of rescues, both she and Steve are not getting any younger. They are starting to notice the effort of picking up and carrying 30-kilogram-or-more kangaroos caught in fences or hit by cars, or wombats in this case. But that's still said as an aside.

We talk about her animal patients and their personalities. "Every animal, every kangaroo, wombat, possum, they all have different personalities," she says. "It's very prominent in the Eastern Greys because they are such emotional animals – they really do relate to humans.

"That's the sad thing because when they develop a bond with you, they love you, and it's such a shame they are treated so badly because they are an animal that develops a very strong bond. Wombats and wallabies once released tend to become wild. But the Eastern Greys, I've got animals down there [at the release site] like Lindsay who came in as a teenage kangaroo with a head injury, a broken arm, a fractured pelvis, she'll come up and give you a big cuddle. You call them and they'll come over and give you cuddles. It's just beautiful, I love it."

I note that while I'll provide a sanctuary, a supplementary feed and a friendly voice, I haven't progressed to physical contact. Rosemary admits that it's the carer role, often from infancy, that would lead to cuddles. "I'm like their mother."

Elaborating on the voice recognition, she tells me that at another release site she may not have visited for six months, "I'd just stand and call for 15 minutes and then I start seeing little heads popping up, and they'd stand and watch me and listen, and then eventually I'd have 30 animals around me".

She tells me a touching story from the neighbourhood that involved a very big male kangaroo who got caught in a fence. To gain release he almost ripped his ankle off. He was very incapacitated and became very agitated when any rescuers came near. "The lady from the property was so upset, she really loved this kangaroo. And he knew the voices of the family. When this lady talked to him, he calmed right down – totally different body language." She kept him calm as the decision was reached to euthanise him. "That family was devastated, it was very sad," she says.

WEEKLY TALLY OF TRAUMA INTERVENTION

Rosemary gave me a glimpse of the grim reality that Possumwood experiences on a regular basis.

"[In one week] we had a 60kg male motor vehicle accident at night; a very wild young male caught in wire; a hypothermic 2kg joey with bilateral tibia fractures [he had been lying in a paddock in heavy rain all day]; and a poor mother who had been shot in the face by a landholder on Bungendore Road.

"The wound was seething with maggots and she was blinded by the bullet as it exited the face. Her joey was still alive but emaciated and severely dehydrated. A similar case from the same area a couple of weeks ago presented a kangaroo with its jaw blown off – it died.

"The killer tells people he has tags [permission issued by the NSW National Parks and Wildlife Service] and it has been reported that he goes out at night on his quad bike and shoots anything he can find.

"[A fellow kangaroo defender] darted the mother and she seemed relaxed in our peaceful enclosure with the other kangaroos. Little Ian her joey required intensive fluid treatment and nutrition."

Rosemary tells me later that both mother and joey did not survive. Complaints to the National Parks entity that hands out shooting tags about the incompetent shooting went unanswered as did complaints to the animal welfare organisation RSPCA.

"Steve and I have done so many rescues over the past 15 years. Some of the rescues are difficult and dangerous but they are the easy part of the work we do. It is the care and treatment of the rescued animals which is time consuming and challenging. At least in my day job [as a general practitioner and locum for aged care facilities in Canberra] I don't have to catch my patients before I treat them!"

A SURGEON FOR ALL SPECIES

Howard Ralph, based nearby, has been indispensable to local wildlife carers and they all call him Howard. not 'Dr.' He goes where other veterinarians don't or won't go, and he has an awesome lifesaving track record. He is over six feet tall. His hands are commensurately large. It's hard not to marvel at how he does such delicate surgery on some pretty small or challenging anatomy.

One wildlife carer, who over the years had taken many wombats to Howard for treatment, recalled how he fixed the back leg of an eight-year-old Eastern Grey kangaroo that had hit something and dislocated her back leg. "It was completely facing the wrong way. Other vets would just have euthanised her, but Howard managed to pull the leg back into the socket, which wasn't easy, tighten up the ligaments which he then stitched up, and splinted and bandaged the leg."

Post-operative care often poses the biggest challenge. In this case it worked because 'Tinkerbell' was fairly habituated to humans and did not stress in confinement. Wild adult kangaroos are amongst the most challenging cases because of the need to restrict the patient in post-operative care and the stress that it causes. The operations Howard calls standard, but the post care is not, because kangaroos die of stress.

Very many of his patients are the victims of cars – with large numbers of broken kangaroo legs, broken tortoise shells, lizards with back injuries, baby wombats with run-over mothers. He has resuscitated a kangaroo in cardiac arrest. I saw a little possum that was picked up from a Sydney street with an ulcer on one paw (now covered by a big, white bandage), a bad skin rash, and liver damage.

All manner of birds are also brought in, like the tawny frogmouth that was completely paralysed. Howard treated him for several different infections of the brain and he recovered. The doctor does a lot of surgery on eye injuries and cataracts, because most wildlife cannot survive blind.

His admirers say he's never turned a person or an animal away. His clinic largely relies on a fund-raising charity and other donations, and the considerable support to the practice of his wife Glenda, who works as a physio and nurse (also both human and veterinary) in Braidwood and in Queanbeyan.

Howard's training as a paediatric anaesthetist came after he was already qualified in veterinary medicine. (He says part of the reason he got into human medicine is that he could then help out his elderly parents.) The infant anaesthetist training honed his skills in getting tubes down narrow and short throats that often present in wildlife work.

"He could have had an easy and wealthy life as an anaesthetist, but instead he's chosen this. He's saved thousands of lives," says one of a small cadre of dedicated volunteer assistants. The volunteer says the doctor now gets constant calls to give free veterinary advice to people from all over the country and even overseas.

'Mum' is a Bare-nosed ('common') wombat, resident at a sanctuary near Braidwood NSW.

WOMBAT BRAIN SURGERY

Asked to recount a recent challenging case, Howard tells of a wild-life carer who brought in a 2kg baby wombat which looked alright, but had a terrible smell coming from a small hole in its head. It was infected, and on examination related to a compound fracture of the skull which was starting to destroy the brain.

Several multi-hour skull operations were followed by a post-operative period just like a human case, with tubes and monitoring. The wombat survived and is now doing well.

Howard says he is busting the myth that wildlife cannot be treated successfully. He chose to dedicate himself to that arena after seeing the effects of the 2000 bushfires on the South Coast of NSW.

He later volunteered following floods in Queensland and after the Black Saturday bushfires in Victoria. Those had a horrific impact on wildlife (Swamp wallabies with their eyes burned out, faces burned off, and so forth) with very minimal help available.

Howard and Glenda's wildlife clinic is tucked away on an old farmstead dominated by remnant bushland, not far from Braidwood. As I arrive for a catchup interview on a Sunday morning, I encounter a man from somewhere north of Tamworth (an eight-hour drive of about 900 kilometres) who arrived with a joey suffering from fractures to both back legs due to car strike.

Glenda had warned me that the doctor was up until 4.30am the previous night performing surgery. Post-op care with a volunteer nurse was going on and Howard would not be with me for another 45 minutes. (Later he joked that the couple had lost all their friends because these unexpected emergencies were the pattern of their life.)

The three-hour operation on the young Eastern Grey kangaroo repaired the fractured tibia bones and undid some crooked healing that had already taken place. The patient had splints on both legs from hip to toe and was expected to make a rapid recovery back at the carer's place in northern NSW.

These days Howard is consulted by other veterinary surgeons and carers from around Australia. Despite increasing interest, there are still varying opinions amongst veterinary practitioners about the value of treating wildlife and also there is still a widespread lack of experience in dealing with the more complicated surgical cases – coming after many decades marked by the common practice to simply shoot badly-injured wildlife. The money is another issue. Howard's clinic is supported by fund-raising, by community volunteers, and by the work both he and Glenda do in human medicine. It's barely enough to cover the need. But most vets don't have such support – the government does not subsidise as for human medicines and they are expensive.

So it is not unusual for Howard to receive an unexpected patient from far away, as on this day, or from even further afield. That's in addition to the flow of local wombats in particular, or of kangaroos or other wildlife that have come off second-best tangling with humans and their machines or fences.

As he trains nurses and veterinary students, Howard thinks that there is a turning tide in Australia of better understanding and appreciation for the wildlife and what is being done to the animals. On the other hand, he has also received death threats and promises of violence. He sees enormous forces still arrayed on the side of traditional views and against defenders of wildlife.

DUCK HUNTING SEASON – WHAT'S HE DOING HERE?

Howard's been told on numerous occasions that he's wasting his time. For example, by duck hunters who enjoy blasting the fragile life flying overhead and don't appreciate the volunteers who try to help the wounded on the ground, notably in Victoria.

He has seen volunteers roughed up, taunted and threatened. It has also happened to him as he prepared to help critically-injured wildlife in the aftermath of horrific bushfires that destroy a lot more than human property. He's been pushed around by property owners who say the only concern has to be humans.

And criticism comes not only from frightened property owners and duck hunters. Howard often hears a familiar narrative from people who say they are environmentalists or scientifically trained. "People say to us, firstly what you're doing is a waste of time. Secondly, it doesn't consider the survival of threatened and endangered species. Both of those things are not true. And thirdly they say, from a biological perspective, we're not really interested in 'a' kangaroo, we're interested in a population.

"Well, we are interested in individuals, and guess what: individuals make up communities. Because our patients are part of a group, we feel protective for the species and its survival. We've taken over their environment, and then people say, there are 'too many'. Well, it's just because we've destroyed where they would naturally be."

What he wants to emphasise on this Sunday morning is his sadness at the disrespect shown by too many Australians to native fauna. That is particularly an attitude towards 'common' fauna like the wombat or the kangaroo species or the Brush-tail possum, let alone lizards, snakes and spiders. "All living things need to be treated with some dignity and respect, that is our guiding principle. Our charter is we will help any living creature at all who is in distress."

Howard has travelled widely and knows that in many places there is no wildlife left. He has hosted international veterinary practitioners and journalists. "You talk to people from other countries and they are always astounded at how disrespectful we are to our precious wildlife," he says, noting Australian domestic narratives about wildlife remain a hangover from the colonial days.

Many people have only a fuzzy or non-existent understanding of ecology, the web of life, and how plants, animals (including all the micro-organisms) and the landscape that we depend on, have co-evolved. There is just a bedrock belief that technology will save us regardless of what we do, he says.

WHAT ARE KANGAROOS LIKE PERSONALLY?

I ask Howard what is his experience with macropods, the kangaroos, on a personal, behavioural level? They are all different, he answers – physiology, behaviour, different age groups, and response to treatment or anaesthesia requiring different levels of sedation and post-operative care – which makes his work such a specialised field.

"They are all individuals, not just a furry opportunity to kill something. Talking about Eastern Grey kangaroos, being the ones that get the worst rap usually, they're lovely creatures in fact. They are quite endearing, very gentle in their behaviour. Just because some large male kangaroo that is protecting the mob gets cranky when people invade – that's normal.

"From our perspective, we're dealing with them all the time, they are very gentle and quite tuned into human behaviour and needs. Even though they come from the wild, in a very short time they adapt to what we need them to do, with feeding and so forth.

"The other thing is that they are very sensitive creatures, so that if they are not treated with some dignity they really do suffer badly from a number of well-known conditions that occur and that can be fatal, like myopathy. We see it all the time and it's a lot more complex and wide-spread than you would see from a text book.

"Any significant stress or upset can precipitate them going into skeletal or cardio myopathy in particular. Then they die of heart failure either straight away or in a month or two months' time and kidney failure. It's quite complicated.

"They have a very definite and complex social structure. If you disrupt that either to an individual or as part of their society, then it has profound effects on their survival. The way I or you approach them makes a huge difference."

I tell Howard that I talk to the kangaroo family of mothers and joeys that stays close to the house, and even to those further afield. They have come to recognise my voice, visibly relaxing when this human shape in front of them talks in a friendly fashion or copies their body language, like a bend-over scratch. They come off alert posture, and return to feeding or stand around and scratch too. I jokingly ask whether I'm putting them into stress by saying 'no' some days when they come around to be fed?

What he does know for sure is that as a medical practitioner, the way he approaches them makes a huge difference to their outcome. Not rushing in, for example, to stick something in their ear "which I wouldn't do with any patient – be it a dog or a small human primate that we call a child. Same applies to little kangaroos, little echidnas, birds, or whatever".

He says he always talks to his patients before he does anything as he would with a human. "I'm sure they take comfort or dislike from the tone of your voice. And they suffer from all the psychological impairments that we do, like stress, anxiety, fearing pain, becoming depressed – even though some people may not recognise that."

Later, when I meet up again with Rosemary and we talk about her extensive work in animal first aid and rehabilitation and the research on post-traumatic stress, she agrees that it is voice that the animals recognise over mere physical presence. The uncertainty is compounded when the costume changes, as when she is dressed for her day job in the city as a human general practitioner. "They don't recognise me. But as soon as I talk they relax."

Stress and pain management are major things to concentrate on with wildlife medicine, continues Howard. They suffer pain just like any creature with a nervous system. They may not show it as we do by screaming and yelling. The body language is very subtle and that comes from living in the wild. "If you have a sore leg, you don't want to alert a predator that you're the one that is hurting."

Birds too are very susceptible to stress, he tells me. "You go to the duck shooting – and they shoot everything that moves, darters shot out of trees and pelicans shot out of the sky. Some birds will cope with the stress of being shot at in the sky, like Grey Teals and Pacific ducks, but you get little Pink-eared ducks that always die, even if they are not shot, just from the disruption of their environment with 3000 shooters opening fire before dawn in the middle of the wetlands – the birds just die from stress."

CHALLENGING CASES, MELODY'S STORY

What was a particularly challenging recent case? I ask Howard. He recalls the case of a young adult female who was brought in after being hit by a car. Rosemary brought in the young doe, one of two female kangaroos with joeys in pouch, both hit by a vehicle at a major interchange outside Canberra.

One mum didn't make it, but the other, Melody, as this patient was named, was rescued by a good Samaritan, risking his own life against the commuting drivers, some of whom didn't want to swerve for animal or rescuer. A couple of army personnel also stopped to help get the dead and injured off the road.

Melody was having trouble breathing and was in significant difficulty. It turned out that she had a ruptured diaphragm. This is called a diaphragmatic hernia, in which abdominal matter has worked its way into the chest cavity. Gradually more and more of the stomach, bowel and liver can work their way into the chest and impact the lungs so the patient can't breathe and dies.

In the course of a four-hour open chest cavity surgery, Howard performed the challenging business of removing the stomach material from the chest cavity and repairing the hernia, after finding and accessing the tear. The anaesthetic was difficult because in this case the lung had to be ventilated and procedures instituted to ensure the lung did not collapse. "All in all a fairly complicated thing," he says with trademark modesty, adding that this method is standard medical practice for all creatures. In his clinic it's all part of demonstrating daily that the same works for wildlife.

Other challenges are met in different ways. Like the case of one baby wombat, one of many whose mothers are killed on the road. This baby was in the pouch, but the legs were protruding. A fox came on the scene and began eating the baby, starting with the feet. A good Samaritan rescued her and brought her in. She had fairly significant damage to two feet. "So we repaired that. She was only little, so we knew she'd have to come back. When she was about a kilo she came back because her claws were distorted and she couldn't use one front foot and couldn't dig."

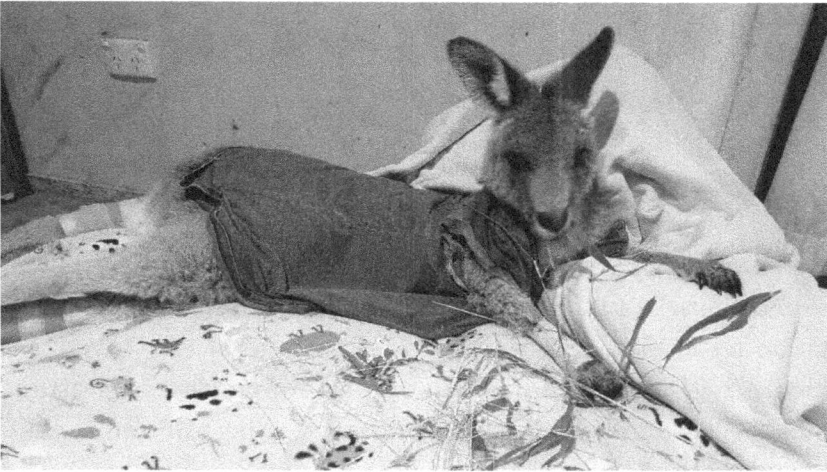

Melody recovering.

Howard and his nurses reconstructed her 'fingers' on the front foot, having to lengthen some and reduce others so she eventually ended up with a normal foot. She grew up to be a normal functioning released wombat.

Many wildlife carers have been trained here how to keep going with medications, dressings, and monitoring in the recovery stage. Here again, stress more than physical response can be the killer.

LIKE BEING IN A WAR ZONE

Turning to human stress, we talk about the pressure facing the relatively small number of activists, rescuers and animal first responders in a society that officially does not share these values. It is often like being in a war zone, concedes Howard.

"I've known people in my medical career that have been to things like the duck shooting. Facing shooters on any front and the negative, aggressive, hostile contact they can face really does take its toll. Attending things like these so-called culls [as in neighbouring Canberra] and seeing the end result and rescuing those that are not dead yet ... these people do suffer things like post-traumatic stress, coping with the awful things they witness.

"I know three people during duck shooting who were shot. Two I referred to the local hospital and to the local police who were not the slightest bit interested because we were rescuers."

It's not an easy experience for those citizens who have volunteered to fill the void created by poor or non-existent government support for all of the nation's wildlife. Animal rescue and rehabilitation tends to take over people's lives, the need is so great, and increasing. It comes with challenges and down-sides, not least the personal economic cost and the necessary setting aside of freedom to come and go.

There is the ever-present question about how and where to release rehabilitated wildlife, and the eventual realisation of personal burnout. As with other national volunteer organisations (not least the voluntary fire services) the average age of wildlife carers is in the 50s, 60s, and 70s. Will there be a new generation picking up the pieces when these baby boomers retire for good, or can this generation finally hope for true conservation in public policy?

Despite the cost, Howard lives in hope that those rescuing and defending wildlife have increasing influence in Australian society. He sees it on the veterinary front. Following the 2020 catastrophic fires and wildlife destruction, time will tell. Perhaps the 2020 duck hunting season in Victoria, that politicians waved through despite calls to stop it under the circumstances, was a harbinger: very few ducks and very few hunters. Of course, affecting human activity in that year was the global virus pandemic linked to other human mistreatment and exploitation of wildlife. But that is another story.

EDEN LOST: WHAT THE EARLY EXPLORERS SAW

"The original inhabitants of the south-west of Australia, the Nyungar, lived, hunted and foraged over a land among the most bountiful of Australian tribal areas. Kangaroos roamed in herds of 500 or more, flocks of cockatoos, parakeets and pigeons darkened the sky. Ducks appeared in great numbers on swamps and pools and the rivers teamed with fish and crustacea and the rich marine life of salt water estuaries supported immense numbers of teal, brown ducks, swans and pelicans. Edible roots, nuts and seeds grew in abundance along watercourses and in the bush."

— WILLIAM LINES, *TAMING THE GREAT SOUTH LAND.*

There are modern arguments that native animals in Australia, particularly the large hunted species of kangaroo, have never had it so good, and therefore are now "overabundant," "in plague proportions," and other similar terms. This is said to be thanks to the settlers' improvements of land-clearing, fertilised pastures, and new dams and watering points.

It is possible to acknowledge this population density argument for the semi-desert interior and west, in country now called the sheep rangelands, where the settlers' cleared native shrub in favour of grasses, and drilled bores – underground water sources. These changes may have attracted a higher density of mammals and birds.

It is also likely that native animals migrated as they were pushed west from earlier settled areas.

But what about the more fertile parts of the country before white settlement? What was there in vegetation, fauna, and water sources before everything was altered? Explorer records, marvelling at the park-like grasslands and woodlands they found, provide ample clues for what was once there.

The early explorers and surveyors were focused on finding pastoral country, with profit in mind. Some doggedly pursued the dream of inland seas and yet more grazing land. Their journals rarely dwelt on natural history or in-depth wildlife observations. They celebrated seeing intermittent rich country with soft soils, extensive grasslands (downs), clear rivers, chains of ponds watering the grassland, and treed riparian meadows.

Some also recorded the variability of the climate, particularly inland with drought drying out the landscape, overturning seasonal good times. But the explorations were in the cause of looking ahead to the advent of English-style farms, villages, and road systems. 'Improvements' would overcome the dry times.

The early explorers and some early settlers testified to seeing a profusion of water birds on rivers and lagoons, emus and brolgas – dubbed Native Companions – and large numbers of kangaroos, in mobs – not all the time, but often. Kangaroos were described in such terms as 'flocks' and 'herds', recognising that here was a social, herd animal.

The presence of large numbers of native grazers is a logical connection with other descriptions from the first explorers and settlers, who found many well-watered grassland and woodland ecosystems east of the Great Dividing Range. A NSW Farmers Association publication gathered explorer testimony. A typical example from John Oxley at the Hastings River in 1818, passing through open forest country noted: "The whole face of the country was abundantly covered with good grass which having been burned sometime, now bore the appearance of young wheat. Six miles down the river it was joined by a fine stream from the southward, apparently watering a spacious valley."[1]

Veterinarian John Auty, a defender of Australia's kangaroos and critic of their industrial-scale slaughter, in 2005 collated many early descriptions of encounters with kangaroos to show that they were naturally abundant in Australia prior to settlement. For example: "By 1794 John Macarthur was taking 300 pounds of kangaroo meat a week using one hunter and six greyhounds at Parramatta. At Sutton Forest to the west of Sydney James Macarthur saw kangaroos in immense flocks in 1821." In Tasmania, kangaroos were also harvested early for human consumption and described as "in abundance" in the early 1800s. But by 1850 hunting had driven them to the edge of extinction.[2]

In the south-west of the continent as well, explorations during 1829–32 recorded "numerous herds of kangaroos," "kangaroos and birds in abundance," "saw many large kangaroos on the plains," "great numbers," and "plenty" and "numerous" were frequent adjectives for kangaroo numbers in south and northern WA.

Auty compiled additional records from observers of eastern Australia. Surveyor Thomas Mitchell, who travelled throughout the south-east, in his journals refers to the presence of kangaroos and records them as "numerous". Auty quotes the overlander Hawdon who in 1837 saw kangaroos "in great numbers" and South Australian kangaroos as being "in great abundance" and Captain Phillip Mitchell at Port Lincoln also recorded kangaroos in 1836 as being in "numerous flocks". South Australians removed much of this abundance in the intervening years. In the mid-1800s colonial records reported such abundance in Victoria that every grazing or farming property was hunting with dogs. Many Grey kangaroos were recorded in forested areas like the Grampians.

WEEREEWAA: LAGOONS, MEADOWS, BRILLIANT LIFE

Natural water sources were much commented upon by the early explorers. Water would be critical. There's the description of the Lake George (Weereewaa) area between Canberra and Goulburn by Governor Macquarie's party. On Sunday 29 October 1820, riding along what is now in most years a dry and sparsely vegetated lake bed supporting some sheep, they found:

> "A very great extent of flat land, composed of open forest, plains, and meadows for seven or eight miles at least. The soil generally good, fine herbage and full of fine large ponds and lagoons of fresh water.
> "These ponds were full of black swans, Native Companions [brolgas] and ducks and when we came to the south end of the lake it was covered with innumerable flocks of black swans, ducks and seagulls."[3]

Macquarie changed the native name of the lake, Weereewaa, to honour his monarch, King George IV – described as a terrible choice given the king was a self-indulgent food, alcohol and drug addict who is reported to have ended up insane and a recluse before dying in 1830.

From west of the Blue Mountains this description by Governor Macquarie marked 8 May 1815: "Both these Valleys are remarkably well watered by large Ponds at regular distances contiguous to each other, which are even full of Water at this extraordinary dry season."[4] This may be a reference to the chain of ponds structure of creeks in many grasslands, now laboriously being re-created by graziers exploring soil and pasture regeneration along natural lines.

THE KIMBERLEY: LIKE AFRICAN SAVANNAH

William Lines introduces his 1991 history of Australian colonisation with idyllic accounts of growing up near Fremantle,

Western Australia before roads and development ripped down the surrounding bush, and recounts the great deforestation of that state (in the millions of hectares) during the 1960s for wheat farming. He wrote the description at the head of this chapter of pre-settlement in the southwest of the continent.

Lines also found colonial reports of the wildlife bounty in the Kimberley in the north of the state as the first sheep arrived in 1879, to number 100,000 head by 1890. Absentee owners and speculators quickly grabbed millions of hectares of land, including the grassy plains of the river valleys that Lines compared to the African savannah in their pristine state. A profusion of wild pheasants, along with lizards, kangaroos, wombats, and other small marsupials greeted the invaders. Flocks of cockatoos, flying foxes, ducks, and other water fowl filled the skies.[5]

Regardless of this half-buried historical evidence, some contemporary pastoralists, politicians, scientists, and media reporters claim that everyone knows large kangaroos have become unnaturally abundant. As justification for ongoing extensive killing this argument rests on a view that combines colonists' improvements with the cessation of hunting by Aborigines and by dingos – that have themselves been persecuted since settlement. I'm not convinced. Drilling further into Australia's colonial and post- colonial history, it is clear that in 250 years, modern humans have more than replaced the activities of First Australians and dingos in regard to macropod numbers – indeed wiping some out.

At least one well-accepted history of Aboriginal lifestyles claims that the people rarely hunted large kangaroos. The large Red and Eastern Grey males can be taller than six feet, with heavy muscle to match. With firestick farming methods (and the frequent need to carry the catch some distances), people more often relied on catching smaller kangaroos and wallabies, as well as possums and other marsupials. All were subsequently decimated by pastoralism.[6]

BEFORE DAIRY FARMS, A BOUNTIFUL HOME OF PLANTS AND ANIMALS

When settlers arrived, between Lismore and Byron Bay in NSW and further north into Queensland lay an irreplaceable sub-tropical rainforest, with many plants harking back to pre-historic origins, and immense trees that the settlers dismissively called brush and then scrub and cut down or ringbarked wholesale for dairy cattle and other farming.

In the 1840s, Clement Hodgkinson, a surveyor working for the NSW government along the coastal rivers, described the rainforest as "gigantic green walls on both sides of the river. It grows on the richest alluvial land and consists of trees of almost endless variety and very large dimensions … the popular names of the most remarkable brush trees are as follows – red cedar, white cedar, mahogany, tulipwood, rosewood, ironwood, lightwood, sassafras, corkwood and the Australian tamarind box."[7]

The story was taken up again 130 years later. Long after the land had been cleared, Harry Frith, CSIRO Wildlife Research Division chief, whose family was from that part of the country, lamented the culture of destruction for what turned out to be short-term gain for one or two generations of immigrants. "Even the hardwood ridges," he wrote, "where the immense blackbutts grew on poor shallow soil were looked upon as potential pasture for cows. The trees were ringed and killed. They still stand and the pasture is poor. Few farmers would spare even a few square metres for a garden or shelter belt around the house; all land was to be grass."

He asked his grandfather why he had not preserved a few acres of his holding under rainforest, and the reply was that despite good intentions, when the next piece of forest came into consideration it was always considered "rubbish."[8]

Frith recounts the abundance and diversity of the wildlife that once inhabited that landscape that interspersed rainforest with eucalyptus-covered ridges and open grassland. Surveys of remnant marsupial fauna indicate a rich diversity that included marsupial mice and tiger quolls, bandicoots, possums and gliders, kangaroos and wallabies. There were also platypuses and echidnas, bats, rodents, and dingos, with an equal richness of birdlife.

Within a few years the Big Scrub was gone. Few native animals survived when the clearing was finally completed, a situation that overall remains in that landscape, along with depleted soils, the occasional giant dead tree, and a widespread weed invasion of exotic shrubs and vines.

As environmental historian Michael Williams put it: "There was a direct connection between the butter that British families spread on their toast for breakfast and the destruction of the great trees of the forests of Australia and New Zealand."[9]

TURNING EDEN INTO WASTELAND

Photo: Maria Taylor

Sheep in southern NSW during 2018 drought.

In similar vein, the stark, treeless nature of much of Australia's southern grazing lands is the legacy of relentless expansion for sheep pastures across what is now NSW, Victoria and South Australia. In contrast, before millions of sheep were encamped, frequently-quoted Surveyor General Thomas Mitchell enthused so much about the grasslands of Western Victoria (as just one example), that he called them 'Australia Felix' – a land of beauty, worthy of civilised man.

He saw woodlands with "exuberant" soils, temperate climate, traversed by mighty rivers and innumerable streams. Mitchell and his party of 25, loaded with all the cumbersome baggage of Victorian exploration, were guided by First Australians following their songlines. Mitchell recorded fertility and beauty, plenty of water, abundance and rich pasturage. Yet despite much evidence to the contrary, he reportedly called the land "without inhabitants". Mitchell reported back enthusiastically and settlers from NSW were soon pushing flocks of sheep along his trail.[10]

Others were opening up Victoria too. Second generation Australian John Batman, now celebrated as one of the founders of Melbourne, sailed from Tasmania in 1835. Around Port Phillip, at the mouth of the Yarra River, he described the land he saw as rich, covered with kangaroo grass two feet high, the acreage dotted with sparse trees of wattle and she-oak. Batman saw rich sheep country before his eyes.

Looking up Batman, I find a man badged a "pioneer" and "entrepreneur." His earlier history was not widely commented on until recent years. Being an entrepreneur in Tasmania, he had negotiated a land grant in return for rounding up Aboriginal people, combative and otherwise, during that state's genocidal push against the first Tasmanians. His party shot at a group in a camp, wounding many, and he later killed two wounded men.[11]

At Port Phillip he attempted a treaty with the local people, offering blankets and axes for 500,000 acres around the bay, an agreement later voided by the colonial government back in NSW. Many have noted that this low-grade treaty was the only such effort in Australian colonial history. Having reported back on the landscape subdivision possibilities and the friendly natives willing to easily give up their land, Batman fuelled a new land rush from across the Tasman. Twenty thousand sheep were brought across in 1836 and, by 1837, 300,000 grazed in the district.

Two years later, the new settlers had extended their reach by 500 kilometres and the number of sheep had tripled. Lines makes the general observation that many vast land seizures and pastoral empires were speculative. Investors – including British gentry, army officers, and lawyers – stayed in the cities while indentured servants, sometimes convicts, shepherded the flocks under basic conditions in the start-up years.

A hundred and seventy years later, sheep grazier, regenerative farming innovator and author Charles Massy described what became of the landscape that enthralled Mitchell and Batman south-west of Ballarat. It was still accessorised with ornate Victorian homesteads. But the land that had been cleared, ploughed, poisoned and eaten out was now given over to cropping with massive industrial size machinery and chemical farming.

"This was country that between 1850 and 1870 had been one of the great sheep walks of the world, bringing wealth to the graziers and to the nation with Merino breeding and wool refinements," Massy writes. But then "the sheep ate the heart out of the country and its vast swathes of diverse, long-adapted natural grasslands". The breeding operations were moved further out, and the land exploitation and degradation cycle started again.[12]

He visits a couple in that area who in the 1980s took possession of part of a family property that was settled in 1839. They found no hint of what Mitchell saw. Treeless paddocks, no remnant bush, sour and swampy vegetation, compacted soil, and eroded water-courses were their inheritance. They studied and researched what might have grown there pre-settlement.

Over the years they laboriously returned wattles, casuarinas, and banksias to their land. By 2017 they had effected a remarkable transformation, with riparian corridors, shelter belts, and other planted vegetation that brought back other native plants and animals, particularly the birds and aquatic life.

Massy farms on the Monaro south of Canberra distinguished by largely treeless grass plains, or 'downs' as the settlers called it – irresistible to sheep grazier eyes. Today, regenerative and 'natural sequence farming' attempts to re-establish the ecology of such areas. Among other strategies, the work is to reconstruct the natural water flows of chain-of-ponds recorded on the Monaro plains in the mid-1800s.

CHAIN-OF-PONDS, AS THEY ONCE WERE

By the 1860s, sheep overstocking, often to pay off land debts as more individual farms were encouraged by governments, had taken its toll on the Monaro. Prior to that time, a settler described his local creek.

> "A succession of deep waterholes, there being no high banks, and grass grew to the waters' edge. Hundreds of wild ducks could be seen along these waterholes and platypus and divers were plentiful. Five years after [a government land sale act] the whole length, instead of being a line of deep waterholes, became a bed of sand, owing to soil erosion caused by sheep. The water only came to the surface in flood time, when it spread the sand over the flats."[13]

Delving into such histories convinced me that the fertile belt of Australia once teamed with wildlife, closely associated with the richness and diversity of the vegetation, soils and life-giving water.

William Lines summed it up in his history:

> "The fecundity of water and land awed the early explorers and squatters on their advance through south-eastern Australia: lavish fish catches, great masses of shell-fish, yabbies and eels, vast flocks of waterfowl and other birds, substantial numbers of emus and large populations of kangaroos, wallabies, possums, bandicoots and wombats, an abundance of yams and huge stretches of reaped grassfields" harvested by Indigenous people.[14]

The richness was systematically and stubbornly cleared away for a different vision that all Australians have now inherited.

FUR AND FEATHERS: AN EXPOSE

"By 1890, two years after Australia's centennial, over 100 million sheep and nearly eight million cattle grazed over much of the continent ... Most of nineteenth century Australians, even native born, referred to Britain as home and looked on their own country as real estate, a camping ground for money-making purposes."

— WILLIAM LINES, *TAMING THE GREAT SOUTH LAND**

Jock Marshall had no doubt why governments of the day supported the slaughter of koalas and kangaroos, large and small, or the Tasmanian Tiger. Votes and money, he concluded. He saw that the Australian states and the federal government through the 1960s (and as it turned out for decades longer) still perceived themselves as part of the British imperial and economic project, tied to the export nation narrative that came packaged with the first sheep.

---

* Renowned Canadian biologist David Suzuki wrote in a foreword to William Lines' book *Taming the Great South Land*: "My grandparents were driven out of Japan by poverty at the beginning of the 20th century. They came to Canada to seek their fortune ... [they] were aliens in an unfamiliar landscape with which they had no historical or cultural link, let alone a sense of reverence for its sanctity ... the land was a 'commodity' full of 'resources' to exploit."

As more and more white settlers pushed across the continent, bringing British Victorian beliefs about private property land ownership along with the call to install a superior European civilisation and an export economy, the on-ground effects were seismic. Some citizens recorded the homicidal mistreatment of Australia's First Nations people as the land grabs and dispossession continued. And some natural scientists and international visitors voiced their shock or disquiet at the treatment of the new society's most defenceless of all – the unique native animals. In successive eras, these voices have been drowned out by the clamour of farmer, miner, and other economic lobbies.

Removal and containment of not only the original human inhabitants but also the natural plant and animal communities were believed to be necessary 'improvements' – essential both to embedding superior and enlightened civilisation and to making money along the way. Australia was sold to immigrants as a blank slate awaiting a radical makeover to a European landscape. Legacy ideas about triumphing over nature and wrestling the land and its former inhabitants into accepted conformity remain drivers of the national self-image.

Nevertheless, in the last 50–60 years the passionate defence of the natural Australian world and its First Nations people has grown, sometimes voiced with refreshing directness from unexpected quarters. In this vein, I came upon the work of a man whose remarkable personal life and determination were only matched by his outspokenness on behalf of the dispossessed.

Alan John 'Jock' Marshall wrote and edited *The Great Extermination* in 1966, during a post-war era of more housing, roads, and business development pushing across the land. Then, as in the colonial era and in the present day, people by and large accepted all the killing as part of the march of progress. Marshall's book is almost unfindable in Australia today, perhaps because it uncomfortably renders the holocaust that was visited on native species with the coming of white settlers and presents an unvarnished view of why it happened. His book is subtitled *A Guide to Anglo-Australian Cupidity, Wickedness and Waste*. There it is.

Before introducing this World War II hero and founding zoology professor at Monash University, here's a glimpse of the enquiring journey from the world today. Looking to buy Marshall's book, I searched for available copies on the internet. Only Amazon US had a second-hand copy being sold by an individual from Adelaide, Australia. Australians couldn't buy hardback books from Amazon US. It's about shipping. I resorted to asking a friend in Seattle to buy the book for me and ship it across. Fortunately, the University of NSW library carries a copy and lends it out.

Similar was the search for William Line's 1991 history, quoting many original sources about Australian colonisation and development and with a foreword by world-famous ecologist David Suzuki. This too was almost impossible to find in Australia. *Taming the Great South Land*, now out of print, can be found in US second-hand bookshops, but hardly here except for some library collections. I managed to locate a copy at a rare book shop in Victoria. His book reminds me what the first settlers found, with memorable descriptions of an abundant country and animal kingdom, quoted in the previous chapter.

Both Marshall and Lines wrote as citizen historians, documenting what British and European values of the time brought to bear on colonised lands. These values left an enduring legacy on how Australians think about things, including the belief that Australian 'nature' and wildlife need to be tamed and exploited for commerce.

A WILD COLONIAL BOY

Jock Marshall was born in Redfern, Sydney in 1911 to a working class family. Nicknamed 'Jock' for a childhood aspiration to become a jockey, he spent much of his youth riding a horse, shooting rabbits and rambling through the countryside rather than focusing on book learning, as did many young blokes of his generation. His independent spirit and determination became clearer when, at age 16, he blew off his left arm by careless handling of a shotgun. Refusing to wear an artificial limb, he taught himself to ride and shoot one-armed.

Later, taking up bird specimen collecting for the Australian Museum, he also taught himself to expertly dissect one-handed. His biographers note that he said the accident was the best thing that happened to him: forcing him to look ahead and make something of his life.[1]

This can-do attitude came good again in New Guinea in 1945 where Marshall was stationed with a small Australian Army reconnaissance team. Despite his one arm, he had convinced the Army to take him based on his previous tropical experience while bird collecting in Vanuatu and New Guinea. The reconnaissance unit was gathering information behind the lines on Japanese movements. They resourcefully sent intelligence back to headquarters using carrier pigeons. The daring foray was nicknamed "jockforce".

Before the war, he returned to more formal education at Sydney University with practical training in zoology. While there he wrote a column for the *Daily Telegraph* and did a weekly broadcast for the ABC. Moving steadily upward in science academe (for a student who never matriculated) he was accepted at Oxford after the war and by 1956 had completed two doctorates specialising in zoology and comparative anatomy. After 10 years teaching and research in the UK he returned to Australia to help establish Monash University, where he became Foundation Professor of Zoology.

Never shying away from a battle for excellence as the university developed, he also fought for the retention of native trees on the campus. For a man of his determined and adventurous spirit, it was apparently no big deal to ensure there would be no building over a patch of remnant bushland. Reportedly under cover of darkness, he removed all the surveyor pegs. The area remains a nature reserve, possibly the one that bears his name.[2] He continued with collecting and research expeditions into the Australian inland throughout his tenure, also taking more personal trips with friends like the painter Russell Drysdale.

With this background, it would be hard to challenge Marshall as a sheltered ivory tower academic, a person who had no relationship with the real world of developing Australia and what was required to install 'civilisation' and prosperity. Or what Europe was like in comparison. He saw it first-hand as well as through research and connections. He recorded in *The Great Extermination* the fate of Australia's marsupials and birds with European settlement and edited the book with additional chapters focusing on forests and woodlands, reptiles, and sea mammals. Fifty years later, this volume is a historical document worth studying.[3]

Foreshadowing the rejoinder still heard today when people who don't live on an agricultural property criticise what some farmers do, he wrote, in the direct style that characterised his work:

"A feature of the reaction from the people who are making the money or who in any case condone the killing, is an angry and usually illiterate letter declaring that kangaroos (for example) still exist in countless thousands and that anyway these city people 'don't know what they are talking about' ... Lest any angry bumpkin should be tempted to answer this chapter in such terms, let me say that I am of the fourth generation of country folk and that I live in the country myself.

"And further, that in the whole wide area between Cooper's Creek and Broken Hill, we (of a Monash University party) in 1963 counted precisely 280 kangaroos, including joeys just out of the pouch. The two biggest of the mighty herds still ravaging the poor sheep farmers grass numbered ten and eleven animals respectively. Admittedly the census was made by day. We saw only 77 emus."

Marshall the zoologist pulls together the history of what happened to Australia's globally unique marsupial fauna and birds, much of it deliberate and commercial, while habitat also disappeared after 1788 with the spread of white settlement (or invasion, depending on your point of view). Today one might keep this in mind as we blame the fox and the cat – immigrant imports – for the extinction of small native animals. Humans were already doing a pretty good job without their help.

Marshall's 1960s perspective provides a historical thread that continues to the present day, with the kangaroo slaughter for skin and meat and just plain removal, looking back at koalas that never recovered after massacres that culminated in the 1920s and the continued victimisation of other common native animals, including the wombat and the emu.

The connecting themes for killing marsupials and birds are fur and fashion, a lack of respect for the extraordinary land and its inhabitants, and the desire to recreate European landscapes and agricultural livelihoods with maximum profits on often unsuitable soils. All the while the habitat – the 'bush' – continued to be removed.

"The bush, to our great-grandfathers, was the enemy: it brooded sombrely outside their brave and often pathetic little attempts at civilisation; it crowded in on them in times of drought and flood," Marshall wrote in his introduction. "… [T]o those who can see little beyond the soft and tame beauty of bluebells and beech-woods (with a pretty little thatched cottage, and the comfort of a tea shoppe around the corner) the grandeur of range and plain is disconcerting."

Marshall describes the variety and magnificence of Australian vegetation that met the first settlers: from fern valleys in Tasmania, majestic jarrah forests in WA, soaring Mountain Ash in Gippsland, rainforests, and the park-like woodlands and well-mulched friable soils of NSW and Victoria – all due to the legacy of Aboriginal management and the activities and soft feet of native animals.

THE MARSUPIAL CHAPTER

Marshall starts his marsupial chapter, named with ironic under-statement 'On the Disadvantages of Wearing Fur,' emphasising, as have many other biologists, the uniqueness of Australia's marsupials and macropods that evolved after the continent's isolation about 100 million years ago.

"Thus, from an ancestral kangaroo-like creature there developed the big, lithe Red Kangaroos that bound over the inland plains, and the Great Grey ones that live in the forest. Heavy-footed rock wallabies also evolved, as well as a variety of small swift things that haunt tussock and undergrowth. Wallaby, Wallaroo, Tungoo [rat-kangaroo], Paddymelon, Potaroo [and Quokka]: these are all kangaroos springing from one or perhaps two kinds of ances-tors ... long before the evolution of [other] mammals [like] apes and Man in countries beyond the sea-barrier."

More than 60 species of macropod inhabited Australia at the time of European settlement in 1788, in most major habitats. Counts seem to vary between non-government groups and official numbers, but roughly one quarter of that pre-settlement number are now classified as either nationally extinct, regionally extinct, or they suffer greatly reduced numbers and habitat and are listed as threatened.

1800s animal studies.
Clockwise from top left: quolls, wombat, hopping mouse, red kangaroos, native tree rat. Gerard Krefft manuscript and pictorial collection, ca. 1856–1895, PXD9, courtesy of Dixson Library, State Library of New South Wales.

The family of kangaroos are browsers and grazers, as are the marsupial wombats, while possums, gliders and koalas evolved in the trees. Native carnivores like quolls evolved alongside. Settlers called the slow-moving koala 'native sloths' and likened wombats to badgers as they tried to describe what they were seeing.

The monotremes, echnida and platypus, were even more disorienting, combining attributes of being mammals with laying eggs as reptiles do. Australia's bird species also developed their own unique lines over millennia. Bats, rats and mice, and the dingo are more recent arrivals.

Marshall wrote that we still have no idea of how populous the Australian animals (or for that matter the first Australian people) were when the settlers started arriving in 1788 and the colony of NSW was established. "We do know however that 'kangooroos' were abundant around the shores of Sydney Harbour and Botany Bay and that the 'Coola' (Koala), Duck-billed Platypus or 'Paradox' and many other less spectacular animals were common nearby."

In 1837, kangaroos and emus were still reported to be plentiful around the settlement of Melbourne, although the emus were already "fast retiring before the white population and their flocks and herds". Brolgas and bustards were also commonly seen in that marshy environment. Marshall relied here on James Backhouse, a member of the Society of Friends, for what he saw in the 1830s.

Quoting other colonial sources, Marshall notes the abundance of platypus in Blue Mountain river pools in 1815, but that by 1852 they were considered extinct in regions frequently crossed by settlers. The colonists used its "deep chocolate pelt, heavy and water resistant" for slippers and rugs. It took 50 or 60 skins to laboriously make a rug.

The early colonists also ate the marsupials and birds for food, and hunted them for sport and then a dinner. This was native game, and was often compared to old country fare in the reports from that time – for example from John Gould, well known for his bird and mammal illustrations. Gould travelled widely in Australia in 1838–40 and collected specimens.

From 1815 on the explorers, followed by land takers and 'squatters', were able to push across the Great Divide and establish sheep runs. The bigger native animals were already becoming scarce along the coast, reported the young Charles Darwin who was travelling as naturalist on the brig *Beagle*. He rode over the Blue Mountains in 1836 and was invited to a kangaroo hunt on a sheep run.

Darwin had a bad day, seeing little opportunity for sport. "The Grey-hounds pursued a Kangaroo Rat into a hollow tree … A few years since this country abounded with wild animals; now the Emu is banished to a long distance and the Kangaroo is become scarce." He had the good fortune to see several platypuses.[4] (Reportedly seeing the notably different Australian species prompted some of Darwin's thoughts on the theory of evolution.)

FUR AND FEATHERS FOLLOWED OIL AND SKINS

Starting around the 1850s, a fur trade upped the indigenous animal mortality rate and range of victims. It was augmented by a thriving trade in stuffed animals displayed in cases and bird feathers for hats.

The fur trade on land had already been preceded by a horrific slaughterhouse visited upon fur seals and elephant seals that started in the 1790s on southern Australian islands, and on Tasmanian and New Zealand beaches, for oil, skins and furs. Locally this was spear-headed by British seamen, merchants, and settlers seeking a quick profit. As would happen with other exhaustive wildlife butcheries, the sealers worked year-round, paying no heed to breeding seasons and leaving orphaned pups to starve.

By 1820 it was all over. Southern seals would never recover previous abundance. By then the British, the Americans, the French and the Australian colonists were going after the whales.

Whale watchers of today could barely imagine the spectacle of marine life that met the first ships. The southern oceans then were still an undisturbed haven for whales, already being hunted towards extinction back across the Pacific. Around Australia, sperm whales and right whales congregated in their tens of thousands, migrating from Antarctica to mate and calve in the bays of New Zealand and Australia.

With trademark colonial determination and efficiency, and the lure of profits, by the late 1840s large marine mammals had been decimated to the point of being hard to find in the southern oceans.[5]

By that time, back on land, the fine pelt of 'flying squirrels' (or gliders) came into demand for hats; possums were hunted with dogs or 'sportsmen' knocked them out of trees with sticks, shot them, or cut down the tree; bandicoots and rat-kangaroos were cut out of tree hollows or dug out of the ground. Marshall quotes an 1827 travel report: "In this way you may return home after a few hours pastime loaded with a dozen opossums, squirrels, bandicoots, kangaroo rats and native cats (quolls) if the forest has not been much hunted in."[6]

"Platypus, Possum, Flying Squirrel, Kangaroo, Wallaby, Koala and Bilby – everything with a marketable fur was slaughtered in order to eke out a supplementary living on selections all over the country," wrote Marshall. By 1863 naturalist John Gould was worried about the wanton killing of platypus and its possible extinction. Kangaroos and emus continued to disappear everywhere settlers abounded in the southern states, along the fertile fringe. Matching the fur trade was the destructive extraction of fine wood from trees like the cedars.

Animals were still abundant inland where the First Nations people took only what they needed, as they had always done. All this was about to change however, with an era of deliberate extermination. Marshall doesn't hold back: "For this the sheep farmer is almost entirely responsible." But first, there was gold fever.

THE GOLD RUSH CHANGED EVERYTHING

The inland was invaded in a big way with the gold rush of the 1850s. Adventurers arrived from around the world, coming particularly from the British Isles in their millions. Australian laborers, failed graziers, and freed convicts joined them. They swarmed across the country like ants. The diggers lived precariously, shooting any native animal they came across and eating anything they could find.

The goldfields were soon denuded of trees. Short-lived canvas villages, complete with pubs and churches, cropped up everywhere, including in my general region with a road called Macs Reef (that being a gold reef).

Homevale National Park.

On a recent trip to the picturesque Homevale National Park in north-east Queensland, I found the following legend on an educational display at the site of the mining community of Mount Briton, describing the valley that the first miners saw. It read, "One of the early gold miners, the Hon Harold Finch-Hatton described these mountains in his book 'Advance Australia' in 1886 thus:

"The diggings were very prettily situated in the centre of a horse-shoe, formed by a spur running out from the main range onto the plains ... Vast ranges of mountains rise up all around the slopes of which are covered with forests of gigantic trees and patches of dense scrub. The summit of the range is formed by a crown of cliffs, which rise sheer from the slopes below ... the red and yellow tints of the rocks contrasting beautifully with the sombre mass of dark-green woods below them ...

"The first time I saw the valley of Mt Britten (sic) was about sundown and I never remember a more beautiful sight ... A soft blue mist, the smoke of many a campfire was rising and creeping gently up the valley."

The next image shows a bark hut village with a miner panning for gold. Gone the many campfires.

Finch-Hatton was a well-educated English aristocrat who had come out to visit his brother and try to make his fortune in the Mackay district and Nebo goldfields. His book, *Advance Australia*, notes the Queensland Marsupial Act of that time. Under this political umbrella, marsupials were hunted and destroyed to increase fodder for the introduced stock. Meanwhile, thousands of the introduced stock animals were boiled down to make tallow, he reported. The tallow industry boomed for a while with the over-breeding of sheep and cattle.

Finch-Hatton's writings also offered candid remarks indicating that early British settlers saw little difference between dispossessing, disrespecting, and enslaving – and sometime killing – humans and their campaigns against the native animals. Either way they showed no mercy, he reported.

HOW TO RUN SHEEP ON MARGINAL LAND

As the gold rush petered out, the former gold diggers started squatting under fee or lease on new 'runs' of less fertile land further inland to run sheep. These properties became the inland 'stations' of today.

North-western NSW shows how marginal lands were set up for sheep. The early runs were concentrated near the watercourses that punctuate the otherwise flat ancient seabed terrain of that countryside. There was water but intermittent, and there was native vegetation for grazing wildlife dominated by saltbush and acacias and some grasses, much of it since altered in composition and health.

A 1995 *Australian Geographic* account of what happened around Broken Hill puts it clearly: with their drive to open up land and "tame the wilderness," they [the settlers] "didn't understand that native wildlife evolved to use vegetation that sprouts, grows, flowers and seeds in a few short weeks after rain – without destroying it." The wildlife evolved with boom and bust.[7]

On country that averaged less than 200mm of rain a year, sheep overcrowding and overgrazing spread outward from the water-courses. The settlers upped the ante with artificial watering points from ground water. Within 20 years there were 15 million hungry mouths and trampling hoofs.[8] In the drought of the 1890s, millions of sheep died of starvation. Graziers were ruined. Dust storms raged. The land did not recover much for 50 years. Stocking rates thereafter went up and down with the wool market. Remaining graziers in this marginal western region continue to agitate loudly that kangaroos must be removed as competition. As I saw in 2018, politicians were still ready to comply.

Before pastoralism around Broken Hill and north, the region supported 20 species of marsupial and five species of rodent. In 1995 only six marsupial species and one rodent species remained.[9] The extinct desert marsupials of this country – like the Burrowing Bettong, Eastern Hare wallabies and bandicoots – had their habitat (food and shelter) destroyed by stock and then came rabbits. As Marshall also documented, hunting of all native animals continued, including then by cats and foxes.

While the inland Indigenous people had been kind to explorer Charles Sturt and his party, the favour was not returned. Armed killings and disease (smallpox, measles, flu) rapidly decimated the inhabitants of the arid rangelands. Back-to-back private property sheep runs became inhospitable to both wildlife and traditional hunters.

ON OUR SELECTION, GRASS IS EVERYTHING

The new generation of inland graziers set about clearing and killing, exactly like those who had settled earlier on better soils. Marshall wrote: "They were brave and resourceful men but the sole ambition of the squatter and selector was to 'make a do' on the land and this meant to run at least as many sheep to the acre as Dad and Dave were doing on the next selection, two things had to be done. First Dad and Dave (and often Mum and Mabel too) set about ringbarking every tree on the place including those near their slab or mud-brick hut … so more 'feed' would grow."

In NSW between 1788 and 1921, 35.5 million hectares were ringbarked or cleared, corresponding to almost half of the area of the state that originally had forest or woodland or 'scrub'. In perspective, this represented an area greater than England, Scotland, and Wales together, cleared by hand. One study estimated that 95 percent of what is now the NSW sheep and wheat belt was cleared or grossly modified.[10]

CLEARING AWAY SOMEONE'S HOME

"With the trees and the undergrowth went the flying squirrels (gliders), the bilbies, the bandicoots, the potoroos, the paddymelons and all the other smaller marsupials," wrote Marshall. Habitat loss did its work against all the ground dwelling and tree-dwelling native grazers. Lack of regeneration, thanks to how sheep eat, and then setting fire to the landscape completed the job on the sheep run. When modern conservationists bemoan the world-class demise of Australia's marsupials in 200 years, seldom is the colonial and ongoing native vegetation clearance accorded equal agency with the fox and the cat.

As one allotment was degraded, the settlers simply moved to take up more land to clear, plough, and graze. By 1890, 98.5 percent of NSW as the earliest colony had been alienated through land grants and sales.[11] Private property thinking, allied with the demand for land 'improvement', set the baseline: native vegetation and native animals are 'owned' and can be disposed of at will. Recent deregulation of clearing rules and reversion to colonial-style wildlife removal seem normal to succeeding generations who think that way.

In Marshall's book, in a chapter titled 'The Decline of the Plants', botanist J.S. Turner described the inland districts that have been a wildlife battleground for a century to accommodate sheep grazing on marginal land. Turner describes a semi-arid belt (to the east of the Broken Hill region topography described above) that in places is covered with mulga, myall, ironbark, callitris, Sandhill pine and Grey Box woodlands, and cleared intermittently from north-central Queensland down through central NSW. He asks whether the sparse vegetation that remains on thin red and white soils that sustained some 60 million Merinos in his day, the 1960s, can possibly do so in the long run. I saw a lot of destocked country in 2018, and ground with rocks not vegetation remaining after the sheep left.

Turner quoted former CSIRO ecologist Francis Ratcliffe's 1930s warning that the inland is in danger of conversion to true desert, as the fodder resource nowhere matched the demand placed on it by European grazing activities.[12]

In context, it was not just the settlers' God-sanctioned search for maximum feed and profit that governed land clearing. In the 1800s, colonial government land grants were often subject to conditions that included vegetation clearing, particularly of the dense coastal 'scrub' (including rainforest), woodland, and other forested areas. This called for massive investment of labour – the so-called 'improvement'. I described earlier one thus-vandalised irreplaceable landscape of flora and fauna, the Big Scrub – a lowland subtropical rainforest on the eastern seaboard.

KILL THE BIGGER NATIVE ANIMALS, REPLACE THEM WITH RABBITS, FOXES

After clearing the vegetation, continued Marshall, "the thing to do was kill all the bigger native animals on the place. Before modern pastoral research, it was good country indeed that would in many districts run even a single sheep to the acre. And so it was understandable that the early settlers would wish to kill off kangaroos. What was inexplicable was that these people savagely butchered *every* kangaroo on the property and every koala, paddymelon, bilby and bustard too".

The kangaroo round-up was called a 'battue'. The white settlers learned the Indigenous peoples' idea of funnelling kangaroos into dead-end spaces for convenient mass slaughter. That was the battue. The difference was the industrial scale that the Europeans applied to their killing, then and now.

In 1863, naturalist John Gould saw what was coming. "Short-sighted indeed are the Anglo-Australians or they would have long ere this have made laws for the preservation of their highly singular, and in many cases noble, indigenous animals … [if they don't] the remnant that is left will soon disappear, to be followed by unavailing regret for the apathy with which they were previously regarded."[13]

Gould also regretted the work of the so-called acclimatisation societies and individuals bent on bringing a wide range of foreign plants and animals to Australia – not least the fox that was released for sport after the squatters tired of hunting dingos, and the rabbit that was introduced for food, cross-bred with English wild rabbits and then deliberately released for sport. The rabbits would soon cause the pastoralists much more loss of pasture grass than any native animal did.

Poisoning of introduced 'ferals' followed, and took more of the smaller slow-breeding native animals with it – a danger that continues to this day, with the spreading of the horrendous 1080 poison aimed at wild dogs, pigs, and sometimes wallabies, and that takes native carnivores and birds of prey with it, as well as pet dogs. At the same time the native animals can't compete with the breeding output of rabbits, foxes, pigs, or goats.

FEARS FOR THE RED KANGAROO STARTED EARLY

Marshall turns again to Gould and the latter's observations, more than 150 years ago, at the "wanton manner" in which the "noble" Red kangaroo was relentlessly killed with "powerful and well-trained dogs" as men moved their immense flocks into the kangaroo's inland habitat. Gould feared that without legal restraint, the Red kangaroo would soon be gone. But Marshall thought the final loss would take a little longer. His 1966 foreboding sends echoes into the present.

> "For another century [after Gould's comment] the big Red buck and his graceful consort the Blue Flier, would remain plentiful in the more arid lands far beyond the pastures with which [Gould] was personally familiar … Now however, the spot-lighter and sheep farmer have banded together for the benefit of themselves, the city traders in pet food, and the exporters of sub-standard sausage and other meat to West Germany, Hong Kong, Singapore and Japan."[14]

Eight years before Marshall wrote, the commercial kangaroo trade for pet food and sausages had got underway in 1958 along with the continuing skin trade, accompanied by government applause at this burgeoning export industry. From the beginning, questions were raised about the food hygiene aspect of bush meat slaughter far from processing facilities, an issue that had significant impact by the 2000s as we'll see.

Marshall caustically notes the unsavoury outcomes at the time of shooting wild animals in the field. He recounts that the 1961–62 value of the trade dropped because "Germans ceased to be amused by maggoty and putrid meat sent from this land of health and hygiene".

He describes how the killing is done, and how the kangaroo's natural 'freeze' reaction to bright spotlight makes them an easy, defenceless target. His description is heavy on blowflies, crows and maggots that get most of the carcass, while the shooter might take the skin and mostly the 'butt' – the top of the hindquarters which is boned by the processor and sold as meat.

By the mid-1960s tens of thousands of Red kangaroos were killed weekly in inland Australia, he reported. In 1966, 50 professional shooters were operating in just the Broken Hill district, with 25,000 Reds said to be shot per week in western NSW at the time. Some testimony regarding that time further describes what was happening in the 'Outback', well out of the public's sight.

A friend told me about going along to a kangaroo shoot in South Australia on country where the animals had not seen many humans. The shooter pulled up to a group of Red kangaroos that quietly observed their arrival, and pumped bullets into the upper legs of maybe half a dozen before the rest fled. He then approached the immobilised victims, caught one after the other by the tail and with a heavy hacksaw-type tool beat into their skull areas until they were dead. Our friend said that this shooter believed a headshot would distribute blood throughout the carcass, spoiling the meat.

In 1973, a traveller reported in a national magazine:

"The track to (Telephone Bore station) was lined both sides with kangaroo legs. We drove for an hour maybe … We passed the freezer van standing on empty drums. The roo shooter's house was still a few miles on. On both sides of the track, as though the ground were covered by some plant or vine … as though the ground were

covered by some grim parody of a garden, there were the kangaroos'
legs. Cut off, and left there. In the end I felt as though I had been
shot and beaten at the full of the moon … At night they chase the
kangaroos with their spotlights … for sport or pig feed … last of the
Reds allegedly killed to feed 'tame' wild pigs."[15]

It wasn't just Jock Marshall sounding the alarm from the scientific world. By 1969, CSIRO's Harry Frith and John Calaby were
warning the hunting to that time had reduced the Red to a fraction
of its former numbers.[16] There would be related genetic health and
population impacts, warned these scientists. By the time Marshall
published in 1966, about a million kangaroos were being killed
annually in eastern Australia, focused first on the Reds. Despite
the early concerns and warnings, the officially-encouraged kill
numbers were destined to increase dramatically across commercial
and non-commercial arenas in the following decades.

The enduring public mythology of plague numbers promoted
by both government and graziers was alive and well in the 1960s.
Marshall wrote: "As recently as July 1964, newspaper reports from
Mildura said that Red Kangaroos were being shot at a rate of 200,000
a week in south-western New South Wales. 'They still appear to be
increasing,' local sheep farmers told a reporter, as though marsupials were flying in from Mars."[17]

WE LOVE 'EM AND KILL 'EM PROPERLY – PLUS MYTHS FROM SHEEP FARMERS

Documenting the remaining large kangaroos' post-WWII fate of
dispossession and treatment as hunted fugitives, Jock Marshall
paused for an anecdote featuring rural people, who saw killing
wildlife for money as the only work option.

A central Queensland woman told Marshall she and her husband
shot kangaroos because it was the only way to make a living,

(a situation I would hear again in central Queensland in 2017 and recount in a later chapter). They made sure the animal was properly dead as painlessly as possible. Others shot hundreds in a night, but didn't check bodies on the ground.

She said they came across kangaroos that had been dying for a week. In my exploration I was to hear more eye-witness cases of mis-shootings and extended suffering that did not stop in the 1960s. For instance, Terri Irwin told me that in 2000 when she and Steve bought a grazing property between St George and Roma, planning to turn it into a conservation reserve, she witnessed similar heart-breaking scenes.

"I've seen really sad things with kangaroos," Terri told me. "Horrendous wounding. Kangaroos dying for days." (More about the Irwin's story and successes with that property in the Sharing chapter.)

These personal accounts refer to an industry backed by governments and farmer groups who to this day claim 98 percent successful death-dealing headshots at night, at 100 metres, often further. Honest shooters told me that this is impossible as an average.

The sheep graziers who didn't love the kangaroos in the 1960s, or before, or since, have always had a narrative to justify their extermination. In 1966 it was said that one kangaroo eats as much as eight or nine sheep (a claim I heard repeated as 'fact' by a television breakfast talk show host in 2020). The actual comparison is just the opposite.

Contemporary research found one sheep needs about as much forage to maintain body condition as do five kangaroos collectively. It was claimed that kangaroos foul paddocks and cause erosion, when again that is more likely sheep or cattle. Knocked-over fences were another grievance, as was water use. There was always the animal's reputed ability to migrate in plague proportions to anywhere that green pick sprouts.

Marshall called most of this nonsense and challenged any claim to special knowledge by sheep farmers. Marshall also knocked the myths about prolific breeding and flying plagues. He noted that kangaroos have home ranges and rarely travel more than 30 miles (or about 50 kilometres), and are rarely seen in congregations of more than half a dozen on a daily basis in their traditional habitats.

The death. Samual Thomas Gill circa 1860, courtesy of Dixson Library, State Library of New South Wales.

A PICTURESQUE HISTORY OF KANGAROO KILLING

The advent of the commercial industry in the 1950s came on the heels of a previous century or two of cultural ideas about the kangaroo species as targets for human sport. Recently, two University of Melbourne researchers analysed paintings and other depictions of the colonial kangaroo hunt. The hunt was depicted as a good, fun, bonding and community-building activity for the more affluent settlers or squatters of British heritage. "Squatters bred packs of hounds and wealthy locals and visiting dignitaries would be invited to join in the hunt and all the social occasions that went with it," so the researchers found.[18]

Researchers Ken Gelder and Rachael Weaver noted that the killing of kangaroos by Europeans began at the same time as the species was first identified, as soon as Cook's *Endeavour* got stranded on a reef in far north Queensland in June and July 1770. Within 30 years there would be gentlemen hunting the large kangaroos with greyhounds, wolfhounds and crossbreed dogs, attended by conscripted convicts and Aboriginal guides. These were depicted in various 'idyllic' paintings from the early 1800s on. More formal colonial hunting clubs were set up across Australia in the 1830s and 1840s.

The researchers quote one Foster Fyans, the Police Magistrate of Geelong, who helped oversee the dispossession of Aboriginal people across the western frontier district. In his words: "A noble pack of hounds was kept up by gentlemen squatters who met every season ... hunting twice or thrice a week, and meeting at each other's houses, where good cheer and good and happy society were ever to be met." Celebrity English visitors, including Charles Darwin in 1836, the Duke of Edinburgh in 1867 and the novelist Anthony Trollope in 1871, enjoyed a kangaroo hunt. Reportedly the Duke shot 30 kangaroos trapped in a yard at close range and souvenired the skins and claws.[19]

Trophy hunting and collecting remain alive and profitable today. Often a dead piece of animal is all a tourist will see of that animal. I was informed at a leather shop in the village near me that in either 2011 or 2014, when President Barack Obama visited Australia, his people (according to this shopkeeper) were sent out to buy purses made from kangaroo scrotums as souvenirs for the staff. Seeing kangaroo paws made into key chains started that conversation. Toy koalas made with kangaroo fur rested on a shelf in the background.

Mount Abrupt in the Grampians, write Gelder and Weaver, was the subject for a painting series from 1864 by Nicholas Chevalier. It showed 'before and after' landscapes: first showing a peaceful Aboriginal family camped in the valley, then no family but horsemen with powerful dogs sweeping across the scene chasing kangaroos.[20] These painting and other images on museum walls are enduring cultural symbols of power, and of settler freedom to do what they want with the land and what inhabits it. Gelder and Weaver were left in no doubt about the continuum of kangaroo persecution in Australia up to the present.

They also found that empathy occasionally cropped up. In a poetic hunting depiction published in an 1805 newspaper, sympathy was extended to a female kangaroo, possibly with joey on board, that is pursued and trapped by a hunter and dog. "Fatigu'd, broken hearted, tears gush from her eyes" as she realises her fate. A hundred years later, with Ethel Pedley's 1902 children's book *Dot and the Kangaroo*, tears again flowed for native animals and the loss of the bush as a result of white settlement.[21] For some native animals however, the trauma was just gathering speed in 1902.

KOALAS, EARLY VICTIMS OF THE FUR TRADE

"The organised savagery with which kangaroos are being hunted today is equalled in our history only by the appalling massacre of koalas in 1927," wrote Marshall.[22]

Koalas had been killed for their fur from the earliest colonial times. The sleepy, slow-moving koala is a sitting duck for anyone with a rifle or shotgun. Coastal ranges and flats are favoured koala habitat, but those richer soils were also favoured for the dairy industry with settlement. In the NSW Bega Valley for example, the valley forest was cleared after 1830 for grazing cows and the timber industry got busy on the slopes of the nearby mountains. Hares, rabbits and foxes were introduced.

Photo: Maria Taylor

Present-day researchers propose that the numbers of large marsupials fluctuated widely during the 1800s as Aboriginal people were dispossessed – meaning less Indigenous hunting. But settlement also meant loss of habitat, widespread extermination, plus whitefella hunting.[23]

Animal populations were catapulted out of previous stable environments. For grazing wildlife and birds, extensive clearing at first meant the appearance of new green grass and possible tasty crops, and also concentrated remaining habitat. Traditions of counting 'plague-proportion' marsupials may well have started with short-term changes following clearing. Just as with kangaroos today, the settlers appeared to think the koala supply would never end.

By the 1920s, the slaughter of koalas for their skins was reaching a peak but focused primarily on remaining populations in Queensland. In 1924 more than two million koala skins were exported, but called 'wombat.' Wombat in turn may have been variously called 'Australian beaver' for overseas consumption, as was the Brush-tail possum, also widely hunted for its fur before and after World War I.[24]

Marshall notes that establishing the Kangaroo Island koala population was a belated gesture by the South Australian government after the animals were essentially exterminated in that state by 1923. There, as elsewhere, no scientific study or ecological data were collected before the animals were wiped out.

AS KOALAS FALL OVER CLIFF, THE PUBLIC IGNORED

The notorious 1927 Queensland open season on koalas put the final nail in the coffin of this iconic species, and it has never recovered. The state government sold licenses to 10,000 'registered' trappers. Within a few months 600,000 koalas were massacred as a result.

Fearless as ever, Marshall named the politicians responsible so that they, if not the koalas, as he put it, would be preserved for posterity. In that spirit, one can name Forgan Smith and A.J. Jones who were acting premiers at the time, the latter also Minister for Agriculture and Stock. Marshall quotes the media of the day on this matter. Those reports provide a cultural record of the official excuses that always claim evidence of high populations, echoed with today's kangaroo slaughters. The newspaper record also provides evidence that there was opposition from the public.[25]

Brisbane Courier July 8 1927: "It had been strongly represented by trappers, and this was supported by official evidence, said the Minister, that native bears [koalas] were to be found in large numbers in certain areas, due, probably, to the fact that the season for trapping this native animal had been closed for eight years ..."

Acting Premier Forgan Smith told the newspaper a week later that the fur industry was valuable to Queensland, and claimed the revenues would be spent on fauna protection and sanctuaries. On July 18 came a letter of protest from a Catholic or Anglican church archbishop, citing many citizens who were offended by the slaughter of koalas.

A letter to the editor of the *Brisbane Courier* on July 13 1927 reflects community protest. "Those of us who are interested in the preservation of this wonderfully interesting and harmless little animal are wondering what has transpired to give the Minister reason so suddenly to alter his very necessary and wise declaration of last year. As far as can be learned, no advice on this matter has been sought from the Department's biological officers or rangers ... As the only way bears can contribute to the revenue is by dying and handing over their skins, dead they have to be." Mr Geo H. Barker, Member of the Committee of Advice on Native Birds and Animals.

Marshall records that at the time, only two of hundreds of letters agreed with the government's position. Nor did editorials agree. The *Courier* editorialised that declaring the open season would simply encourage immediate slaughter, weeks before the season's commencement, and indeed it did.

The letters supporting the killing made arguments still used today. The koalas had to be killed to save them from disease (these days it's about saving kangaroos from starvation). The fur industry, wrote one person, was at the time more important in the state than mining.

The same writer, Mr. Thos A. Foley MLA, also claimed that koalas bred like bacteria and their abundance was evident from the fact that in 1919 the open season bagged one million koala skins, notwithstanding that the animals only had an 18-month rest from a previous open season. Much the same abundance arguments are today put forth for killing kangaroos: that they breed like rabbits, if not bacteria, and they are always there to be slaughtered in vast numbers.

Not all the opponents to koala slaughter lived in towns. Marshall quotes one bushman on July 25 in the *Courier*'s ongoing debate saying true bushmen of that era called koala killers 'crawlers,' and, regarding the disease argument: "He might as well suggest that we all commit suicide so as to preclude the possibility of dying from cancer." He also ridiculed the Acting Premier's pretensions of being a country bushman.

The open season went ahead after the Acting Premier charged that protesters were acting with "political malevolence" and that there was no concrete evidence to support a stop to the killing. More than a million possums and 584,738 koalas were slaughtered for their fur in August 1927. Marshall noted that the Queensland government's subsequent inability to calculate its royalties on the haul at 5 percent showed its arithmetic was no better than its humanity. Possums fetched 59 shillings per dozen and koala skins 56 shillings 9 pence per dozen.

In Marshall's view, the fact that any koalas remain in Australia to delight tourists is because the state governments finally decided the votes of outraged citizens outnumbered the shooters and skin dealers. In 1956, David Fleay, pioneer of captive breeding for endangered species, wrote that "the pathetically harmless little fellows with their slow rate of increase have never recovered".[26] The situation has not improved for koalas who are now officially 'endangered'.

After once numbering in the millions in Queensland alone, the koala population was about 80,000 nationwide prior to the 2019 bushfires that took a heavy toll.[27] South-east Queensland and northern NSW had offered the best remaining sanctuaries for the koala, although few people saw them. But with rapid suburban development and continued habitat destruction, the nation has seen pathetic images of koalas, who are quite attached to a home range, cowering or dead on roadsides, clinging to light poles, or on someone's back porch, as their trees are cut down and they try to stay or return to an area. In NSW in early 2020, warnings of statewide koala extinction by 2050 were circulating.[28]

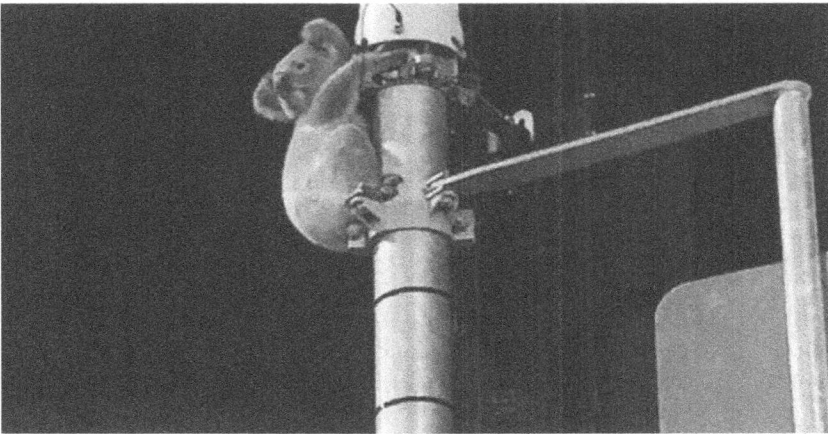

Photo: Wildcare Australia

Koala on lamp-post.

Marshall, ever alert to the ironies of Australia's wildlife management, recounts that in Victoria, after the great northern slaughter period, koalas were re-introduced to Phillip Island and protected. But at the same time, he wrote, the state government was employing professional trappers at a bounty of 10 shillings a scalp to kill at random the equally attractive wombat. The wombat is the closest marsupial relative of the koala.

The wombat's sin? Being built rather like a bulldozer, they plough through fences that often were established to keep out the rabbits that the settlers let loose in Australia. With bounties, there were no baseline biological or ecological studies conducted about the animals the farmers wanted wiped out. Were they strongly territorial? No one knew. But if they were, it would have been cheaper and more humane to just remove those with burrows near fences.

EXTERMINATING NATIVE GRAZERS BECOMES LAW: THE BOUNTY ERA

Pademelon and wallaby shoot, using Beagle dogs, Bega NSW. At Work and at Play, 1880–1940 (FL1680042), courtesy of State Library of New South Wales.

Bounties were extensively applied for three quarters of a century against native grazers large and small, labelled pests and vermin, and against birds like the emu, demonised as a crop pest. In NSW in the 1870s, the Legislative Assembly heard that marsupials were overrunning many parts of the colony and "rendering land virtually valueless." As a result, kangaroo species were declared to be 'pests' to the pastoral industry.[29]

Ten years later, eastern Australian states had enacted legislation encouraging the eradication of kangaroos and wallabies that were declared "vermin" – a quaint old term for noxious pest. The NSW colony was divided into sheep districts, with boards of directors who would pay the bounties. In 1884 in the Tamworth district alone, 260,780 macropods were killed, and bounties were paid for some 100,000 kangaroos for each year of the early 1880s in this district.

Across the state, in that same year of 1884, more than 250,000 bounties were paid for kangaroo scalps and more than 86,000 bounties were paid for scrub wallaby (Red-necked wallaby) scalps. In Queensland, nearly eight million of kangaroo species were killed from 1877 to 1907 as part of a bounty program and 65 million kangaroos are said to have been killed in various pest programs in Queensland during the century from 1877 to 1987.[30] The slaughter was not restricted to the larger kangaroos.

Approximately 3 million Bettongs and Potoroos, related rat-kangaroos, were shot for bounties in NSW between 1883 and 1920.[31] Three of the five species of these are now extinct in NSW, with the help of habitat destruction and fox introduction. Belatedly, their environmental contributions are being recognised. The Brush-tailed Rock-wallaby was pushed close to extinction in NSW thanks in part to the fur trade. Between 1884 and 1914 the Pastures Protection Boards in NSW paid 640,000 bounties for this species and researchers suspect the slaughter was much greater.[32] The Brush-tailed Rock-wallaby is now absent from most of its NSW range and subject of an expensive recovery program.

Keeping the tradition of direct state killings alive today is the annual destruction of Eastern Grey kangaroos on public reserves in the national capital, Canberra. If there is irony in this slaughter, it is with a tax-payer-funded experiment to reintroduce the colonially-slaughtered Bettong into a small idealised woodland setting behind 10-foot fences in the city – while healthy Eastern Greys willing and able to co-exist are shot around the perimeter.

The ACT has also used kangaroo carcasses as bait – joining other state government agencies – in poisoning dingos, foxes and dogs and any native mammal or bird bycatch – again on behalf of graziers. At the same time, governments routinely tell the public a lack of both predators and Aboriginal hunting are reasons that lethal management of 'too many' kangaroos is necessary.

The sorry history of state killing and bounties was compiled in a 2012 research paper focused on the legal position of contemporary kangaroo management. Legally or by purpose, little has changed since Marshall's time. Keely Boom and colleagues at the University of Technology Sydney's Centre for Compassionate Conservation didn't doubt what had been the driving force since the 1800s:

"The primary justification for this mass killing was the protection of the pastoral industry which was regarded as playing a central economic role, especially in terms of exports. One NSW parlia-mentarian stated that he had killed 18,000 kangaroos in the early 1890s because they were eating grass that [he thought] would have supported some 30,000 sheep. Another advocated killing all native animals to prevent them from 'using up the grasses of this country upon which our salvation almost depends."[33]

FATE OF THE BILBY, AND MORE FUR TALES
Not caught in bounty nets but still early victims of the settlers' habits were many of the smaller marsupials that today inhabit the extinct or endangered species list. The bilby is one example. Australians have taken the bilby to heart as an endangered species,

and in chocolate form as the Easter Bilby, as distinct from the reviled rabbit. But the bilby did not fare well for long under the early colonists.

Bilby.   Rufous Bettong.

Close to the ground and with long ears, the bilby was also called the rabbit-bandicoot or native rabbit. It was widely eaten, including by the naturalist and ornithologist John Gould who commented on it in 1863. In some districts in the early days the bilby was even protected as a house pet by people who recognised its usefulness in the destruction of mice and insects. That protection did not last. Jock Marshall describes their demise in his roll call of extermination: in the latter 19th century, the species was slaughtered for its pelts "and marketed in very large numbers in the skin sales in Adelaide. They were maimed and killed in steel traps set for rabbits, and likely many fell victim to poison baits".[34]

Such treatment was not confined to South Australia. Add to that the introduced fox and rabbit populations that competed for breeding burrows, and you have an endangered species. The last-known pair in NSW lived on a rocky hill in an experimental farm near Wagga until 1912 when they were shot by townsfolk.

South Australia may come into more than its fair share of shame and blame in Marshall's history, but the examples of marsupial extinction are arresting. Marshall sketched the cases of the Toolach wallaby and the Southern Hairy-nosed wombat, and the smaller marsupial rat-kangaroos. The source for the history is anatomist and naturalist Frederic Wood Jones's telling of what happened to the mammals in that state.

The Toolach wallaby lived only in the south-eastern part of South Australia, and was noted for its distinctive beauty, swiftness and abundance. "Its chase was at one time a very popular form of sport and its beautiful pelts have been marketed in very large numbers in the sale rooms of Melbourne." When Wood Jones wrote this in the early 1920s, he noted there were still five or six individuals left, exhorting that a vigorous "saving" campaign should be undertaken. Unfortunately, the Toolach did not survive to be pampered as an endangered species.

The Southern Hairy-nose wombat was hunted with spotlights, like present-day kangaroo hunts, and made into stew and 'ham'. Marshall notes that when he and artist Russell Drysdale (a good friend) crossed the Nullabor in 1958, there were still many wombats.

In 2019, media reports showed how little has changed for native grazers. The Southern Hairy-nose wombat appears to have made some comeback in South Australia, and soon graziers were reported to be calling for a cull. An image accompanying this call shows a primary producer on a wide expanse of treeless and grassless red dirt, beset by drought, possibly having been overstocked, but as usual blaming the wildlife.[35]

Then there is the fate of the once abundant rat-kangaroos. The Tuft-tailed rat-kangaroos remained abundant across much of South Australia into the early 1900s. However, wrote Marshall quoting Wood Jones: "The dealers in Adelaide did a great trade selling them by the dozen at about ninepence a head for coursing [meaning being hunted with greyhounds] on Sunday afternoons. It may surprise people who remember those days that there is not a preserved specimen, not even a skin of the animal, available for scientific study in South Australia today. In the same way it will one day surprise the rising generation when they realise that the few native animals they are now familiar with are gone forever."

Other rat-kangaroos now on death row due in part to habitat destruction are the Potoroo, known in colonial days as the Long-nosed rat-kangaroo. It was plentiful in low scrubby lands from northern New South Wales to South Australia and Tasmania. In the 1960s it was reported as extinct in South Australia, and rare everywhere outside of Tasmania.

The same fate awaited the cute Rufous rat-kangaroo, also known as Rufous Bettong, that was once common along the coast of New South Wales and southern Queensland. Marshall wrote that in 1966 it was found only in isolated colonies and was in danger of extinction. Rat-kangaroos need protective cover.

Other ecologically useful native animals that became scarce with the clearing and burning off are the numbat (or banded anteater) which is now extinct in most of Australia but still survives in parts of WA; Fat-tailed mice or dunnarts, now considered vulnerable to cats and foxes. They first became scarcer as they had nowhere to go when their habitat was razed or burned. The little marsupial survived under logs and rocks, or in holes, feeding on grasshoppers, cockroaches, beetles, centipedes, and other insects. A hopping mouse, *Notomys*, of northern and central Australia, was another attractive native that may be extinct in the Northern Territory, and endangered in South Australia, while still enduring in Queensland.

Marshall briefly apologises for picking on the South Australians, but then reminds himself that as he was writing in the mid-1960s the state government of Sir Thomas Playford remained among those obstinately deaf to any entreaties for a moratorium on the slaughter of kangaroos – "at least until zoologists gather concrete data on their ecology in relation to that Sacred Cow of Australia, *Ovis aries*, the domestic sheep".[36]

It would be another 50–60 years before studies showed that kangaroos and sheep rarely compete directly, except in severe drought; that, as a yardstick, one sheep needs to eat as much as 5–7 kangaroos together to retain condition, (more so for cattle and horses); and that kangaroos, unless hemmed in, do not denude the ground as sheep do.

Marshall finishes his chapter on the marsupials with the fate of the singular marsupial 'wolf', known more popularly as the Tasmanian Tiger. It was still common in 1863 in Tasmanian forests, but was marked for extinction with increased settlement on the island, and with sheep farming. No captive breeding or sanctuary was offered.

VOTES AND MONEY DRIVE THE CARNAGE

Marshall had no doubt why the governments of the day supported the slaughter of koalas and kangaroos large and small or the Tasmanian Tiger. Votes and money, he concluded.

He saw that the Australian states and the federal government through the 1960s (and as it turned out for decades longer) still perceived themselves as part of the British imperial and economic project, tied to the export nation narrative that came packaged with the first sheep. He recognised that state legislators support wildlife 'management,' particularly kangaroo slaughter, in a bid to win country votes and that the commercial industry 'harvesting' of kangaroos was part of that 'help the farmers' pitch.

He recounts that when a "fauna protection association" request arrived during the second term (1949–1966) of the Liberal Party's Sir Robert Menzies, asking for a moratorium on the prevailing open season on kangaroos for export, he passed the buck to the states, although the federal government rules over the export of native species. That divide continues.

With koalas, small landholders and farm workers wanted the money (as supplementary income) and the politicians wanted their votes. With kangaroos it was – and is – the votes of graziers on marginal land, or those with traditional beliefs and understanding of Australian conditions, who have a profit motive and are beset by weather problems. Today the farming and grazing lobby, and the politicians who represent them, most often through the National Party, exert the same inordinate influence on behalf of export agriculture as the ones in 1870s NSW or in Queensland in 1927.

Marshall concluded his scathing narrative on the demise of the marsupials, and the lack of biological research or evidence-gathering on this unique sector of the animal kingdom, with these words: "I could go on and on with this tragedy of greed and misery, stupidity and callous political expediency." He contents himself with a modified list of endangered or extinct mammals, in 1966 numbering about 30, with another dozen unknown enough to be uncertain.

HAVE YOU SEEN AN EMU, BUSTARD, OR LYREBIRD? FOOD, FEATHERS, AND FASHION

With a focus on wildlife, it's hard to skim past (but also hard to look at) the horror that the settlers inflicted on Australia's endemic birds: early on for food, then for monetary gain, akin to the koala, possum and kangaroo slaughters for skins, or for no discernible reason other than eliminating them, for example shooting every land and sea eagle. The killing was conducted with a thoroughness that matched that of the sealers and whalers of the time. In some cases the perpetrators *were* the sealers on Australia's southern islands. The history here is sourced from another chapter in Marshall's book.

As with the removal of cover for marsupials, sheep grazing destroyed the habitat for ground-dwelling birds, including the unique mallee-fowl that incubates its eggs in soil burrows. Australian birds also fell victim to the feather trade, recreational hunting and collecting, and cropping. Emus, bustards, and lyrebirds once so plentiful are today a rare sight.

When walking in southern woodlands or forests today, a high-light for some like me is hearing and glimpsing that talented mimic, the lyrebird. I was also delighted to see groups of emus in central Queensland. My delight was tempered by the vision of many running up and down the kilometres of new wildlife exclusion fencing erected by the latest generation of cattle and sheep graziers, including large corporate operations.

Photo: Maria Taylor

ROLGAS

Grus rubicunda

and elegant, Brolgas
e through grasslands,
edges of billabongs,
swamps being preferred

ir trumpeting calls are
n heard in unison, both
n in flight and on the
nd.

iding 1-1.25 m tall, their
jspan is up to 2m.

BUSTARD

Ardeotis australis

Up to 1m tall , the Bustard or Plains Turkey is solidly built and walks with head held high in a slow and stately manner.

It usually ranges silently through the grasslands and open scrublands, but gives a harsh barking croak if alarmed.

It runs before taking flight on broad wings up to 1.20m in length.

and Bustards are often seen on the plains between Nebo and Glenden

Educational board with image and text about brolga and bustard.

The Australian bustard, which looks somewhat like a crane or two-coloured brolga, was called the plains turkey by the settlers, and was once common along coastal regions. It was first spotted and eaten by Captain Cook in 1770. The English immediately thought of the soon-to-be-extinct bustard of their home country, and the Australian version was considered a good eating bird. Bustards were soon killed wherever they were found, and by the 1960s were extinct in Victoria and in other southern regions. It could still be seen in remote regions of central and north Queensland, and in the Kimberley.

There were voices – citizens and overseas observers – who protested at bustard and other bird killing and pushed for government and public enlightenment, just as happens today, and were accorded about as much respect by authorities. Marshall wrote, "I made a vigorous protest against all this [the killing of bustards] through the Zoological Society of NSW, but we had no way of knowing whether this had any effect. On a journey in a 'good year' from Melbourne to the Simpson Desert and return by way of Coopers Creek, a recent Monash University party saw only one Plains Turkey".[37]

WAR AGAINST BIG BIRD

Emus are the second-tallest living bird, after the ostrich. Flocks of them were once plentiful around Sydney. While some of the fearless birds were eaten, others were made pets. One anecdote from 1798 described the scene in the Domain near Government House, where some tame emus, described as "noble birds," marched with measured step as if keeping pace with the guards on duty. The emus even mingled with crowds that came for festive occasions to the Domain, and in one recorded incident playfully ran with a wary group of newcomers, removing the hat from the head of one gentleman to everyone's amusement.[38] This charming (mostly) live-and- let-live attitude was not to last.

Emus, Kinchega National Park, NSW.

Sealers wiped out the numerous emus on King and Kangaroo islands for food by the 1830s. Wrote Marshall: "Contemporaneously the Anglo Tasmanians were ferociously exterminating both their Emu and the native people" including successive waves of emus introduced from the mainland.[39]

By 1860, a contemporary observer reported that emus were only seen in the far interior of the mainland, and were invariably killed when seen. Often it was for emu oil, extracted by boiling the skin of a dead and plucked bird … The oil was used for lamps and seen as a good emollient for sprains and bruising. But, Marshall added, the birds also were killed for no reason at all. In fact, their troubles had only begun, as they were increasingly scapegoated in the agricultural landscape.

The emus in Queensland had a bounty placed on their heads and eggs in the 1920s when country people there suspected that the seed of the wildly invasive prickly pear, (an exotic species introduced by Europeans as natural fencing material and to establish a dye industry) was being spread by the big birds. In two years, two shillings and sixpence were paid for each of 317,768 emu scalps, and one shilling each was paid for 109,345 eggs.

"While this holocaust was in progress, an entomologist found 2,991 injurious caterpillars in the stomach of one emu," reported Alex H Chisholm in his 1929 book *Birds and Green Places*.[40] Meaning that the emus were conducting good crop pest control.

Next it was wheat growers in Western Australia who went to war against the emus, in one case literally. In Western Australia, as elsewhere, new land was opened up for soldier settler allotments after World War I. Again, pressure was brought to bear on native species and their habitat as land was converted to farms. In hindsight, many soldiers (after a horrendous war) and their families may not have been cut out for the rigors of pioneer farming, but governments were adamant. Carving up the landscape for more private property meant more control.

In 1932, the Great Emu War pitted a Commonwealth defence department- sanctioned machine gun detachment against a claimed 20,000 emus ravaging WA wheat-growers crops across 40 square miles.

As Marshall tells the story, the troops were accompanied into action by a special correspondent, and by a motion picture war photographer. The commanding officer was a major, who arrived with a sergeant and a gunner. The latter took to the field with two Lewis guns and 10,000 rounds of ammunition. Fifty settlers organised a drive of emus for twenty miles into a dead end – the rabbit-proof fence – where the birds were supposed to gather and be shot.

"History does not record the name of the Emu C.O. but he must have been a good chap because the preliminary skirmish on the first day accounted for only about 12 birds out of a platoon of 40 ... It was soon realised that the hoped for open warfare would not eventuate, because the Emus obeyed the infantryman's first law of preservation, 'don't bunch!' and split up into innumerable small patrols."[41]

So it continued. An ambush at a watering point netted another 12 birds, and then the gun jammed. By the time another 50 birds were shot, some 2500 rounds had been discharged. After a week of this, when the situation began to draw comment and satire in Canberra, the then federal Minister for Defence, Sir George Pierce, ordered a strategic withdrawal.

Vividly demonstrating the ongoing influence of agriculturalists on various political parties and departments, the Emu War continued with federal defence department help for some time thereafter, without a great body count. More effective were the wheat growers themselves who killed 57,000 birds in six months from August 1835. By 1943, the West Australian government was giving free ammunition to local 'vermin boards' for distribution against the emus. In 1944, the government escalated the war to placate rural voters.

Australia's other emblem on the national coat of arms, next to the kangaroo, was declared 'vermin' throughout that vast state – the emu's last stronghold.

Naturalists and other citizens protested vigorously and managed after three years to get the bird back to protected status in the state's southwest corner. In the mid-1960s when Marshall wrote, the Central Vermin Fund was still paying bounties accounting for hundreds of thousands more dead emus and destroyed eggs.

Today the emu is a 'protected native species' and considered 'common' as distinct from 'threatened or endangered'. Common means that native animals can still be killed by property owners and their shooter friends, or by their cluster fences, as currently is occurring in Queensland. Or have their eggs cooked by poorly-timed fire regimes in the far north. With a total estimated population no higher than 750,000 birds, you will rarely see an emu in the south-east of the country.

THE DEPTHS OF FASHION: LYREBIRD, EGRET, AND ALBATROSS PLUMES

Fashion and the turn-of-century millinery industry picked up where land conversion paused. A main target in Australia was the forest and woodland lyrebird, so called because the male's tail feathers resemble the curves of the classic Greek instrument. In the 1860s the bird was reported to be common in the southern ranges and tablelands. But already tail feathers were being "detached" from the bird and sold in Sydney shops at increasing prices as the lyrebird population fell.

Journalist, author, and amateur ornithologist Alec Chisholm, who described the assault on emus in the 1920s, also wrote about what happened to lyrebirds in southern Australia a few decades later, and Marshall draws on his account.[42]

Lyrebirds, who lay only one egg a year, would be hunted down for their tail feathers for more than 100 years. Habitat destruction for development went hand in hand with hunting, the introduction of foxes, and the activities of domestic and feral dogs and cats. Aboriginal people, who had rarely troubled the bird prior to white settlement, were paid and sometimes supplied with firearms to bring in the treasure. (One story has it that in 1840, when Aboriginal people were issued with bird-killing muskets, they turned them against white settlers in what is now outer suburban Melbourne).

"Along with carved Emu eggs and stuffed parrots, it was fashionable to display lyre plumes in bush inns and household parlours.

A lyrebird tail, it would seem, was a fitting gift for a colonial gentleman of fashion to present to his lady," reported Marshall.

The feathers were abundant in Sydney shops in the late 1880s, as well as being hawked on the streets. Being put on a postage stamp by NSW and given protection by Victoria did not stop the slaughter, nor that of the northern Regent and Rifle birds for their plumage to grace European hats and dresses.

Chisholm sends an echo down the years about the greenwash of 'protected native species' when he writes: "Not the least extraordinary feature of the whole sorry business was the lethargy of governments ... Lyrebirds were protected in three States, yet never once was an official finger raised to check the men who, though perhaps relatively few in number, were creating a national calamity by their campaign of murder."

Finally, when the Royal Australasian Ornithologists Union got involved and started protesting around 1911 about the thousands of lyrebird tails being sold and exported annually, politicians once again began to notice that the votes of concerned citizens might outnumber the votes of the traders, and moved to more effective protection of the greatly depleted survivors.

Nor were these the only birds slaughtered for the hat trade. Nesting albatross were assaulted and sometimes plucked alive. The feathers of tens of thousands of courting egrets caught in breeding colonies were sold as batch lots in London as 'osprey plumes' and the osprey sea hawk itself was killed in large numbers. When the adult egrets in the breeding colonies were shot, their young slowly starved to death. And this is only in Australia.

We cannot follow Marshall on his account of the hat decoration plumage slaughter in New Guinea. Suffice to say this was another face of colonialism, as "white men everywhere engaged in the trade. Even government officials and missionaries dealt in feathers and made easy money".[43] The final word to this sorry tale is that the slaughter stopped not because of governments but because fashion changed and the demand went away.

The live bird trade did not escape Marshall's attention either. Grass parrots were particularly fancied, and declined in the 20th century. Parrots and cockatoos, brush turkeys, Bronzewing pigeons, bowerbirds, even Cape Barren geese were caught and sold. In 1959, before the federal government prohibited the export of fauna for commercial purposes (while states could still export to zoos), about 400,000 birds were trapped, of which maybe 100,000 survived for export – stuffed into overcrowded boxes through hot and cold. Marshall called the state-based bird trade nasty and lucrative. (Later, I catch up with an iconoclastic avenger against the live native animal trade who did much to expose corrupt dealings between government bureaucrats and commercial wildlife traders, including the kangaroo trade.)

Ruminating about the rhetoric of abundance, Marshall noted: "Nobody thought that the Fur Seal of Bass Straight was in danger but it was exterminated in the Furneaux Group." He offered the cautionary tale of the American Passenger pigeon. In the 1800s Passenger pigeon flocks, multi-million birds strong, darkened the skies of the eastern United States. The last individual died in the Cincinnati Zoo in 1914.

In Australia, the Harlequin or Flock pigeon (Flock Bronzewing) that appeared in massive numbers also suddenly disappeared. Discovered by John Gould in NSW in 1839, these are seed-eating birds of the arid country. They once travelled in immense flocks, millions in total, breeding only after rain and fresh grass appearing. They disappeared in the 1920s. What happened? Sheep and cattle herds prevented grass from seeding and caused erosion. Different vegetation, like spinifex, took over. The ground-breeding bird's eggs and young were trampled. The adults were shot in great numbers. With declining numbers, climate variations, drought, and possibly disease did the rest. When Marshall wrote, the bird seemed to be recovering, and today is considered to have stable populations, no longer in the southern pastoral country but in the far north and in the centre.

Influential scientific voices of the 19th century found Australia's indigenous animals to be interesting but "useless," providing but "a little sport and the occasional meal," as one member of Melbourne's scientific community reportedly put it.[44]

The reaction was to agitate for introduced animals through 'acclimatisation societies' that successfully imported dozens of species, many that are today combatted as 'ferals.' They have included starlings and Indian mynahs, carp, goats, donkeys, horses and camels, prickly pear and blackberry – not forgetting the rabbit and the fox.

GOOD AT SWIMMING AND BALL GAMES BUT NOT HABITAT PRESERVATION

Marshall concluded this roll call of disaster by saying what other independent biological scientists have repeated since: habitat is key to survival of wild animals and wild plants. Now, with a human population more than double that of the 1960s and increasing, and development pressures and weather pressures across the land, this has never been truer. There are more national parks. But compared to the extent of privately-managed agricultural land blanketing Australia, the reserves and parks that have been set up since 1966 remain fragmented and tiny as habitat. The non-productive mountainous areas that have been traditionally set aside are not the only or ideal habitat for marsupials and the large birds of the plains like emus and brolgas.

"Until recently I tended to put most of the blame on our British ancestors," concluded Marshall, "but that simply will not wash. We modern Australians do not shoot Aborigines as our forebears did, nor do we present them with treacle laced with arsenic. But there is still today an appreciable proportion of the sheep farming fraternity which would extinguish the Red Kangaroo, as our great-grandfathers did the Tasmanian Aboriginal."

In 1970, about the time Marshall's book appeared, the number of sheep in Australia peaked at 180 million.[45] Australia was also celebrating 200 years since Captain James Cook "discovered" Australia, as the national narrative had it. Every town and village staged colonial pageantry. The British Royals visited for months, touring and taking homage. Civic leaders and media owners were still overwhelmingly of British descent and framed the glorious Australian story of improvement, development, progress, and overcoming hostile natives. Despite Marshall's hopes for change, fifty years ago Australia was still very proudly a colony.[46]

AFTER CRIMINALISATION AND DISPERSAL

Viewing colonial settlement, it is impossible not to notice the parallels between how the Europeans thought about and destroyed the native plants and animals in the name of improvement and profit, and what they did to the First Nations people. Harold Finch-Hatton reported in his 1885/1886 book that either way, settlers showed no mercy or respect.

While others have covered what happened to the First Australians extensively, and the theme of this book is wildlife, the two are linked in the culture of brutality, exploitation and indeed extermination – that have left a legacy with present-day Australians. Cases I saw in the course of my research provide some idea of what was happening on all fronts in those early decades.*

* More on the mistreatment and genocide of First Australians is in the appendix at www.mariataylor.com.au, injustice-appendix

Private property wildlife management: Narrandra NSW Kangaroo and Emu hunt 1946.
Photographed by Norman Herfort, 30 April 1946. Collection ACP Magazines Ltd photographic
archives 1930s–1980s, courtesy of State Library of New South Wales.

WHISTLEBLOWERS AND GOOD PEOPLE STIFLED
FOR CONFORMITY

I learned throughout this exploration that with both the human dispossession and massacres, as with the wildlife, there were records of witnesses and whistleblowers and newspaper efforts to disclose and stop the killings. These were overridden by social and economic silencing, and demands for conformity of thinking. The same values still rule and silence people today. Extermination is still justified by the incentives of commerce and money.

Maintaining those traditional values requires deployment of the classic propaganda technique of demonising in order to de-sensitise the public. They called the First Australians 'savages' and other labels the Europeans considered the opposite of 'civilised' and Christian. It continues with the labelling of kangaroos, emus, or other inconvenient wildlife, as 'vermin', 'pests', and 'plagues' that need to be lethally managed. The disrespect that tourists notice comes with those attitudes.

Nevertheless, in the years after Marshall's expose, the fight was not over. Starting in the 1970s, the free-living kangaroo – as the outstanding victim of this colonial legacy – gained a number of notable new champions. I discovered that they enjoyed a measure of political success for a while, and also took the fight overseas.

VOICES FOR THE VOICELESS, 1970s–90s

"In some areas of Queensland far west, there are a few medium to large mobs of kangaroos of about 400 to 500. These mobs are on the move because of severe drought and because they have lost most the grazing land so essential for their survival. The kangaroo has been forced to become a fugitive in its own land."

— ARTHUR QUERIPEL, FOUNDER OF THE AUSTRALIAN WILDLIFE
PROTECTION COUNCIL, IN A LETTER TO THE *HERALD*, AUG 12, 1985

Arthur Queripel operated a petrol station in Mildura in the late 1960s, but his heart was always in the bush. If broken hearts are possible, his became so from what he observed over his lifetime – but it also spurred him to start one of Australia's seminal wildlife advocacy organisations.

Born in Western Australian in 1911, Queripel's bush childhood and later life journey contribute a documentary record bridging the earliest settler days, when Europeans took over the most fertile grassed and treed lands before spreading to more marginal grazing land, and then to the 20th century cleared and developed landscapes Queripel experienced, Jock Marshall recorded, and we see today.

167

Queripel wrote of the early days in Western Australia: "My parents lived on a small 20 acre property about 15 miles southwest from Pinjarra. We lived among huge Jarrah and Karri forests. The birds and other wildlife along with the wildflowers were prolific, whilst the air and spring water were fresh and invigorating. It is so sad that now much of this paradise has been destroyed by the European invader."

Worse was to come after his parents moved to Victoria in 1921, where his father started a tire-re-treading business.

He recalled witnessing the clearing of the Mallee 'scrub' after World War I (primarily mid-size acacia species adapted to a sandy soil). He later recorded what he saw: the massive round-up of kangaroos, emus, and other native animals. He watched their carcasses burn on the smouldering vegetation. He described what he saw in later submissions on behalf of the kangaroo.

"I travelled the outback country, where I found that for many hundreds of miles the stations [ranches] adjoined each other to the north, south, east and west. The kangaroos that had originally and for time immemorial occupied this land had not been left one acre as sanctuary.

"The brutal manner in which I found the native animals being treated and continually being referred to as 'vermin' upset me a great deal and it all made me realise how unfair and greedy the European settlers and stock agents were.

"Because these unfortunate animals could not understand what had happened, they repeatedly tried to recover land by hopping from one property to the other [so] the vermin brand was placed on them.

"The general public were in the process of being trained to hate the kangaroos as the insidious propaganda was circulated far and wide. I could see the terrible injustice of this as I also witnessed the never-ending atrocities being inflicted upon these innocent and unique marvellous animals."[1]

Outback ethos. Photo by Jock Marshall's friend, herpetologist and defender of Australian nature, Eric Worrell, 1960s. Arthur Queripel used the photo in a newsletter commenting that the only change was that the hunters no longer brought cameras.

A decade earlier Jock Marshall had exposed what was happening on the ground since settlement, and now Queripel was seeing the legacy up close in rural Victoria. He witnessed the evolution of the industrial scale killing of kangaroos that ramped up in the 1950s as a skin trade with meat on the side. With Australian governments and individuals having brought the koala close to extinction by the 1930s for the same export 'product', the remaining larger marsupials had offered an easy alternative source.

He didn't know what to do. He recalled that he kept silent as most people do and worried over it for a long time. What finally set him into action was a day in 1969. A truck rolled up to his petrol station, and he was asked to service it. On closer inspection, he found that it was full of kangaroos bound for an interstate pet meat processor. He found many of the roos were being kept alive (for freshness) with their legs broken to stop movement.

Looking back on his decision right then to sell up and start a life of activism, Queripel also described the casual remarks of a man he employed who was telling a kangaroo shooter about how he 'had fun' with a joey by burning it with a lighted stick. "I sacked him on the spot," he said. A single man without a family to worry about, in 1969 he moved to Port Elliott in South Australia and started the Australian Wildlife Protection Council (AWPC).

The AWPC told a 1981 Royal Commission into the meat substitution racket prevalent at the time (kangaroo meat sold as beef, an official concern being the bushmeat quality of the outcome) that after seeing the truckload of tortured kangaroos with broken legs, "outraged and disgusted Mr Queripel reported the incident with no satisfaction. The RSPCA, the police and the Fisheries and Wildlife Division (of the state government) all divorced themselves of any responsibility".[2]

RECOGNISING WILDLIFE MANAGEMENT IS NOT NEUTRAL

Queripel and his band of growing citizen supporters realised that the parts of society that were treating kangaroos so badly also had very strong representation in the country's parliaments. He concluded that to have any influence, they had to intervene in the political process.

The fledgling AWPC had attracted 'name' supporters, including philosopher Peter Singer as patron, some federal and state politicians of the day, scientists including David Croft, and words of encouragement from Paul and Linda McCartney. They contacted the then Labor opposition spokesperson for foreign affairs and trade, Dr Jim Cairns. The AWPC proposed they would campaign for Labor at the 1972 election in tandem with a campaign for kangaroos.

The payback came when the Whitlam government swept into power and banned the export of kangaroo products. The AWPC asked that the ban stay in place until state governments took the necessary action to curb cruelty to kangaroos, and to protect them with establishment of more national parks. (For example, NSW in the early '70s had only three reserved parks for a fledgling National Parks and Wildlife Service that started in 1967.)

Three years later came the historic dismissal of the Whitlam government. The following Liberal–National coalition government led by Malcolm Fraser reverted to business as usual on behalf of commerce. Australia's treatment of kangaroos was about to get worse again.

Even so, the 1972 political action was groundbreaking for an animal welfare group, as Queripel wrote. "We mounted a most outstanding campaign in all capital cities under the banner of 'Cast your vote for the Kangaroo'." The outcome was legend. "We were accused of 'making conservation a political issue' but what we had really done was show how the conservation movement was tied up in politics."[3]

Those were prescient words. Australian mainstream conservation organisations – while first strongly backing the protection of kangaroos, and being at the forefront of an effort in the United States to stop imports of skins, as I describe shortly – by the mid-1990s had fallen back to a position of silence, or moderately backing the commercial slaughter of millions that ensued.

Making a change of perspective easier for environmental groups, and other Australian non-government entities, was Australian wildlife science. Applied ecology all along was lending its credentials to 'managing' kangaroo populations to help agriculture. The cloak of science made conformity from politicians, conservation groups, media organisations, and the general public much easier. A science badge sanitised more of the same: demonisation and blame, pest destruction and/or commercial exploitation.

Five years after the euphoria of the Whitlam years, the kangaroo was being officially designated a unit of trade, like a wool fleece or a lump of coal. Still Queripel battled on from his small acreage in Port Elliott, with support for the AWPC growing around the country.

From direct outback experience, he also waged a battle on behalf of Australia's first people – their cruel dispossession, poor health outcomes and ongoing discrimination and marginal living. For him it was all part of the "hideous" and "barbaric" outback he had observed. Indigenous people and animals received the same immoral treatment.

UNJUSTLY ACCUSED FUGITIVES IN THEIR OWN COUNTRY

If this perspective clashed uncomfortably with the favourite mainstream narrative of valiant (white) Australian men and women battling and conquering a hostile bush environment, Queripel remained undeterred, brandishing uncomfortable truths. He pointed out that, like the early Aborigines, the Australian wildlife – and in particular the large kangaroos that had survived the initial colonial onslaught – were left as fugitives in their own country.

In an August 1985 letter published in *The Herald,* he rejected complaints against competing wildlife from "those who have taken up farming in those notoriously drought-stricken outback areas of Queensland." Or there were those in the Victorian Mallee, the destruction of which he had witnessed, who were now screaming for drought relief "after clearing and converting much of the land into desert" – and, as always, blaming the kangaroos.

Reliable reports received by the Australian Wildlife Protection Council, he wrote, indicate that in some areas of far west Queensland in 1985 there were a few medium to large mobs of kangaroos of about 400 to 500. "These mobs are on the move because of severe drought and because they have lost most of the grazing land so essential for their survival. The kangaroo has been forced to become a fugitive in its own country."[4]

He and later others of the growing AWPC helped make the nation aware of the land and soil destruction being wrought by over-grazing marginal country, and the price the wildlife was paying as the scapegoat. With publicity, they pushed authorities towards some action to curb the worst cruelty abuses still rampant in the mid-20th century.

Ten years earlier, in 1975, Queripel had told the *Adelaide Advertiser* that he just spent $1,000 on a national advertisement on the plight of Australia's kangaroos. He would spend $50,000 of his own money during the following decade. The paper reported that "the advertisement, accompanied by a photograph showing a row of dead kangaroos mutilated by poor shooting called on the public to support retention of the Federal Government's [then] ban on the export of kangaroo products" – soon to be lifted with the ousting of Whitlam and the advent of the Fraser government.

Queripel was hopeful but realistic. "I'm wondering just how much good it will do. The Federal and State government have put an 'industry' tag on kangaroo slaughter and they are trying to show by cleverly concocted figures that the 'industry' can be run on a commercial basis without wiping the kangaroo out." The government-supported Rural Industries Research and Development Corporation activities in the following 30–40 years exactly bore him out.

The newspaper report continued: "Mr Queripel said he had not 'been bush' recently but it was obvious governments were not sincere in claims of 'culling' kangaroos merely to keep populations from getting out of hand. If that was the case they would employ expert shooters to kill only the older animals ... Instead these amateur butchers go out and slaughter wholesale the younger animals with better class skins so they can make golf bags and other disgusting things.[5]

By 1981, the AWPC's Royal Commission submission noted the latest 12-month open season on kangaroos in Queensland coinciding with the "promotional requirements of the Commonwealth Games ... it is ludicrous to think that thousands of live Kangaroos will be destroyed to make souvenir toy koalas and replicas of the games mascot Matilda," wrote then AWPC President Peter Preuss with long-time activist and later president Maryland Wilson.

CRUELTY TO THE MOST DEFENCELESS

Queripel was tormented by the rampant cruelty to the most defenceless: the dependent joeys. He had witnessed some skinned or gutted alive, to save the shooter a bullet, after they spent a night wounded. Most frequently their heads were bashed in, a practice that is considered an advisory (i.e. without legal force) 'code' today. This code applies whether in the commercial slaughter or the 'conservation' programs practiced by the rangers of the Australian national capital and sometimes in national parks of Australia.

Where possible, according to this lethal management framework, joeys must die along with their mothers. Leaving them to fend for themselves has been termed a longer-range death sentence as, lost and bewildered, they die of starvation, pneumonia, wild dog attack, or car impact. The collateral damage to individuals and wildlife family structure has dismayed ethical and humane citizens like Queripel and many others. But having an advisory welfare code to killing is one of the modern innovations that lull the public into acceptance.

'At work and play' images of rural life 1880–1940. Captioned kangaroos shot for meat any joeys saved and hand-reared. Courtesy of Dixon Library, State Library of New South Wales.

Later, veterinarian John Auty advised and worked with AWPC and other citizen wildlife campaigns in the 1990s and early 2000s. He knew all about the welfare code and the fate of dependent joeys in the kangaroo killing fields, whether commercial or overseen by government departments. He had been employed by the Commonwealth Department of Primary Industries to oversee the federal responsibility for animal welfare. He knew fairly quickly that the kangaroo industry resisted government input into how its business was conducted in the field and that the managing author-ities were complicit.

He recounted in a 1994 letter to the AWPC: "My first under-standing of the likely outcome for kangaroos was when attending an interdepartmental committee to discuss the impact of the documentary *Goodbye Joey* when a senior officer of the Parks and Wildlife Service said: 'there's no cruelty; only a roo being finished off with a club.' At that time, two Victorian farmers were in jail for the same crime."

Peter Cunningham, former ABC cinematographer and later film-maker with the Defence Department, made the documentary *Goodbye Joey* in the early 1980s. He interviewed Whitlam's Deputy Prime Minister Dr Jim Cairns as well as representatives of the meatworker's union and the RSPCA. They roundly criticised the institutionalised mistreatment of Australia's unique wildlife and nature and confirmed the complicity of governments in the whole-sale slaughter of the kangaroo.

Cunningham himself told an animal welfare group for its newsletter that what he saw and heard put him off eating meat forever. He hadn't gone in as a conservationist, he said, but found the kangaroo industry to be the most disgusting and covered-up situation he had ever heard of. I couldn't find an archival copy of *Goodbye Joey* anywhere in Australia.*

In his outback work, Auty learned what other observers including myself have seen: 'At-foot' joeys are a constant companion to their mother and depend on her for continued milk supplementation in the first year, and rely on her for protection from hypothermia, predation, and for learning the ways of the world for much longer.

In one of many personal communications on what he learned, Auty wrote: "The nature of ex-pouch young [the 'at-foot'], with the clear cruel practice involved in making them orphans when most are unable to survive without their mothers, would result in the outlawing of the kangaroo killing industry in a civilised country."

He told a 2002 Tribunal considering complaints against the NSW kangaroo industry: "The parties to defence at the tribunal ignore two completely unacceptable practices innate to this industry, the bashing to death of in-pouch joeys and the orphaning of immature ex-pouch joeys." Describing photos submitted to the tribunal: "The grey joey shows the fate of probably one million ex-pouch joeys

* A scan of the newsletter article about the film *Goodbye Joey* is in the appendix at www.mariataylor.com.au, injustice-appendix

orphaned each year in the legal and illegal shoot. It is already disoriented and over subsequent days will suffer hypothermia, starvation and will almost certainly fall prey to foxes and feral dogs."

AGENTS OF COMMERCE

During 60 years of activism, Queripel learned the disappointment of those who expect government action in the public interest to follow evidence, but are obstructed when private property and commercial interests stand to lose. Wrote his friend Peter Andrew in Queripel's obituary: "He saw State and Federal wildlife departments as essentially 'agents of commerce' and once commented that elections would be more honest if we were to vote for our favourite financial institution, bank or treasury official."[6]

When he died in 2000 aged 89, his obituaries also noted that his crusade won him many ordinary citizen admirers but few friends in high places. His defence of wildlife cost him a six-figure sum – much of it for newspaper advertising campaigns and for other AWPC activities. He never gave up hoping for a more compassionate world.

A SCIENTIST STEPS UP FOR THE VOICELESS

Just how deeply involved federal and state governments had become in treating the national emblem as an export 'resource' became apparent in the 1980s, with the effective action of a new battler on the side of the hunted fugitives – this time a biological scientist.

In 1983, La Trobe University zoology senior lecturer Peter Rawlinson very boldly (for an academic) took on federal and state authorities, and the then $19 million a year kangaroo killing industry, in a personally-delivered submission in May of that year to the US Fish and Wildlife Service. He had become an outspoken supporter of the AWPC, and in 1983 was also elected to the council governing the Australian Conservation Foundation, where he served as kangaroo spokesperson.

"When the history of this century is written it will show that those who lived in it were such lovers of material things, so selfish, and caring so little for future generations, that they persistently violated natural law and largely destroyed the world in which Man was intended to live in harmony and beauty:

Arthur Queripel
ORIGIN, March 1971

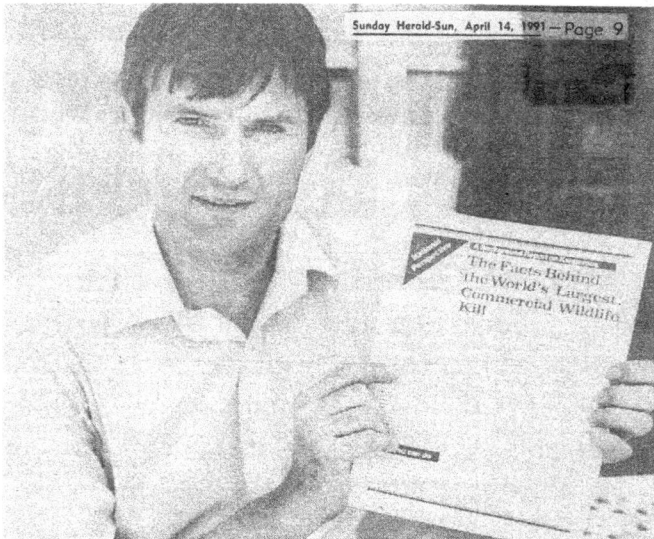

Arthur Queripel (top) and Peter Rawlinson (bottom). AWPC archive.

At stake in the US was the proposed lifting of a 1974 US ban on the importation of kangaroo products. Heavy lobbying from Australian federal and state government officials was being directed across the Pacific to re-open a skin market trading in Australian marsupials since the 19th century. Meat was also on the agenda.

Rawlinson's submission revealed that, at the time, the Commonwealth had no conservation management program in place (as required by both Australian and US law) before embarking on a kangaroo export trade. In fact, there were no legal provisions in place for the establishment of a kangaroo industry. It was all ad hoc.

In 1974, the US Fish and Wildlife Service had put the three largest species of kangaroo (the Red and the Eastern and Western Greys that are hunted) on their threatened species list and banned all imports due to lack of a conservation plan.[7] The US, except for the state of California, finally removed bans in the mid-1990s as Australian conservation groups went silent.

The US ban was in reaction to previous bad experience with wildlife from other countries. US law required foreign wildlife to be listed as threatened if the exporting country could not provide a conservation management plan. Threatened species in this context did not necessarily mean close to extinction.

AUSTRALIAN POLITICIANS DISDAIN AUSTRALIAN WILDLIFE

Describing the domestic policy arena in 1983, the quietly-spoken 40-year-old Rawlinson told US officials about leading Australian politicians' attitudes to the country's wildlife that underpinned this trade. "Apparent dislike and intolerance of kangaroos and other Australian wildlife is often expressed by parliamentarians," he testified. He quoted the then Australian Minister for Tourism J.J. Brown, telling a newspaper that not only was Australia not a land of the kangaroo, but 'the koala myth' needed to be exploded too.

He said Americans needed to learn that the koala was not a cute, cuddly, little bear but a "rotten thing" that is flea-riddled, stinks, and scratches and piddles on the unsuspecting tourist who might want to pick it up.[8]

A related view of Australia's unique marsupials – as simply trade units like coal – inhabited both Australia's major political parties. The federal Hawke Labor government had just been voted in. Rawlinson told the Americans that the new federal environment minister Barry Cohen had endorsed the previous Liberal–National party government's activist role, petitioning the US in 1982 to have these same kangaroo species removed from the US threatened species list.

A kangaroo management plan had been cobbled together in 1980, but it was focused on starting up a system of commercial quotas. It was not a conservation plan. But under heavy lobbying from the Australian government brandishing this management plan, a year later the Reagan administration was proposing to lift the ban. By 1983, Australian wildlife managers were offering up to three million kangaroo lives a year to commercial processors.

It was time to set the Americans straight. Rawlinson and conservation groups built up the evidence of how Australian governments were massaging the kangaroo narrative.

DISHONEST POPULATION COUNTS

Even more damning than not having a real conservation plan, in the view of the Americans in 1983, was the Australian government's dishonesty about their population counts – an arena that has drawn criticism right up to the present day.

Alleged total population numbers are the basis for killing quotas and for claims of sustainable 'harvest'. Environmental impacts like prolonged drought, flood, and disease epidemics (and now the weather effects of climate change) were and are barely reflected in counts that rely on sampling and mathematical extrapolation across whole states – as if there is no landscape-wide agricultural or urban development that would yield very few kangaroos. Rawlinson referenced "extensive, expensive but otherwise uninformative aerial survey techniques". He told the US authorities the species were hunted with continuing ignorance of on-ground conditions and longer-term population impacts.

Rawlinson and conservation groups in June 1983 were able to spotlight the fraud. The federal Australian government had encouraged US investigators to believe the population of the three 'harvested' species was almost twice what a more accurate survey between 1980 and 1982 showed it to be (19 million nationwide versus a claimed 32 million). Allegedly, Queensland numbers had been double counted. The first population count had also failed to take into account the guaranteed high mortalities during drought.[9]

At that time, eastern Australia was coming out of a prolonged drought. Surveys from the eastern states showed kangaroo populations had fallen by 50–70 percent within a couple of years.[10]

Rawlinson told the Americans the hastily cobbled-together first National Kangaroo Management Program was a de facto large pest control scheme. This would change in rhetoric and emphasis by the end of the 1980s, with support from the applied ecology fraternity to a new commercial narrative: harvesting a natural resource for the good of farmers, the national economy, regional jobs, saving degraded rangelands, even eventually saving whole ecosystems.

In a statement made for his 1983 Australia Conservation Foundation (ACF) Council candidacy 'Let's Fight for the Fighting Kangaroo', Rawlinson identified concerns that have continued unabated despite protest for three decades and more. "Very serious moral, ecological and evolutionary issues are raised by the kangaroo industry; however, these are virtually ignored by our wildlife authorities in favour of a simple set of questions – how many kangaroos are there and how many can be harvested?"

ZOOLOGICAL SCIENCE AGAIN MEETS AUSTRALIAN FIRM BELIEFS

Speaking in 1984 to the Melbourne *Sun* newspaper, he said that two years earlier he had no more interest in kangaroos than in any other species. "Like most other people in Australia, I firmly believed that governments had it all under control and the kangaroos were shot because they were pests to farmers … but then at the urging of some of the conservationists, I had a harder look and I was appalled."

By 1988, writing on behalf of the ACF and ANZFAS (the Australian and New Zealand Federation of Animal Societies), he charged that wildlife management in Australia remained highly compromised. Up to 10 species of macropod – including large and small kangaroo species and wallabies – although legally designated as 'protected native species' were still being killed by the millions in commercial or pest management programs, legally and illegally.[11]

Three years earlier, federal and state Nature Conservation Ministers (CONCOM) had met to grapple with the already low bar of 'protected native species'. They approved an updated "National Plan of Management for Kangaroos" involving the 10 species. Pest management to benefit agriculture was upheld as the umbrella rationale, but now adding a 'wise use' commercial return on the killing.[12]

Rawlinson in 1987 was one of the first to publicly point out the lack of evidence of direct competition between kangaroos and domestic stock for the same grazing plants, bar extended drought or confinement – since supported by other researchers.[13]

Forty years later, these research findings did not deter a Victorian Labor government from again bowing to agricultural lobbying and 'wise use' philosophies to re-establish a commercial kangaroo pet food trade, soon pushing human consumption too, again targeting kangaroos described by rural politicians as "out of control" on farmer paddocks.

From his training as a zoologist, Rawlinson also warned that wildlife 'management' of kangaroos was proceeding without understanding the likely long-term impact of killing millions every year. Either the shooters focused on males – particularly the bigger males who are more attractive targets in a commercial sense – or, they shot females and juvenile males as the big males become harder to find.

That meant killing twice as many smaller animals for the same yield. With bad publicity about the plight of joeys, the industry pivoted at times to targeting males almost exclusively. How such distinction could be made in the dark at 100 metres, except for a few large alpha males, appears a mystery, partly explained to me by an ex-ranger who said you can tell the females apart because they almost always have a young joey besides them.

Rawlinson knew that in taking out the largest and fittest there is a genetic cost for the population going forward, not least losing the stabilising role of an alpha male in the mob. In a situation of constant shooting with a male bias, kangaroo numbers can increase because of the high female to male ratio and a bias towards younger breeding animals in a degraded, unnatural mob structure. This in fact has been observed in Queensland and elsewhere after 30–50 years of shooting.

Where the shooting is instead called a 'cull,' everything is shot and the net effect may be population collapse, also foreshadowed by Rawlinson and by experiments conducted elsewhere. A classic example of what happens was demonstrated in a northern Victorian national park in the early 2000s.*

---

* For the 2006 shooting experiment in Wyperfeld National Park, see the appendix at www.mariataylor.com.au, injustice-appendix

Rawlinson reported in the 1980s, and Jock Marshall before him, that no state authority conducted baseline ecological studies of wildlife populations or their health before they were, and are, allowed to be killed en masse. Other native species threatened by human activities attract equally few baseline studies if they are not yet labelled 'endangered'.

A WIN WITH ENVIRONMENT GROUPS ON BOARD

Rawlinson's 1983 overseas testimony was given much credit for the US decision to delay taking the kangaroos off the US endangered species list for at least another two years – and, as it transpired, for longer.

The state of California had separately banned the import and sale of kangaroo products as early as 1971. But the ban was temporarily lifted around 2007, allowing sports shoe manufacturers like Nike and Adidas to increase the demand for kangaroo leather.[14]

In 2015, Australian and international animal welfare groups came together to counter another Australian government tax-payer-funded public relations effort. With the ban about to be re-imposed, the Australian government was pushing for the Californians to instead permanently re-open the market.

The Australians and their PR firm came armed with familiar narratives of super abundant animals and farmer hardship. Later, I look more closely at that overseas campaign and its outcome. One thing was clear from 2015: Australian foreign service officials and top politicians had not given up on the idea that this is a must-have market for Australia.

Dr Peter Rawlinson told his La Trobe campus newspaper that what is happening to Australia's wildlife and natural systems boils down to human value systems. In the end, the kangaroo issue came back to fairly basic moral principles, a message he continued to deliver from his Australian platforms working with the Australian

Wildlife Protection Council and also with the more prominent Australian Conservation Foundation.

The ACF then was in no doubt that the Kangaroo Management Program was no 'conservation program' for the species as required by the Australian National Parks and Wildlife Act 1975, as well as by the US government for any export business.

A June 1983 editorial in the ACF magazine *Habitat* did not pull punches: "A fraction over every 10 seconds, every minute of this year, a kangaroo or a wallaby will die, under quotas for the commercial 'harvesting' of kangaroos announced in January by the former Australian Government ..." The 1983 'harvest' quota was 3,143,000 animals.

The ACF editorial continued: "As this magazine goes to press, Commonwealth and NSW wildlife officers have been in America defending the soundness of Australia's kangaroo slaughter ... If it is allowed to continue on this scale, it will suggest that our sense of nationhood should be listed as endangered and our national conscience may already be extinct."[15]

REPORTERS GOT THE STORY

Rawlinson and the conservation groups were good at marshalling mainstream media articles at that time. For example, an informative piece from 1986 by journalist and author Tony Horwitz described a trip to the "gothic" outback, a $15,000 livelihood killing kangaroos, and what officials thought about it all.[16]

Hortwitz reported that the 30-year-old shooter Trindall supported a wife and five children in or near Walgett NSW on the nightly slaughter. But it was poor pay. After a night's shoot his truck would sway off, festooned with a dozen kangaroo bodies. He aimed for males, each having earned him about $50. Still, he bought the government's argument that its either a commercial kill for some income or wholesale genocide instituted by farmers.

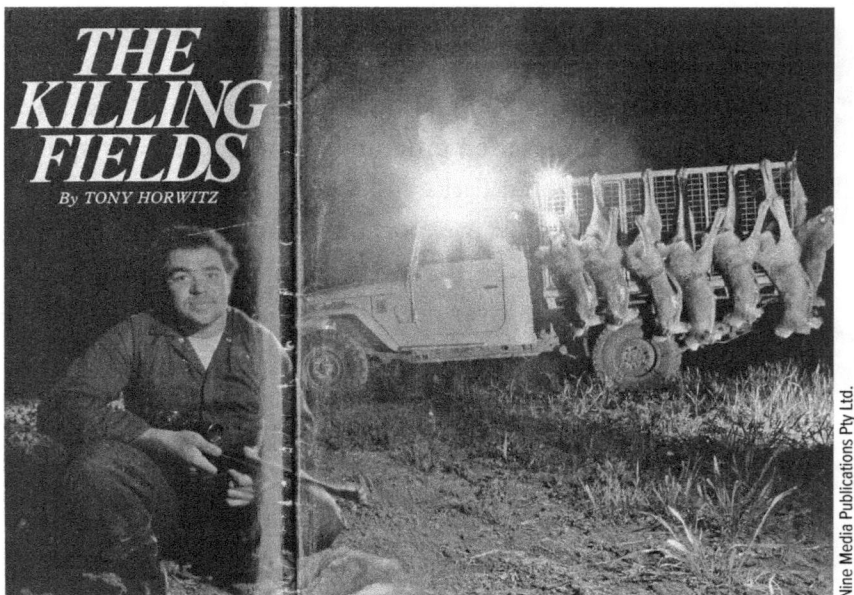

A $15,000 livelihood.

The article examines the lax or non-existent oversight and record-keeping that applied to the export of skins and meat. A customs officer is quoted as saying that in 20 years he's never seen an officer check for correct skin numbers being exported. That officer gave his testimony to the Senate Select Committee on Animal Welfare (1985–6) where Tasmanian federal Democrat Senator Norm Sanders was listening. He told Horwitz he believed his government didn't have the foggiest notion what is being killed or where.

I found a letter in the AWPC archive in which Sanders wrote to Arthur Queripel following these committee hearings (chaired by an equally dismayed Senator George Georges). Sanders was hoping for an overhaul of the whole kangaroo killing system based on the evidence. "I am aware of the corruption of government officials, criminal activity, deceit, and the threat of decimation of kangaroo populations due to culling," he wrote.

That translated to 'the rules are a bit stretched, but if we don't kill them, the farmers will' in the official response and shooter rationale, reported Horwitz. He talked to Dr Jack Giles, then assistant director of the NSW National Parks and Wildlife Service, calling him a leading expert on kangaroo management. Giles was one of the officials who had been petitioning the US to overturn its ban a few years earlier along with Federal environment minister Barry Cohen, also interviewed.

PERCEPTION THING IN THE BUSH

Giles told Horwitz the state governments like NSW had to do this, regardless of the facts behind charges of pest and competition. It was about "the perception thing in the bush … even if kangaroos ate stones, cockies would still think they hurt their crops [or pastures]. To stop the 'cull' would be to risk a rural revolt," he said.

Five years later, the quota had only gone up: now standing at four million. The government and industry were making a renewed bid to overturn a US ban on leather and meat imports. A 1991 editorial in *Mainstream*, the magazine of the Animal Protection Institute of America, reported a clear-eyed view of where Australia sat on the global stage of animal killing.

"It is like going back 100–150 years to an America where birds were slaughtered to make feathered hats and millions of bison were wiped out to make rugs and robes. Wholesale deliberate slaughter of wildlife for commercial purposes on this scale just doesn't happen anymore – except in Australia."[17]

Peter Rawlinson's sudden death in 1991 while on a field trip in Indonesia, reported as a heart attack, was a tremendous loss not only to fellow animal crusaders but also for the kangaroos themselves, who too seldom – before or since – have enjoyed a credentialed advocate who was so fearless, relentless, and effective.

AUSTRALIAN CONSERVATION GROUPS ON FRONTLINE ...
AND THEN

Rawlinson might have been dismayed that by 1993 the Australian Conservation Foundation, with a change of leadership, had withdrawn from that strong advocacy role for elements of Australian land-based wildlife. As Australia's biggest environmental group in the 1980s, the ACF had, along with Greenpeace, been pivotal in exposing not just dodgy population counts but a direct lie by government officials lobbying for the kangaroo trade.

In 1983, Greenpeace, in its magazine, posed the question that reverberates still today: "We still do not learn from our mistakes of the past and carry on regardless, oblivious to the signs ... Must we have a re-enactment of the whale saga, koala, platypus etc etc before government bodies bring about stricter controls on the kangaroo slaughter?"

In a 1996 book, *Smuggled-2* (an account of the relationships between some wildlife officials, Australian wildlife smugglers, and also the kangaroo industry at that time), Raymond Hoser describes a bit of tricky business that had driven the Australian conservation groups and also the RSPCA to come together for kangaroos.

Hoser recounted that when in 1983 Jack Giles from the NSW National Parks and Wildlife Service and the federal Minister for Science and Environment Barry Cohen went to Washington to lobby that the ban on kangaroo imports be lifted, the officials claimed that the major Australian conservation groups supported their position. They almost succeeded in convincing the Americans.

But Peter Rawlinson stepped in with his 1983 trip and testimony. Later he mobilised six environmental groups – including ACF and Greenpeace as well as wildlife defenders – to make it clear they did not support the government's position. Instead, they wrote a damning letter in February 1987 informing the US House of Representatives of a litany of problems headed by the "complete breakdown" of the National Plan of Kangaroo Management.

Furthermore, there was evidence of massive illegal kangaroo meat trading, particularly through Victoria, and there was evidence suggesting that the Australian National Parks and Wildlife Service and the Australian government had (repeatedly) misled the US government and the European Parliament on population figures.[18]

After Peter Rawlinson died in 1991, the biggest conservation groups gradually backed off. In 1995, the US federally rolled back its ban in a victory for the 'harvest,' following a petition from the Keating government.

Two years earlier, Australian Wildlife Protection Council head Maryland Wilson expressed her disappointment to the ACF executive director – reflecting the previous closer relationship between the two organisations. "The Wildlife Legislative Fund of America which is a hunting and shooting organisation and the Keating Government have been successful in this petition. With Peter dead, not a word from you as there was in 1983 from the ACF."[19]

Geoff Mosley, ACF executive director between 1973 and 1986, and a continuing member of its council thereafter, told me that things did change after Peter Rawlinson died and his influence at the organisation stopped. Internal politics, as anywhere, set future directions. Environmental and animal welfare spot fires everywhere demanded attention and campaigns.

Issues considered politically divisive might easily slide down the agenda. Lethal treatment of some common native species – kangaroo, wombat, emu, dingo – no doubt falls into a divisive basket – conflict with farmers and governments guaranteed. But contemporary silence by some big environmental and welfare organisations on the treatment of 'common' native species left the door open to public enlightenment by government and industry propaganda headlining yet another narrative: killing kangaroos was a way to relieve and rehabilitate depleted grazing lands.

INCONVENIENT TRUTHS IN 2006

Twenty-three years after Peter Rawlinson revealed to US wildlife officials that Australia lacked a species conservation plan or any baseline studies, there still were none. This again became apparent in 2006.

That is when Glenys Oogjes, Executive Director of animal welfare group Animals Australia, publicised some alarming findings from that year's federal State of the Environment report. Biodiversity was taking a hammering from human land clearing and development. As alarming was what she revealed about the kangaroo meat and skin industry.[20]

She said that according to the federal environment report: "Government decisions relating to wildlife are being made devoid of any substantive data and are having a dire impact on the welfare and numbers of Australian wildlife."

The report noted that "there are insufficient data available on actual kangaroo populations and population characteristics to demonstrate that harvesting does not have a detrimental impact either on the harvested species or their ecosystems". In particular, it pointed out that there was not enough information on population trends, structure, or distribution to show a sustainable industry.

After Oogjes contacted government officials to enquire about the ethical and environmental implications of this assessment, she says that the report was altered. "We believe that the report was changed after pressure from the [responsible] minister and possibly interests within the commercial kangaroo industry," she told the Canberra media.

The same inconvenient 2006 analysis indicated that between

1991 and 2006, actual 'harvesting' numbers did increase by nearly one million, and by 2006 were at their highest levels ever.

The revised final report no longer included the concerns noted by Oogjes. It claimed that commercial harvesting had been sustainable for 25 years and that management plans "incorporate provisions appropriate to the current drought". In fact, annual federal quotas and harvest figures showed no change in methodology and did not bow to population drops clearly correlated with the weather. I reported on this saga in 2012 using the environment department source documents and Oogjes' testimony.

The cumulative statistics show that as another severe drought hit in the early 2000s, government killing quotas stayed high. Between 2002 and 2003, federal counts (based on state by state figures) again showed a population drop of about 50 percent in just one year. Yet quotas and harvest numbers did not budge. About four million kangaroos were slaughtered in 2002. In 2003 almost as many were shot according to official figures.[21]

More extraordinary, by 2017 and 2018, five years of severe drought in Queensland reflected no population drops in the national total counts – instead one finds population increases of 30 percent a year and more, and related kill quotas in Queensland and parts of NSW, despite terrible on-ground conditions. (I come back to this in a later chapter with a look at how the counts are achieved.)

IT'S CULTURAL – THE DARK SIDE OF COUNTRY LIFE

A cultural wall of silence, argument, and denial have ensured visual evidence, even more than written testimony, is scarce to non-existent. You're unlikely to find film of a modern kangaroo or wallaby hunt, or wombats trapped, or possums and dingos or introduced animals systematically poisoned with horrendous 1080. The grim realities have been avoided by the mainstream media.

Historical material is no easier to find. I searched in vain for an Australian copy of the 1984 documentary film *Goodbye Joey*, finally tracking it to the British Film Institute (https://www.bfi.org. uk/films-tv-people/4ce2b72031445). Viva!, the UK animal welfare organisation, had archived some footage on YouTube showing a brutal kangaroo killing scene by adults accompanied by children. Teaching the next generation.*

One of the most graphic depictions of a culturally-accepted institution, the 'sporting' kangaroo hunt, comes not from documentary film but from a feature film directed by a Canadian, based on a book written by an Australian journalist. The raw world of small 20th century country towns and 'The Outback', the landscape Arthur Queripel grew up in, was depicted in harrowing detail in Kenneth Cook's 1961 novel – and then the 1971 film – *Wake in Fright* – based on Cook's journalistic experiences working in Broken Hill in the 1950s.

In a heat-struck outback mining town, a kangaroo slaughter is the highlight of a 'lost weekend' of drink, gambling (greyhound racing along with two-up), and increasing degradation for the 'city boy' school teacher who loses his money gambling and gradually his thin veneer of civilised life. The local boys bring their new 'mate' into the fold with mind-bending quantities of alcohol. He comes to think it's a good idea when he and the other men barrel into the surrounding arid countryside in an old sedan, loaded with 'piss' and rifles for a round of fun spotlighting.

The ensuing brutal and gruesome slaughter of the innocents pinned in the headlights' glare, shot and then knifed for bravado, is relished by the mates as real man stuff. Kangaroo balls for breakfast the next day is part of the ritual for some.

---

* See the Viva case study in the appendix at www.mariataylor.com.au, injustice-appendix

From Page 5

ARE WE UGLY AUSTRALIANS?

59   Walkabout, March, 1972

42   Walkabout, March, 1972

Are we ugly Australians?

MALE BONDING

Conformity is the name of this game and the complicity of violence marks a dark picture of Australian male bonding. The story also explores elements of homophobia and misogyny (you must be a 'poofta' if you like talking with women). Degraded homo-eroticism with a rape under the influence of alcohol completes the picture.

The film, reissued, has been hailed as a masterpiece of cultural realism. Anyone who doubts the inherent brutality of 'hunting' kangaroo families with youngsters at foot might like to watch it, or read the even more graphic description in the book, also hailed as a classic. Author Kenneth Cook told various interviewers that it was all based on what he experienced and saw.

Yes, the kangaroos were harmed in the filming – this was 1971. The film was reportedly rejected in the 1970s by Australian moviegoers because it did not fit the mythology of living in the outback more suitably depicted later in *Crocodile Dundee*. *Observer* film critic Rex Reed in his enthusiastic review of the reissue docu-ments a 13-year search for the original negative that was finally found in a trash bin labelled 'for destruction'.[22]

The March 1972 issue of *Walkabout* magazine asked the ques-tion, "Are we ugly Australians?" – answering that *Wake in Fright* was sadly not just fiction. The same horror waited almost every night for defenceless kangaroos that often are run to exhaustion and sometimes tormented before the final bullets. The hunt of Red kangaroos was documented for the magazine by photographer Jeff Carter, who said the event had sickened and disgusted him.

In an essay-length dissection of the cultural meaning of all this, Australian expat author Kate Jennings described the kangaroo hunt at the centre of the story in an essay for *The Monthly*:

"The kangaroo hunt, which sends audiences out of theatres reeling, is only eight minutes in length, carefully edited to seem much more. The carnage is powerful, stomach-turning, even more so for viewers who have never seen farm animals slaughtered, much less been hunting, which would be most Australians ... the kangaroo Grant chooses isn't fully grown, and he falters at the sight and the pathetic noises the poor beast is making.

"JOE: What's the matter, teacher? You scared?

"GRANT: It's only a baby. It's badly wounded.

"JOE: Have a go, you mug.

"Once the deed is done, slow clapping from Dick and Joe and guns fired to salute him."[23]

Alcohol, often now combined with other drugs, still fuel spotlighting forays to kill and maim kangaroos as a form of ritual Saturday night fun for mates of both sexes. The comment thread to Jennings article gave examples from readers of spotlighting outings in a recent decade. It's not much talked about, with some realisation that in the mid-2000s there are now many people who think this is not normal behaviour.

Some responses on discussion threads after people defend kangaroos haven't diverged far from what Jock Marshall described as the common retort almost 60 years ago: those kangaroo lovers are 'just Greenies' who don't understand the ways of self-described real country folk – even when the animal defenders are from the neighbourhood.

Jennings in her article reflected on the cliché of boredom of growing up in the Australian Outback (defined as anything outside the big cities) that she fled as soon as she was able to. She reported what she heard from men she had encouraged to watch the *Wake in Fright* film. Her question was: does this type of alcohol-fuelled male bonding still go on? Answer: yes, and we know that from the city crimes and from sports too, arguably worse with added drugs like cocaine, amphetamines and ice.

Wake in Fright offered some reasons, focusing on boredom, hardship, and often dangerous, rote work lives, as reasons why humans, mostly men, resort to alcohol twinned with bloodshed as a release from their lives. Here's an exchange from the film:

> TYDON: It's death to farm out here. It's worse than death in the mines. You want them to sing opera as well?
>
> GRANT: And what do you do?
>
> TYDON: I drink.

Jennings, for her part, having escaped the Outback to live in Manhattan, has little positive to say about "stifling" Australian landscapes or the cultural habits that white people use to tolerate residing there. She also inadvertently sheds light on other ways that today's Australians feel comfortable – by not knowing. She writes that kangaroos are no longer killed for pet food or for their skins – leaving out the ongoing Australian domestic and international trade for both.[24]

Alcohol-fuelled animal abuse is not separate from interpersonal relations. Of what he saw in 1971, director Ted Kotcheff told Kate Jennings for her article: "The men are never there. They are in mines or the RSL club or the pubs." He went on to recall doing a play in Ireland and peeking through the curtain and seeing only women in the audience. "Where are the men?" he asked. The answer: "In the pub."

As I mulled over this gritty colonial legacy in Australia, I was reading the 2016 autobiography of Australian rock-n-roll icon Jimmy Barnes. That instantly broadened the arena of cultural habits raised by *Wake in Fright*.

To what extent had old colonial traditions moulded a certain male character – patriarchal, often wedded to alcohol and feeling entitled to bully, sometimes kill fellow creatures – human and animal – while demanding conformity in values from their women and children and the greater society? High levels of domestic violence are one reflection.[25]

Barnes documents how this looks. He describes his childhood in Glasgow and then growing up in the industrial northern suburbs of Adelaide (when there were still factories) as an unremitting round of drinking, violence – including regular domestic abuse – relieved by singing, and then more of the same the next day. And all the Scots that Barnes knew growing up fitted the same subculture. Violence was the way to vent every uncertainty, and alcohol the mother's milk of men who spent their non-working life in the pub with other men.[26]

Another recent account is fashion designer Alannah Hill's horrendous true tale of growing up poor in just such an alcoholic and abusive family, Irish this time, in rural Tasmania. Her Dad didn't like animals, or his children, but neither did Mum. This is surely not confined to the Scots and Irish who came to Australia or to a social class in the new society.

The colonial record shows hunting and killing was second nature to all social classes. Hunting mammals and shooting birds for sport was always a favoured pastime amongst the land-holding class of the British Empire, and in Europe.

Violence to cement settlement with exotic stock and crops accompanied the hardships of often unsuitable terrain. Everything native was alien and a threat to prosperity and well-being. The Indigenous inhabitants, both human and wildlife, would be the scapegoats. Violence as tension outlet was one side of the coin. The British imperial project of commerce and the grasp for profits was the other side.

LAWLESS OUTSIDE THE CITIES

Many thousand acts of individual kindness, animal rescue, and rights organising since Queripel and Rawlinson's time, are still overrun by that cultural and economic legacy – to unleash violence just because people can.

Because the law is on side with private property rights, authorities rarely interfere with what landholders do in a rural environment, even as their activities affect someone else's private property. Many people living on bush acreage say privately that they won't speak out against the killing culture for fear of what the neighbours might think or do in retribution.

A friend emailed me about what she witnessed, and the police response, in her rural residential area near Braidwood, NSW in 2019. This may have been encouraged by the NSW government's program of 'as easy as a phone call' wildlife killing to help the farmers.

"There's new people living on the property diagonally across from me and he is intent on wiping out every kangaroo on the place," she wrote. "Shooting almost every night. Yesterday, I witnessed him run down a roo with his tractor, pin it against the fence and kill it before picking up the carcass in the front bucket of the tractor and dumping it in a ditch – presumably with the bodies of all the other roos he's killed.

"It's tragic – there was a lovely big mob of roos down there. [A wildlife carer] and I have both contacted the police and basically received an 'Oh, well, it's his property and he can kill kangaroos if he likes' response."

Values that say this is normal, that this is what we do on the land, continue the common law tradition that the wildlife 'belongs' to landholders to treat as they wish, particularly outside the cities.

I learned that in Tasmania every year, up to a million wallabies and possums are slaughtered by shotgun or poison bait on public and private land to protect plantation trees and other crops.[27] On the mainland, as the number of large kangaroos declines, or just because the pest label is applied to them, the remaining wallaby species are increasingly hunted everywhere for their coats or pet food.

The culture that spawns a 'yobbo' who uses his vehicle for kicks to run down a mother and joey on a peaceful rural residential road verge (as recently happened in my neighbourhood), or runs down a recovering wombat on a rescuer's property in Victoria, or that encourages a neighbour like that of my Braidwood friend, is not separate in values from Australia's industrial-scale killing arenas – comfortably supported by governments and some sectors of science.

Is the legal field inching towards change? In December 2018, national headlines ensued with the prosecution in Western Australia of four males, reportedly related to a bikie gang, for animal cruelty. More headlines came when the defendants' friends attacked the news media after a verdict for daring to report the case. The charge was punching a kangaroo with knuckledusters before shooting it in the eye and burning it. The judge had no doubt this was sadistic act, but a friend of the defendants explained it as a rite of initiation.[28]

MARGINAL FARMING INFLUENCE ON HOW AUSTRALIA TREATS WILDLIFE

Following in the footsteps of Arthur Queripel, Maryland Wilson was one of the dedicated citizen activists who led the Australian Wildlife Protection Council in the 1990s and 2000s. A tireless advocate for kangaroos and a legend in her own time, Wilson was left in no doubt where the problem continues for Australia's native herbivores and other wildlife. She wrote in a wide-ranging 2006 speech:

"Unsustainable, destructive agricultural practices on marginal, uneconomic land [and] native vegetation/tree clearing have degraded Australia which is divided into kangaroo killing zones." Wilson was referring to Victoria, but the same bureaucratic culture exists in all Australian states. She wrote: "The deeply entrenched colonial mentality 'culture' within [the Victorian state environment department] of unabashedly appeasing the farmer or landholder still prevails."[29]

Two leading conservation biologists who held radically different ideas to Wilson about kangaroo management agreed about the state of marginal farming. This was in the context of their influential ideas that kangaroos should be moved from label 'pest' to label 'resource,' and killed that way, to save the environment and the farmers bank accounts.

They provided financial details in 1999 on the parlous state of grazing enterprises in just two Australian states with semi-arid zones pre-climate change. Gordon Grigg and Tony Pople wrote that high debt levels and other negatives meant possibly only 10 percent of Queensland grazing properties were considered large enough to be viable in the long term under current conditions. Things were equally bad in NSW "with 250 properties inviable in the long term and perenniality of pasture low in many areas with the worst affected no longer capable of sustaining sheep grazing at commercially viable levels". A question that might follow: is it time for land management rethinks that don't involve waiting for the grass to grow after the wildlife is killed?[30]

Attacking the exploitation of wildlife from a different direction was the man I meet next.

WILDLIFE TRADE EXPOSED: A TALE OF MURDER, CORRUPTION AND BOOK BANNING

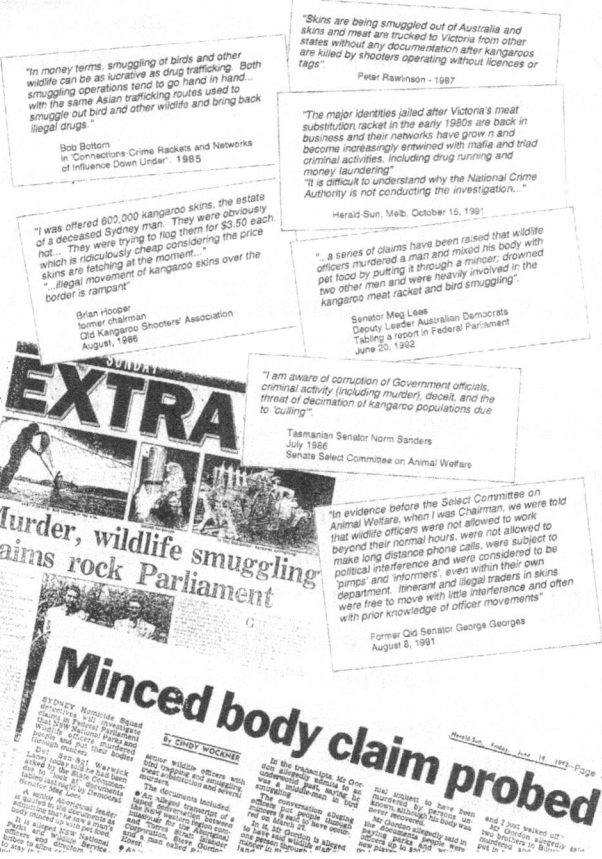

"In money terms, smuggling of birds and other wildlife can be as lucrative as drug trafficking. Both smuggling operations tend to go hand in hand... with the same Asian trafficking routes used to smuggle out bird and other wildlife and bring back illegal drugs."

Bob Bottom
in 'Connections Crime Rackets and Networks of Influence Down Under'. 1985

"I was offered 600,000 kangaroo skins, the estate of a deceased Sydney man. They were obviously hot... They were trying to flog them for $3.50 each, which is ridiculously cheap considering the price skins are fetching at the moment..."
"... illegal movement of kangaroo skins over the border is rampant"

Brian Hooper
former chairman
Qld Kangaroo Shooters' Association
August, 1986

"Skins are being smuggled out of Australia and skins and meat are trucked to Victoria from other states without any documentation after kangaroos are killed by shooters operating without licences or tags".

Peter Rawlinson - 1987

"The major identities jailed after Victoria's meat substitution racket in the early 1980s are back in business and their networks have grown and become increasingly entwined with mafia and triad criminal activities, including drug running and money laundering"
"It is difficult to understand why the National Crime Authority is not conducting the investigation..."

Herald-Sun, Melb. October 15, 1991

"... a series of claims have been raised that wildlife officers murdered a man and mixed his body with pet food by putting it through a mincer; drowned two other men and were heavily involved in the kangaroo meat racket and bird smuggling".

Senator Meg Lees
Deputy Leader Australian Democrats
Tabling a report in Federal Parliament
June 20, 1992

"I am aware of corruption of Government officials, criminal activity (including murder), deceit, and the threat of decimation of kangaroo populations due to 'culling'".

Tasmanian Senator Norm Sanders
July 1986
Senate Select Committee on Animal Welfare

"In evidence before the Select Committee on Animal Welfare, when I was Chairman, we were told that wildlife officers were not allowed to work beyond their normal hours, were not allowed to make long distance phone calls, were subject to political interference and were considered to be 'pimps' and 'informers', even within their own department. Itinerant and illegal traders in skins were free to move with little interference and often with prior knowledge of officer movements"

Former Qld Senator George Georges
August 8, 1991

SUNDAY EXTRA

Murder, wildlife smuggling claims rock Parliament

Minced body claim probed

Composite image of clips and quotes. AWPC archive

Raymond Hoser doesn't shrink from a fight with authorities. In fact, he's been battling wildlife bureaucracies since the 1980s and he's still treated as a troublemaker by government officials. Others know this reptile expert, independent investigator, and author as a tireless crusader for animal justice and against official corruption.

Then *Sun Herald* journalist Fia Cumming, who was introduced to the shady world of wildlife smuggling by Hoser, wrote in a foreword to his 1996 continuing expose *Smuggled-2*: "*Smuggled* [the first book] landed heavy blows on individuals and institutions alike that had treated the law with contempt. Backed by a courageous publisher, Raymond named names which had been whispered in anger and fear for years. Then he stood back to take the inevitable flak."[1]

Hoser had moved to suburban Melbourne from Sydney while writing his books to put distance between himself and NSW wildlife authorities, whom he accused of raiding and harassing him. His current home sits next to a shed full of Australian snakes that he breeds and feeds (with a lot of spares) for his work in educational reptile demonstrations and shows for school children and others.

As we arrived for a visit, he had just ducked out in his other work capacity as snake handler – saving squeamish householders from the wildlife, for a fee. This time the wildlife had already departed.

A 2015 article by a Victorian regional paper gives the flavour of the ongoing fiery relationship with officialdom. The report said an administrative tribunal had just cleared Hoser of charges that he was not a fit person to hold a wildlife handling license. In finding him fit the tribunal noted that Hoser and the department were "vehemently critical of each other" which had led to frequent clashes. Hoser said he would investigate seeking damages, not for the first time. Battles with authorities are expensive.[2] He says he's become a target since writing his anti-corruption books that also included one targeting the Victorian police.

WILDLIFE MANAGEMENT 1970S–90s INVESTIGATION

Smuggled, published in 1993, laid bare the illegal trade in Australian wildlife – supported by corrupt officials – principally NSW parks bureaucrats in Hoser's rendition of that period. He also wrote about the developing kangaroo trade.

A June 1992 *Sydney Morning Herald* article provided a flavour of allegations that had been tabled in federal parliament regarding the kangaroo trade, which were then expanded on in Hoser's books. 'Murder, wildlife smuggling claim rock Parliament' went the headline. "A series of extraordinary claims were raised in Federal Parliament late last Thursday night – claims that National Parks and Wildlife Officers murdered a man and mixed his body with pet food by putting it through a mincer; drowned two other men; and were heavily involved in kangaroo meat rackets and bird smuggling," started this newspaper account.

Australian Democrats Senator Meg Lees had tabled three documents, two transcripts of evidence, and a file note that dealt with wildlife smuggling and alleged corruption in the kangaroo meat trade and the NSW National Parks and Wildlife Service.[3]

The evidence went to the Senator from work done by *The Sydney Morning Herald.* Reporter Fia Cumming gathered much of it after starting an investigative collaboration with Hoser a decade earlier. In a 1993 follow-up, Cumming wrote in a *Sunday Herald* piece that the evidence indicated that: "A syndicate involved in kangaroo meat substitution for export beef, wildlife smuggling and probably drug and gold imports was responsible for the deaths of three, possibly four men in 1979–80 … The syndicate operated with the knowledge of and assistance of senior officials in the NSW National Parks and Wildlife Service and possibly the Queensland Service."

A 1992 account in the Melbourne *Herald Sun* by a different reporter shed more light on what was being alleged. It drew on one of the transcribed conversations that had been tabled in federal parliament. That one was between a NSW western region commissioner for the Aboriginal and Torres Straight Islander Commission, and one Raymond Hoser.[4]

Hoser later described this conversation to me. He was driving a taxi in Melbourne and talking to a passenger and they got onto the topic of wildlife. Transcripts of the conversation that made it to federal parliament reported Hoser's informant had knowledge about bird smuggling and about the kangaroo syndicate referred to by Cumming. He said he had been interested in getting involved with the kangaroo trade and knew the players, including the alleged murder victims.

The informant claimed the murder (followed by mincing) of a major kangaroo processor in Queensland in 1980 was carried out to warn off those who might threaten the syndicate. And he claimed from first-hand experience that bribes of $20,000 to $30,000 were being demanded by certain NSW wildlife service administrative officials to obtain a killing license, which, in the event, he and his group did not get.

The evidence tabled by Meg Lees included a confidential note wherein police repeated rumours that a Sydney underworld figure was involved with the "game meat' and kangaroo meat business, also naming a company.[5]

KANGAROO TURF WARS

The sensational story that a man had been murdered and fed into a kangaroo meat mincer refers to the 1980 disappearance of Queensland kangaroo meat trader Andrew Komarnicki. Maybe he knew too much about 'the syndicate,' or otherwise threatened someone's profits and trade expansion. Two other alleged victims, the Judd brothers, were found drowned in a dam on their property in late 1979. The theory was they had stopped the wrong shooter on their property. These were part of the infamous kangaroo turf wars that erupted around that time.

Killing kangaroos had become a multi-million dollar wildlife trade since the later 1950s. The picture painted by Hoser, Cumming, and others was of a trade where a handful of allegedly corrupt wildlife officials at NSW headquarters had the power to pick winners and losers, to set quotas, and to turn a blind eye to over-shooting or under-the-table wildlife trading across state lines and out of the country.[6]

Hoser and Cumming also raised the lid on allegations that the corrupt kangaroo meat and skin trade was, in the '80s and '90s, part of a web of illegal activities – from meat substitution and wildlife trafficking to drug running and money laundering – operating since the 1960s (Hoser was to note the role of disused airfields in Queensland). This underground economy had continued to export kangaroo meat and skins during the Whitlam era export ban.

Testimony at the time showed how government managers could structure the business to benefit some individuals and businesses and keep others out. Whether or not links to corrupt officials continued beyond the mid-1990s has not been documented. Some think so, others don't. The same companies continued to dominate the industry.

At the time, Hoser's detailed evidence of payoffs from favoured industry operators to limit access to kangaroo commercial licenses did not spur departmental housecleaning or prosecutions. Just the opposite – the NSW wildlife service turned on him. His greater sin was that he had also exposed, through many examples, how evidence about wildlife smuggling was made to disappear before the legal system could get involved.

By 1996, when Hoser expanded on the kangaroo trade in his second book, *Smuggled-2*, naming officials and prominent processers, police had apparently investigated at least the murder stories. No evidence emerged that national parks officials had murdered anyone.

The most suspicious circumstances involving parks officials and a violent human death was the supposed suicide (by a shotgun blast to the face) of a park ranger in north Queensland in 1980. His family always alleged that the slain ranger, Modesto Melino, had stumbled on a wildlife smuggling and meat racket.[7]

ENFORCEMENT STYMIED

Honest officials were victimised in this environment. According to Hoser's accounts, backed by other media reports, NSW National Parks enforcement officers were routinely stymied in their efforts to apprehend wrongdoers, apply regulations or report corruption. These dedicated officials were sidelined or eventually retrenched.

The Australian Senate had also been looking at officialdom and wildlife in those years. Then Queensland Senator George Georges, who was an unabashed champion of Australia's native animals, wrote in August 1991 to the Australian Wildlife Protection Council of what he heard as chair of the Senate Select Committee on Animal Welfare:

"We were told that wildlife officers were not allowed to work beyond normal hours, were not allowed to make long-distance phone calls, were subject to political interference and were considered to be 'pimps' and 'informers' even in their own department. Itinerant and illegal traders in [kangaroo] skins were free to move with little interference and often with prior knowledge of officer movements."

A ranger active at the time, who said he saw no evidence of corruption himself, told me that a big part of the enforcement problem was that police and prosecutors seldom are persuaded to take action. Continuing to this day, laws remain untested and legal authorities can view the field of wildlife crime as too difficult or not a problem.

Journalist Greg Roberts, writing in 1994, detailed testimony to the NSW Independent Commission Against Corruption (ICAC) from several former NSW National Parks and Wildlife Service officers. Clive Bennett, who retired in 1990, tried to launch prosecutions on some 30 cases of wildlife smuggling. Each time, the cases were aborted before going to court after he reported them. He was stripped of investigative powers in 1985 before any further enquiries could get underway. Bennett remained convinced of corruption in the service and spoke of bribery involving sums of $10,000.[8]

Another former investigator, Les McQueen, who retired in 1984, told the ICAC and journalists that he had a copy of a letter from an underworld figure to a senior NPWS official telling the latter to cancel a kangaroo killing license held by a rival. He also noted that murder victim Komarnicki "probably stood on the wrong toes" in the kangaroo meat trade. Roberts' article also details allegations in regard to the multi-billion dollar bird and reptile smuggling trade, fingering Australian Customs Service personnel at the time in alliance with smugglers.

SHUTTING UP THE REPORTERS

On publication of *Smuggled* (the first book) in May 1993, Raymond Hoser became the subject of a determined effort by the NSW NPWS to shut him up – and to restrict access to his book by threatening the whole book supply chain with legal action. This ultimately failed thanks to intervention from the NSW environment minister at the time.[9]

Hoser details this apex of his ongoing legal battles with wildlife authorities in the introduction to *Smuggled-2*. He reports that when *Smuggled* was published it sold out from bookstores within

48 hours, indicating to him that the Australian public had a strong
desire to conserve its wildlife – or maybe the element of crime and
corruption was an equal draw.

He writes of receiving an avalanche of phone and fax messages
containing further allegations of wildlife crime, corruption, and
bureaucratic empire-building showing scant regard for actual
conservation. He was also being approached by many honest and
frustrated officials who wanted to clean up their departments,
prompting him to publish *Smuggled-2* in 1996.

Meanwhile, threats of lawsuits were made, demanding that the
book be banned. Hoser documents that the NSW NPWS threatened
both the small publisher (Apollo/Charles Pierson) and then the
national distributor over the course of weeks, without presenting
a legal cause; the service also contacted major booksellers and
successfully threatened them with reprisal if the book continued
to be sold (with the Co-op chain being the only holdout against the
threats).

Hoser didn't flinch and neither did his publisher. He writes that
since his book was backed by indisputable material, much of it
gained through freedom of information requests over the years (he
gathered material starting in the mid-1970s), individual defama-
tion suits were not pursued. And as Hoser noted, a government
department per se cannot be defamed under Australian law. No
writs were issued.

With a de facto book ban in place, journalist Fia Cumming
continued to raise the issues and agitate against the NSW National
Parks and Wildlife Service's ban-the-book campaign. This culminated with her major expose of the whole saga in Melbourne's
Sunday Herald Sun in June 1993 titled 'Who Killed the Kangaroo
King?' It linked an alleged criminal syndicate, alleged murders, the
testimony tabled in the Senate about corruption in the park service,
and the kangaroo industry.

She and the *Herald and Weekly Times* group were promptly sued in the Supreme Court of Victoria that same month, with kangaroo industry plaintiffs successfully seeking redress for reputational damage. The plaintiffs claimed the article was published recklessly and without inquiry of the plaintiffs, and that it allegedly printed things that were not true.

Hoser and Cumming told me that during the book ban fight they had reason to believe that their personal phone lines were tapped by unidentified agents as they were calling media and politicians to get the ban lifted. Other journalists were warned off the book ban story. Meanwhile the federal Shadow Minister for the Environment, Chris Gallus, lobbied her Liberal counterpart in NSW Chris Harcher to rein in his department. The Australian Democrats Senator Meg Lees continued to highlight the censorship.

Still nothing happened until finally publisher Charles Pierson convinced the editor of *The Sydney Morning Herald* to run a prominent story about suppression of free speech by the parks service. That prompted the NSW Labor Opposition into vocal action and other media outlets to finally run the book banning story. According to Hoser's account in *Smuggled-2*, an ABC *7.30* reporter was threatened by an anonymous phone call, but proceeded with the story. She interviewed whistleblower Les McQueen. The ABC reportedly received calls from others eager to tell corruption stories.

Minister Harcher came on the program the next day to answer allegations of a cover-up and defend his department. But he broke the logjam by acknowledging the department was wrong in attempting to stifle free speech, calling it a basic right in our society. The ban was lifted. The publisher had suffered significant losses and ended up suing the department. Large amounts of taxpayer dollars were spent defending that action. Campaigns to discredit and marginalise Hoser continued.

This saga, with public servants in the wildlife management arena pulling out all the stops to stifle evidence that counters the official narrative on what to believe, had its echoes in Canberra in 2009, where I reported on an extraordinary story, again to do with kangaroo management. But first, a look at the wildlife science that supports the type of wildlife management administered in Australian bureaucracies.

ENTER AUSTRALIAN APPLIED ECOLOGY

"Australian ecology emerged from a background of 'empire science' which began with the sciences of 'exploration': 'the astronomy of the southern skies; geophysics ... and natural history. Natural resource benefits were important to the economics of empire ... Conservation science which emerged later, still incorporated the imperial traditions."

— LIBBY ROBIN, *ECOLOGY: A SCIENCE OF EMPIRE?*

"There is little convincing evidence of substantial damage by kangaroos to crops, pastoral production or rangelands, except in a few localized areas."

— OLSEN P AND LOW T, *UPDATE ON CURRENT STATE OF SCIENTIFIC KNOWLEDGE ON KANGAROOS IN THE ENVIRONMENT*

In 2002, a group of conservation biologists and applied ecologists gathered to consider a different national direction for kangaroo killing. Building on the framework that had moved kangaroos from economic pest to commercial and export resource, many doubled down on the idea that farming of kangaroos would be a win for conservation of the animals, the bank accounts of farmers, and the rehabilitation of the countryside.

However, veteran ecologist Harry Recher wasn't impressed. Armed with a less 'applied' ecological perspective, he told the assembled kangaroo experts:

"Suggestions that Australia can advance the conservation of native fauna by encouraging people to keep native animals as pets and have pastoralists replace sheep and cattle with kangaroos are not revolutionary. As with the preoccupation of environmentalists with endangered species, national parks and wilderness, these are limited options which will achieve little in the way of conserving Australia's flora and fauna. It is far more important to end land clearing and habitat fragmentation in terrestrial environments and to cease building dams, diverting rivers and trawling for fish in aquatic environments."

Not much changed. Seventeen years later came the Darling River catastrophe, marked by a million dead fish, dying terrestrial wild-life, and a shattered ecosystem, reflecting Australia's continuing exploitative path to benefit export agriculture.

Staying with the kangaroo story, ideas about substituting kanga-roos as meat 'product' to replace sheep and thus take the pressure off Australia's degraded grazing lands had been floated within Australian conservation biology since 1988. It wasn't making much headway – more for practical than ecological or ethical reasons. The notion of farming kangaroos was laughed at by the farming commu-nity, and rejected by biologists and veterinarians who understand kangaroo physiology and trauma response to confinement. Add to that the vast numbers of kangaroos needed to yield equivalent meat.

An early proponent of this solution was Gordon Grigg from the University of Queensland – a leading voice on Australian kangaroo management and adviser to governments under the conservation biology banner (a subset of zoology studies often taught as applied ecology). Grigg was joined by some of his former PhD students as well as like-minded conservation biologists from other universities and the Australian Museum. A pulpit for the ideas of conservation biology has been the Royal Zoological Society of NSW. Here are dominant voices on managing common Australian wildlife, particularly on what to do with kangaroos or how to count their numbers.

The 2002 conference where Harry Recher spoke focused on discussion around the theme 'using native fauna to assist in its own survival'. The logic of this theme was as follows: that after two centuries of sheep grazing depredations and macropod persecution, the kangaroo should save its own species, the countryside, and the graziers by dying for petfood, skins, and 'jump steak' in a more organised and commercial fashion.[1]

In this vein, when a 2004 book, *Going Native*, by palaeontologist Michael Archer (best known for his quest to clone the extinct thylacine) and journalist Bob Beale, was reviewed by a Sydney Greens party member, she quickly announced that she ate kangaroo, regularly. And so should the reader. Why?

She had bought the argument that Australians should farm and consume kangaroo in order to save the clapped-out, semi-arid rangelands from total ecological collapse after 250 years of European pastoral management. On the book's back cover, I read that returning to Australian nature as it advocates, includes "the massive health and environmental benefits to be gained from harvesting kangaroos".

The argument was further amplified by media articles and was soon picked up by the kangaroo industry which had been ploughing money into public relations and market research, co-funded by the federal government through the Rural Industries Research and Development Corporation.

The 'trust us, we're scientists' strategy had become a rewarding path to counter public interest arguments, pioneered by the tobacco industry and picked up by logging and other resource battles and prominent in the global warming/climate change 'debate' as conducted by the fossil fuel industry.

Thus a 2005 *Sydney Morning Herald* article reported on an

industry consensus that in order to get Australians to eat the national symbol the industry had to overcome the 'Skippy syndrome'. A good way to do that, John Kelly, Executive Officer of the Kangaroo Industries Association of Australia told reporter Daniel Lewis, was for Australians to learn that prominent scientists such as Mike Archer and Tim Flannery (who had worked with Archer at the Australian Museum) promoted eating kangaroo meat as a way to save Australian ecosystems. The industry's website at the time reportedly did just that.[2]

However, Lewis was even-handed in covering the mantle of science that has obscured the nasty realities of Australia's wildlife killing habits. So, at a book launch for *Kangaroos Myths and Realities* he interviewed macropod biologist David Croft. Croft, like Archer, held a research position at the University of NSW at the time. Croft studied Red kangaroos at the university's Fowlers Gap station in the rangelands north of Broken Hill where there were certainly ecosystems under stress. He told the reporter the notion of eating kangaroo to save the environment was "complete bunkum".

Croft pointed out that pastoralists had not been destocking, and that their view of kangaroos as 'vermin' to be removed often put them at odds with the goals of the commercial industry which would need sustained 'product'. Croft, as noted earlier, has been a long-time advocate of turning the rural pastoral economy towards ecotourism to safeguard the remaining wildlife and offset destocking. He told Lewis that kangaroos "authenticate the whole experience of being Australian and the animals should be visible on every roadside untroubled by a barbaric industry".

In the same year, the national quota of kangaroos that state governments were offering to be killed was 3.9 million – not including the collateral deaths of millions of joeys. While quotas are never exhausted, numbers of that order had annually yielded 5000 – 6000 tonnes of kangaroo meat for petfood and sausages, and up to two million skins used for soccer shoes and other leather products, for annual export. And that was just the legal market.

SCIENTIST PRESCRIPTION MEETS RURAL SCEPTICISM

Looking through more recent newspaper accounts, I saw this industry idea had not died and instead had gained new spokespeople amongst applied ecologists. They have diverted from the idea that kangaroos can be farmed, to double down on commercial harvesting as the way to extend on-farm income and maybe effect some soil conservation. The sub-text is that the wildlife is the property of the landholders.

One of these science voices, often tapped by media and government, is British Isles-trained zoologist and veterinarian George Wilson. Wilson, according to his company's website, has enjoyed a revolving door between academe, industry and government work with experience in Australian applied wildlife management.

A 2014 rural newspaper story featured Wilson promoting commercial hunting at a central Queensland grazier (AgForce) meeting. This was worth a look because of the arguments Wilson made and those he encountered when graziers were asked to mentally shift kangaroos from pest to valuable 'resource' (pointing to other countries with large native herbivores). In this scenario the resource is for hunting and killing, not ecotourism.

The reporter started her account with the ubiquitous claim that Australia had "out-of-control kangaroo populations". She noted that viewing kangaroos as valuable in any way whatsoever "was a topic that was always bound to be controversial – the kangaroo is widely viewed as a menace that is ruining properties and needs to be removed at all costs".

The story cited Queensland's purported 32 million kangaroos in 2013, itself a controversial claim, and the potential dollar income to graziers from a 'harvest' as proposed by Wilson. The rejoinder from the audience was that graziers had no confidence that the despised kangaroo would ever be more than pet food. Wilson expressed astonishment at the hatred people directed towards the national icon.[3]

Five years later, Wilson was still promoting the win-win "humane" kangaroo harvesting industry. If graziers actively cooperated in taking kangaroo meat and skins for profit, they would value the animals, while controlling those alleged rampant numbers. Pointing to these advantages in 2019, he argued that amateur hunters were cruelly killing kangaroos and erecting fences on behalf of graziers. This is true. Therefore, better to leave management in the hands of the commercial industry, he argued. With his Australian National University zoology researcher hat on, Wilson enjoyed a series of national media stories promoting this idea. As commonly the case with Australian media stories about the alleged need to manage kangaroos to help the farmers, there were little to no balancing perspectives.

WILDLIFE SCIENCE AND A SINGULAR MESSAGE

In February 2019 a five-minute documentary drew anger from kangaroo defenders, while being vigorously applauded by right-wing Australian media figures and reported uncritically by other Australian media. The documentary featured credentialed ecologists promoting the same ideas as Wilson's and indeed the film was given his public support. Titled *Australia's Shame*, it was executive produced by two South Australian ecologists. I looked them up and found they also enjoy a revolving door between academe and consultancy in wildlife science.

The shame they were exposing was that 'too many' kangaroos existed and were not being saved from starvation by pre-emptive death, which would also save public or Indigenous land and other native flora, fauna from the native grazers' alleged impacts.[4]

As a scientific effort, numerous variables affecting the state of the wildlife were not discussed when considering Australia's shame. Those might have included extensive habitat conversion and exclusion, influence of the weather on populations, and the whole panoply of colonial and post-colonial destruction of Australia's biodiversity and specifically of kangaroo species. Or that starvation is the natural end for all kangaroos as it is for other grazers as they lose their teeth.

The film's ecologists made sweeping national claims and judgements. But what viewers saw was a narrow slice of South Australia's arid zone and cleared mallee land where these researchers worked to save some now endangered species on degraded soils during dry times.

The remedy prescribed here as ever was "management". Australians should eat more kangaroo meat (as a welfare gesture?), and at the same time revive a flagging commercial kangaroo product industry. Kangaroos would be saved not only from death by starvation but from death by grazier culling. The welfare/ professional management narrative did not mention that the industry had shot out many eastern 'harvest zones' at the level of commercial viability since the 1960s. As this film was released, South Australian-based Macro Meats, the leading commercial processor and exporter, was reportedly exhorting landholders to pick up the phone and get a killing license that easily and the state was considering new shooting zones.

The arguments made by the scientists in these examples fit a long-standing pattern of values in the field of applied ecology and wildlife management in Australia. The brief is to benefit the agricultural and commercial sector. Perceived wildlife abundance supports calls for lethal management and commercial exploitation. I was reminded again of the koala story.

Ironically for me, as someone who wrote a book exploring Australia's climate change uncertainty since the 1980s – as a mainstream science narrative was being sniped at by a cohort of contrarian scientists, in the Australian native wildlife management arena the opposite has been the case. The undisputed mainstream of the science has over time provided arguments for the killing and exploitation of the public's wildlife to benefit commercial interests, with little to no public input.

The contrarian voices here are those advocating a less lethal, more compassionate and purely ecological approach to Australia's unique animals and their necessary habitat. That is those animals not already labelled endangered. Scientists and animal welfare voices who advocate compassionate and non-lethal values and methods have been marginalised and framed as less valid than the rational, traditional (and loud) mainstream.

All environmental decisions are at root cultural and values-based. Millions of 'common' native animals lose their life in the name of commerce and development every year. In the case of kangaroos, the commercial 'harvest' has no more convincing scientific or cultural reasons than those advanced for clubbing baby seals in Canada or harpooning whales by the Japanese and Norwegians.

Which brings me back to applied ecology and its influential advice. Gordon Grigg for example wrote in 2002 that kangaroos 'exploding' in abundance since settlement is a given that everyone understands without need for evidence or detailed geographic qualification. "A small number of species of large kangaroos – the Red Kangaroo *Macropus rufus*, Eastern Grey Kangaroo *M. giganteus* and Western Grey Kangaroo *M. fuliginosus* in particular – have increased markedly in abundance," he wrote. These happen to be the surviving large kangaroos that are the target of commercialisation.

"They are present in vast numbers in many parts of Australia's arid and semi-arid sheep rangelands, a mostly degraded area occupying about 40 percent of the continent, where they coexist with about 15 percent of the nation's sheep flock." Grigg added that sheep graziers are now often adding goats to the production mix, which will do nothing to lessen land degradation.[5]

The vast millions narrative is regularly amplified with government population counts for the commercial 'harvest.' The methods were devised by applied conservation biology mainstream practitioners. But national kangaroo totals gained from surveying harvest zones that blanket the states, raise valid questions of how indeed they get their totals while annual numbers jump around dramatically and increase to fantastic levels even during drought. I drill into that question in a later chapter.

EMPIRE SCIENCE SPAWNED SCIENCE FOR DEVELOPMENT

Development-focused nature research and a specialised understanding of ecology has a long history in Australia as in South Africa and North America. The biological sciences were put to the service of development and 'progress' and commercial gain in the British colonies. History shows us why there are no baseline ecological studies, unencumbered with ideas of 'management' or commercial use, for many of Australia's common native species.

At the same time, modern European countries and their colonies evolved with respect for expert knowledge. What scientists say matters and the context of a narrowly-focused academic field can get lost. In the case of kangaroos, when applied ecologists say that some kangaroos persist in vast millions and populations "explode" from time to time, governments and the media listen.

Conservation biology/applied ecology hang off the broader fields of zoology, botany and population biology. Wildlife management to pave the way for development has been a traditional brief for applied ecology as practiced in Australia.

Since the British dispossessed native peoples and native species and established the private property rights culture, wildlife populations – from the dingo to the kangaroo species, not sparing birds including emus, brolgas, raptors and large parrots, possums, wombats and flying foxes, have been subject to lethal management for agriculture and development on private and sometimes public land. Native vegetation and therefore habitat receive similar management.

Zoologist David Croft, who has long stood in somewhat lonely public opposition to parts of this discipline, told me that before he introduced the seemingly radical idea of wildlife tourism for Australia "95 percent of conference papers were about killing things".

CONQUEST BY INTRODUCED SPECIES

Environmental historians point out that the colonisation of Australia was accomplished not just by humans but by a whole zoo that would take precedence over the natural landscape and animals and that needed biologists to consult on the "acclimatisation", as this invasion was called.

Along with sheep and cattle, came pet animals including the rabbit and the cat, hunting accessories the fox and the hunting dog, crops and ornamental species of plants and, most effective in overcoming human opposition, the microbes that hitched a ride including smallpox, syphilis and influenza.

Today's CSIRO (Commonwealth Scientific and Industrial Research Organization) was established post WWI to support primary industry in Australia and applied biology was central to its mission to foster development, writes historian Libby Robin in *Ecology: a science of empire?*[6] Established in 1926, the Empire Marketing Board as it was called (no, we're not channelling Star Wars) had a big hand in supporting early applied research and early ecology research of the CSIR as it was then called.

Australia's understanding of applied ecology started with agricultural and pastoral pests. While this description refers to corralling escaped introduced plants like the prickly pear and animals, particularly the rabbit, native animals would soon come under the same frame.

There was not then, and inadequately since, an Australian scientific focus, with no dollar signs attached, on the ecology and interconnection of native species for baseline understanding. Except when those species are almost gone and labelled 'endangered', and 'management' is kicked into high gear on their behalf.

Australia's early biologists and CSIRO heads were British-trained through Oxford University, a world leader in applied ecology. This established a shared value structure for the colonies: that applied biological sciences were to be handmaidens to late empire visions of colonial development in agriculture and forestry and that inconvenient natives as a matter of course would be removed. Still, valuable insights into the nature of Australia were gained.

A MAVERICK OF EMPIRE SCIENCE

Biologist Francis Ratcliffe, while of this background, proved more independent in his thinking. He was sent to Australia by the Empire Marketing Board in 1929 to study the biology of the 'fruit bat', flying foxes, which had been labelled a major pest by east coast horticulturalists who wanted to eradicate the species entirely. Ratcliffe persuaded them that this was not necessary as only a few animals caused problems.

He conducted pioneering work on soil erosion, documenting erosion with sheep grazing on boom and bust marginal country. He also thought long and hard about those inland sheep enterprises that to this day spearhead the demonization of native grazers like the kangaroo and emu, rather than considering the basic sustainability of the enterprise in that landscape.

Similar to the reception of Marshall, Auty or Croft in later years, Ratcliffe's conclusion about sheep grazing in inland Australia was not welcomed. "The essential features of white pastoral settlement – a stable home, a circumscribed area of land, and a flock or herd maintained on this land year-in and year-out – are a heritage of the reliable, kindly climate of Europe. In the drought-risky semi-desert Australian inland they tend to make settlement self-destructive," he wrote.[7]

The choices have not changed from the 1930s droughts examined by Ratcliffe: if the graziers meet the inevitable droughts by destocking, they lose their investment and their breeding programs. If they don't, they ruin the land.

Ratcliffe's pioneering ecology career in Australia extended to being a key founder of the Australian Conservation Foundation (ACF) in 1965 with the idea that science and ecology were basic to native species conservation.

Historian Libby Robin, expanding on the theme that ecology in Australia was established to introduce and acclimatise non indigenous species to benefit 'the national needs', concluded that Western thinking within the sciences has been "deeply imperial". Only recently have some biologists started to work cooperatively with Australia's first people to better understand how to live in the unique environments of the country.[8]

Thus, an empire-directed science helped embed a white, European, property-owning class dictating political agendas and ideas about the natural environment. Christian notions of superiority and dominion over nature played a role. Zoos, botanic gardens, and collecting animals and plants, soon to be dead, captured the post-Victorian ideas on nature in the colonies.

CULTURAL BEDROCK

Settler culture morphed to Australian culture, and the same values and beliefs inevitably inhabit many of the scientists who grew up in the culture. What they inherited was imperial dedication to making introduced agricultural species flourish, joined to traditional and colonial ideas about game management and pest management.

From Jock Marshall and those who wrote chapters in his book I had already learned that no scientific studies were undertaken prior to eradication of plants and animals in the new colony. Few original ecosystems were put into reserves before the 1960s. Habitat for animals disappeared along with the plants and trees.

Even Ratcliffe, who was hired by the CSIRO in 1949 to become the first Officer-in-Charge of the Wildlife Survey Section, had to acknowledge little progress eight years later. He noted his department, distracted to deal with the issues of rabbits, had not been able to amass baseline data on the status and distribution of native wildlife nor the biological adequacy of parks and reserves. A survey of marsupials in NSW was the sum of it.

Opinions and assumptions along the lines of 'We've never had so many kangaroos in Australia because they have prospered with our improvements' have filled the void since. Without the early science, the next best evidence on that claim is historical observation and the accounts of explorers and settlers, which document a rich and diverse fauna and landscape, as I described earlier.

WHAT DO NATIVE ANIMALS DO IN THEIR ECOSYSTEMS?

My next question was: what contemporary studies were available on the ecological role of Australia's unique macropods, wombats, dingos, bats, possums, and other common and often persecuted natives?

Still today, the quest leads outside what is considered the mainstream of Australian wildlife research. A small band of newer-generation field ecologists – which includes David Croft, Daniel Ramp, Dror Ben-Ami, Ray Mjadwesch, and Arian Wallach, all who have helped my investigations – say that there is little to no funding for basic ecological research on the ecosystem functions of the surviving common Australia native wildlife, as if there is no role that matters.

These ecologists have testified that kangaroos, like other native grazers, are keystone species in the landscape, whose grazing, under natural conditions, is matched to the needs of other animals throughout the grassland structure – in other words, a true ecological analysis. The nutrient cycling or the native grass seed dispersal role of native grazers is also known from observations, often by people living on the land.

The 2020 ABC natural history program *Australia Remastered*, is worth a mention here for its stunning resurrected documentary footage and intimate home visits with Australia native species. An updated narrative recognises the ecological role of some of the persecuted natives. Wombats, for example, are recognised as essential ecosystem engineers for the grasslands and woodlands they share with other Australian wildlife.

Yet it is not uncommon, as I have witnessed over the years, that the biologists who defend an ecological role for kangaroos in particular but also for dingos and other inconvenient species, or who argue against lethal management, are attacked by mainstream practitioners and have had their evidence discounted and credentials dismissed in legal challenges.

IT'S COME TO THIS: KANGAROOS OUTSIDE OF BIODIVERSITY

With this kind of science history background and their mission to manage kangaroo populations, the Australian Capital Territory applied ecology fraternity and parks bureaucracy began promoting an amazing idea as fact. The idea became justification for the territory's controversial annual 'cull' of Eastern Grey kangaroos. It has been repeated without question in media reports domestic and international and has spread to other public land-management agencies in southern Australia.

The narrative is that these large kangaroos should be treated as something apart from Australian native biodiversity and are indeed a threat to biodiversity. This frame further strips the animals of already meagre legal protections as 'protected native species' and justifies overriding previous guidelines against killing females. The proponents in Canberra of a government cull offer a list of endangered species that they claim, offering no compelling evidence, are threatened by kangaroos.

How applied ecologists in the ACT go about demonstrating that kangaroos are damaging the surrounding environment is revealing: they rely on measuring grass height and mass as a 'surrogate' for measuring healthy biodiversity. (Even a non-expert may suspect the web of life is a bit more complicated than that.) In this scientific method, tall grass is good, and grass grazed down by kangaroos is bad – on paper anyway.

The natural native grass contours – in many areas dominated by tussock species – is a mix of taller and grazed down. The grasses and tussocks have evolved to regrow. Fifty years ago, CSIRO's Harry Frith wrote that kangaroos do not damage their environment but know when to move on, unless confined.[9]

The spread of the novel idea that kangaroos are outside of biodiversity was illustrated in the February 2017 appearance of two articles from the UK media, both from serious, respected outlets – the BBC online and *The Independent*. Each led with a statement that Australia was about to 'cull' a million kangaroos – "to protect endangered grasslands and wildlife" according to the BBC version.

The English media turned for expertise to a research program at the Australian National University Fenner School of Environment and Society. In the BBC article, Fenner's highly-published Professor David Lindenmayer discusses the need to kill kangaroos (apparently the number 'one million' did not faze him). The article illustrates a foreigner's confused uptake of 'facts' accompanying Australia's kangaroo killing programs. Lindenmayer is quoted as saying that it was necessary and people are still too squeamish on the topic of eating Skippy – that the cull was to save ecosystems and endangered species. (The millions already killed commercially did not rate a mention in these reports.)

The professor is quoted as implying the critically-endangered Leadbeaters possum that lives in trees in the Mountain Ash forests of Victoria is a victim of the kangaroos. He doesn't explain how that could be, and it seems a British journalist did not ask. Fire and logging of the possum's old-growth forest habitat do get a mention. A logical person might suspect they are the true threats.[10]

Frequently offered as evidence of the kangaroo danger has been an academic research report by a former Australian Capital Territory government employee. This paper is said to show that kangaroos threaten native reptiles. Its co-author was the government ecologist who first devised the Canberra kangaroo cull on public reserves, as well as Professor Lindenmayer as program leader.

I had looked at that research, as did others who can read an academic report. There was no data involving actual kangaroos, or direct evidence of their impacts, in the rise and fall of reptile populations studied. That did not stop the authors from actively claiming this paper proved kangaroo damage, seemingly guided by an assumption of unacceptable kangaroo number in the vicinity (basically a long-time average number for the regional landscape). The study was offered as conclusive evidence by not only the ACT government but by outside organisations that proposed to thin kangaroo populations claiming to save biodiversity.[11]

Five years after this paper was published, international studies emerged warning that pesticide use, loss of habitat and climate disruption were decimating global insect populations at catastrophic levels. Insect loss would endanger pollination, nutrient recycling, soil health and food for other species like insect-dependent birds, mammals and reptiles. Varying weather and the state of insects were variables not controlled for in the ANU Fenner School reptile study that relied on comparing grass height and wanted to blame kangaroos for reptile declines.[12]

CONSERVATION BIOLOGY AUSTRALIAN AND US STYLE

One of the few academic analyses of conservation biology as it is practiced can be found in the *Stanford Encyclopedia of Philosophy* (both 2004 and 2014 editions). I learned that "Conservation biology emerged as an organized academic discipline in the United States in the 1980s though much of its theoretical framework was origin-ally developed in Australia. Significant differences of approach in the two traditions were resolved in the late 1990s through the formulation of a consensus framework for the design and adaptive management of conservation area networks."

What emerged in this discipline is a largely desk-bound biology with some useful jargon like 'adaptive management,' focused on modelling hypothetical cases for areas that require conservation planning. Computer algorithms trumped field biology. Animals in such a system are units, not living beings with families and social organisation. Some people called such modelling 'playing God'.

The Australian version that evolved is described as radically different to the early ecological and ethical scope of the US version that started in the late 1980s. That was led by scientists like Jared Diamond, E.O. Wilson, Michael Soule, Paul Ehrlich, and Thomas Lovejoy. Soule wrote in 1985 of what he thought would be basic to conservation biology: "In emphasizing the inherent value of nonhuman life, [the perspective is that]: Species have value in themselves, a value neither conferred nor revocable, but springing from a species' long evolutionary heritage and potential or even from the mere fact of its existence."[13]

The Australian variant on the other hand was focused on active species management: completing that imperial project of converting wild country and serving the agriculture that replaced it – a process dubbed "habitat conversion".

The *Stanford* analysis notes that Australian conservation biology has been the handmaiden of cultural values, "socio political factors," and priorities from inception – as in, handmaiden to the values and priorities of colonial settlement – transforming the existing environment, its fauna and flora, for European and British-style farming, introduced species and economic gain.

1080: POSTER CHILD OF CONSERVATION BIOLOGY, AUSTRALIA AND NEW ZEALAND

The lethal approach to effecting conservation biology goals has been accepted as a primary environmental management tool in both Australia and New Zealand. These two former colonies are world champions and still-holdouts in poisoning animals with 1080 baits, often dispersed from the air.

In both countries, killing millions of introduced animals once they are labelled as 'pests' (for example, Australian Brush-tail possums in New Zealand) raises even less debate than killing indigenous wildlife. The practitioners of pest animal eradication and wildlife management of anything not labelled 'endangered' frequently blur. The notion of abundance and tag of 'pest' is all that is needed.[14]

In Australian sheep country, 1080-laced baits are often dropped from aircraft. One example is dispersal in a four kilometre-wide transect of country bordering the 'dog fence' that stretches for

5,600 kilometres (3,500 miles) between the north and the south of the continent.

While the target is dingos and wild dogs, no one knows the total impact, including persistence in the environment, secondary poisoning of scavenger birds or, elsewhere, mammalian native predators. The poison is dropped by government departments on behalf of sheep graziers. Regular government poisoning is conducted on the outskirts of national parks for the same reason.

In the state of Tasmania, industry and government are united, although not necessarily with the public, on the need to poison-bait Brush-tail possums, and poison or shotgun Pademelons and Bennett's (Red-necked) wallabies that nibble on emerging trees shoots.

Developed as a rat poison – therefore a mammalian poison – from a naturally-occurring plant metabolite, 1080 is now tightly controlled or banned in most countries because of its hideous method of dealing death, along with its variable persistence and danger to non-target species, including carrion feeders. The use of this poison as a wide-ranging control method, targeting for a long time now the Australian native dog the dingo (as well as escaped domestic dogs, foxes, cats, pigs, rabbits, and possums) is, simply put, an animal welfare issue.

Most animals that ingest it will die – and worse, they will suffer horribly for up to 48 hours or longer before they die. In dogs, the signs of poisoning are usually noticed within half an hour of ingestion, but can take more than six hours to show up. First symptoms include vomiting, anxiety, disorientation, and shaking. These quickly develop into frenzied behaviour with running and screaming fits, drooling at the mouth, uncontrolled paddling and seizures, followed by total collapse and death.[15]

NSW BLANKETS BURNED FORESTS WITH POISON

Native carnivorous forest dweller, the quoll.

The NSW Animal Justice Party published further facts about 1080, as NSW started what it was proud to call its "largest feral animal control program in the state's history" following the 2019–2020 catastrophic bushfires. This involved dropping poison baits disguised as food for hungry mammalian animals into 60,000 kilometres of the state's burned-out forests over a 12-month period.

Any animal, states the AJP in an available fact sheet, including humans that ingest 1080 will die a slow, painful death. There is no antidote. The toxin also causes birth defects and reduced fertility, as well as damage to the reproductive system, brain, heart and other organs. It works by preventing the body's muscles and organs from absorbing energy, resulting in cramps and failure of the lungs and heart, with a death typically lasting between 8–24 hours for birds and 2–4 days for large mammals.

The possibility of poisoning native non-target species like the endangered marsupial carnivore quoll, ground-digging rat-kangaroos like Potoroos, or omnivorous birds, is strenuously denied by government authorities. People who protest are told that most marsupials are immune to the poison (except, it seems, the possums that are regularly poisoned in New Zealand and poisoned in Tasmania along with the wallabies).

The Animal Justice Party quotes research indicating that Potoroos are more susceptible to 1080 than introduced rabbits. Localised extinctions of Tiger quolls were linked to 1080 baiting 20 years ago when politicians were informed by a government Threatened Species Scientific Committee. And yet, nothing changes. The AJP is under no illusion that lobbying by sheep farmers isn't related to this toxic warfare, noting there are alternative ways to ward off foxes and dogs.[16]

DESKTOP FORMULA TO KILL VERTEBRATE 'PESTS', AND THE NEED FOR PUBLIC PERSUASION

Budget cuts and thinning park service ranks, and a desk jockey approach to ecology have played into the automatic reach for gun and poison as land management tools. Twenty years ago, a conference organised by the Australasian Vertebrate Pest sector discussed the challenges of bringing the public along with killing as the preferred management tool working to a formula. They canvassed the best ways to kill rabbits, goats, pigs, dogs and horses, as well as kangaroos in the South Australian Flinders Ranges national park.

They had a plan to reverse years of introduced stock damage. The plan was to cull Red kangaroos and Wallaroos/Euros down to two and 10 animals respectively per square kilometre, i.e. per 100 hectares (250 acres). These theoretically acceptable numbers, along with culling goats and rabbits, underpinned a desktop formula they developed of 'total grazing pressure' treating social animals as statistical units.[17]

The government scientists compared what they considered alarmingly high macropod numbers in the park (sampled at five Red kangaroos per square kilometre and possibly 10 Wallaroos/ Euros) with more acceptable numbers on surrounding pastoral land, "where there is competition from grazing stock and commercial kangaroo harvests are undertaken opportunistically".

The agenda here, as with the suggestion of farming kangaroos to replace sheep on grazing properties, was recovery of native vegetation and sometimes 'threatened species' after years of stock degradation. These approaches to shield the perceived needs of vegetation and endangered species from the presence of more robust common species have also divided some Landcare affiliates and some environmental groups from wildlife and welfare advocates. An integrated ecological approach is still missing.

Few Australians are aware and might be aghast to learn, that some Australian states routinely kill wildlife, specifically macropods, in national parks. Following a period of severe drought and then bushfires in 2020, activists learned through freedom of information requests that the state of Victoria killed more than 4000 Western Grey and other kangaroos sheltering in western Victorian parks. The government had designated twice as many for destruction. This was not a new trend for Victoria. In the north of Australia, a mix of land managers have eliminated much of the terrestrial wildlife and habitat through igniting annual fires that burn too hot, too late after a wet period, and burn indiscriminately.

WE ALL THINK ALIKE

It does not take long to realise that Australian applied wildlife research is overwhelmingly conducted by agencies funded by the taxpayer. Some of it comes through the commercial-minded Rural Industries Research and Development Corporation (RIRDC). RIRDC reports can be used as science-badged promotions handed out in Australia and overseas. CSIRO applied branches have been another mainstay: lumping some native wildlife in with vertebrate pest research. Some academic departments are on board.

Meanwhile, the CSIRO's on-ground field ecology branches, which did conduct some long-term data gathering, have slowly been disbanded as the organisation moved to require more external, commercial funding to underpin research. State departments of agriculture transparently pay biologists to work on pest management for farmers.

While the claims of scientific expertise in conservation biology and wildlife management come cloaked in the conventions of scientific institutions – the conference, the journal publication, the higher degree – many of its proponents have proven less happy with the open debate convention of science.

"These people were promoting themselves as scientists but using all the tools of propaganda," zoologist David Croft told me. "If they had a critic, particularly anyone with any animal welfare interest they were 'animal rights people', they were not fellow scientists, always extremists, extreme vegetarians. Welfare is considered emotional, not scientific. It was suggested that there was a conspiracy to stop people eating meat because some people who opposed the commercial kangaroo industry were vegans."

Ecologist John Read, who commissioned the 2019 film *Australia's Shame* about starving kangaroos was happy to repeat to me how he characterised the opposition: "Tragically, campaigning against human consumption of roo meat by a fringe minority of ill-informed animal welfare advocates has reduced export markets and ironically reduced the capacity for kangaroo populations to be managed sustainably and ethically. Increasing our consumption of roo meat and restoring export markets will assist in ethically managing kangaroos (according to RSPCA-endorsed guidelines) rather than having them culled by amateurs or left to starve to death."

THE PROFESSIONAL, ETHICAL, HUMANE, KANGAROO HARVEST OBSERVED

Those who promote commercial and non-commercial killing of kangaroos, counter public unease by assuring everyone the hunt is professional, ethical and humane. Most people want to believe that is so and not think about it. But observations and experience relayed by activists and disillusioned shooters, including to me for this book, have seriously questioned whether in aggregate the nightly killing today is any less brutal than in past decades. Neighbours where shooting takes place also have seen the worst.

West of the Blue Mountains in NSW, Greg Keightley and Diane Smith had almost a decade to document the commercial kangaroo harvest along three kilometres bordering their 500-acre property, bought with the idea of owning a conservation property. Three species of kangaroo exist in their area. Little did they dream of the neighbourhood nightmare they would encounter, including threats, because they are non-conforming with the 'harvesting' of kangaroo supported by other landholders.

"We have watched with our own eyes, and it is inherently cruel," they wrote in 2015 to the *Sacramento Bee* newspaper in California prior to that US state's legislative vote on resuming import of kangaroo products (it was voted down).

Night after night they witnessed trucks with bright lights shooting at and pursuing what were family groups of kangaroos.

They testify that they saw and heard many distressed animals that were wounded and not killed immediately. They have found the remains. They have seen the lost and bewildered joeys. They have documented the frequent body-shooting that is almost inevitable. They wrote in their testimony:

> "We have seen hundreds of kangaroo heads that have been butchered and left in the field. Many do not have a gunshot wound to them. The heads are cut off very low down the neck indicating that the kangaroo may have been miss shot, struck by a bullet in the neck or the torso.
>
> "We have witnessed kangaroo heads that have been shot in regions of the head other than the brain case, often in the front of the head. The animals may not have died until sometime after, often showing the signs of gruesome secondary trauma from a length of metal pipe or an axe. Joeys are often not killed with their mothers but ripped from her pouch and discarded into the bushes, not even counted as a statistical 'kill'.
>
> "We hear joeys calling for their dead mothers until the sun comes up. We see them in the mornings lost and bewildered. We may see them again the next evening, but usually never again after that. This is considered 'acceptable collateral damage'.
>
> "We often see kangaroos shot on a previous evening who died on our property while escaping the terror of being continually hunted. We see the trails of blood where the kangaroo has had her throat cut. The body is hung on the back of the truck to bleed out. We see the butchering sites where the shooters stop to 'dress' the kangaroo.
>
> "The group social structure is ruined. The mob is in disarray. The fields smell of death. Such an integral part of the biodiversity of the Australian rangelands – hunted down, killed and then butchered in a dirty, dusty truck bed. Squashed into pet food cans,

or sold as sausage, or to manufacture soccer boots and gloves, or testicle key rings for tourists. It just doesn't add up."

In 2019, Greg and Diane were still documenting the hunt that disturbs their nights, even following the shooter to the chiller box. Diane is now taken up with caring for rescued joeys. Greg told me that the big male kangaroos are all gone, shot out of the area. The bodies going to the chiller boxes are all female, and small and young animals.

The remaining mob's guard is now a matriarch rather than the alpha male kangaroo. The shooters' vehicle is followed regularly by foxes that eat the decapitated heads and other discarded body parts. The couple has not seen any mainstream media outlet in Australia show interest in what really goes on Outback under cover of darkness.

One-time professional kangaroo shooter David Nicholls has written about and also spoke to me about his experiences, and the nightmares he endures from his time in the industry. He remembers the terrible wounding, the "slaughter of the innocents," the "juggernaut that was and is altering the genetic makeup of a marvellous animal," and feels he must bear part of the blame every time there is a wanton act of cruelty to kangaroos. One-time kangaroo shooter Lyn Gynther, to whom I spoke extensively about the situation in Queensland, now runs advocacy group KangaWatch and spends her days as a wildlife carer.

These voices pull the veil from the "humane" and professional hunt advocated by some applied ecologists and wildlife officials. I wonder whether the science badge has convinced the long-silent peak environmental groups and Australia's peak animal welfare organisation, the RSPCA. A spokesperson for the RSPCA hinted at how the slaughter has been rationalised. She told a reporter for *The Sydney Morning Herald* in 2016 that the commercial hunt is more acceptable because the government has set standards and someone is overseeing the activity, so cruel practices are less likely to occur than with ad hoc shooting.[18]

Unfortunately, this is a delusion shared by many. No one – other than citizens who attempt to bear witness like the Keightleys or those who protest at Canberra's government cull – oversees or monitors the nightly commercial kill, or the non-commercial slaughter on grazing properties in every state, or on public lands, barring the occasional ranger.

COMPASSIONATE CONSERVATION: A VIEW WITH ROOM TO GROW

Australia's growing compassionate conservation scientific fraternity has more in common with the US ecological version than with mainstream Australian conservation biology.

As a founding scientist of the Australian Centre for Compassionate Conservation at the University of Technology Sydney, ecologist and wildlife biologist Dror Ben-Ami emphasises that all conservation is about values, that it just depends on the mindset and methods.

"Biology is not mathematics. If you value wildlife, the pest name does not exist. Biologists should be about love of life, not the opposite. It's disrespect. I had the privilege of studying kangaroos for 4–5 years in the wild. Animal protection and animal rights *is* a value."

Still, with the mainstream science firmly behind the lethal management ethos, few scientific voices enter the public conversation saying that lethal management is pointless and counterproductive – whether to boost stocking rates or to find a scapegoat for drought conditions.

One who has spoken out is dingo researcher Arian Wallach at the Centre for Compassionate Conservation. In a media landscape that faithfully amplifies a traditional narrative of 'our poor farmers' beset by unkind nature and wildlife, aided by go-to scientific experts, she raised questions seldom publicly examined.

When NSW decreed in August 2018 that to help drought-stricken farmers the killing of kangaroos and poisoning of dingos would ramp up, she told me: "The announcement to help farmers through drought by making it easier to kill kangaroos and to use their meat to poison dingoes is counterproductive, unethical, and has no basis in science." She can speak from experience, including a two-year period when she and her partner managed a large cattle station in northern South Australia.

She knows first-hand the extreme stress of prolonged hot and dry conditions. It is an experience she won't forget, and it informs her work as an ecologist, marrying the realities of farming in Australia with the desire to preserve the wildlife. In South Australia she also interacted with some neighbouring graziers who are forging their own way in wildlife-friendly farming. They have been running successful businesses, particularly organic cattle farming, while allowing wild animals such as kangaroos and dingoes to co-exist on their land.

She says that wildlife-friendly farming is a movement growing worldwide, with theoretical research supporting it. Ideals of compassion and respect for the individual are central tenets, getting away from treating animals just as management units.

Another theme is restoring a more natural balance in eco-systems by not targeting native predators like dingos for automatic destruction. This is not just a theoretical point. A new taxpayer-funded push of dingo destruction was launched while this book was being finalised, and as I learned of the mega 1080 drops in NSW national parks.

Wallach says research shows that dingo populations that are randomly killed actually increase in number, once the alpha dog is out of the picture. The same is true for kangaroo mobs where the top male is killed. These alpha males keep a sustainable order as they monopolise reproduction.

A similar story was told to me by Terri Irwin from Australia Zoo. From the experience on the family's conservation property in central Queensland, she has learned that dingos and kangaroos reach a stable population if unmolested. The dingos repay their ability to co-exist by keeping the foxes and cats down, she says. They appear to be preferred prey. Dingos there have never been known to pull down a calf on the property.

From Longreach, Queensland, cattle grazier Angus Emmott told *National Geographic* his experience. As he leaves the dingos alone, they form settled packs that permit only senior females to breed and they keep young dogs under control. On his property he too has observed that the dingos keep the kangaroo numbers down and take out feral cats and foxes and goats. He has no doubt the natural balance has great biodiversity benefits.[19]

Nevertheless, cultural and scientific groupthink, intolerance, and even paranoia have continued when faced with alternative points of view on wildlife's place in the environment. This was on full display with a bizarre witch-hunt in the nation's capital starting in 2009 that I reported on at the time and recount in the next chapter.

Back at the 2002 workshop, ecologist Harry Recher reminded everyone of the narrowness of conventional approaches to flora and fauna conservation:

"A real revolution in nature conservation requires a change in national priorities from ones of increasing economic growth, resource consumption and population growth to becoming an ecologically sustainable society.

"Landcare needs to return a minimum of 30 percent of existing cleared land to native vegetation with an additional 20 to 40 percent placed under deep-rooted perennials with a primary objective of providing other species with the resources they require to achieve their evolutionary potential."[20]

BURN THE HERETIC

"Native herbivores such as kangaroos and wombats play a vital role in ecosystem functioning but are often victimised and treated with lack of concern because of socio-political factors and historical value judgements rather than heeding biological and ecological information."

— ECOLOGIST DAN RAMP, IN 'THE ROLE OF BIODIVERSITY
IN CLIMATE CHANGE ADAPTATION'.

"If burning heretics at the stake were still fashionable, and legal, I would be a pile of ashes now," Robin Tennant-Wood told me in November 2009.

Dr Tennant-Wood's sin: a report she oversaw raised some inconvenient truths about the environmental role of kangaroos that did not fit the narrative that had built up in the national capital. The Australian Capital Territory government and its parks and ecology sections were promoting kangaroo killing in Canberra reserves and they did not like conflicting thoughts or evidence.

Tennant-Wood was at the time the Director of the Canberra Environment and Sustainability Resource Centre and a Visiting Fellow at the Australian National University. She had just experienced an incredible couple of weeks.

During that time, the ACT Office of the Commissioner for Sustainability and the Environment, ACT politicians, and ACT science advisors had gone to great lengths to discredit her and a report submitted from the Environment Centre to the Commissioner. This report was on the contributions of biodiversity – i.e., native animals and plants – in climate change adaptation for the ACT.

Tennant-Wood said the territory government's then Environment Commissioner was told from the outset that the report would be compiled by an environmental science student employed by the centre as a project officer, for a cost of $4,500 over a two-month period. I later interviewed the commissioner, Dr Maxine Cooper, and she did not dispute that she had commissioned the report on that basis.

It was to review the research literature on how biodiversity benefits the ACT and might help the territory adapt to likely climate change impacts – including longer droughts and bigger bushfires. Several case studies were included, one of them on the Eastern Grey kangaroo, recently targeted for annual, government-initiated killing campaigns on nature reserves.

The report was lodged in August, the money paid. It was to help inform the next State of the Environment report. Then on 21 October, a page one story in *The Canberra Times* started a major uproar about a leak, and worse. The charge was led by the commissioner's office, with several supporting players.

What was the sensitive information leaked to the Canberra public? 'Roo Cull will increase city's bushfire risk' ran the admittedly provocative headline. The newspaper story reported on the four-page kangaroo case study in stronger language than the actual report, which made the simple case that kangaroos had something to offer as natural grazers in the landscape, kinder on the land than sheep or cattle.

The report noted that compared to livestock, kangaroos cause less erosion which in turn means less silt in waterways, and less disturbed soil where weeds can grow. Kangaroos could keep down growth of dry grasses in a dry environment – and because they don't pull up roots, plants in areas they have grazed could regenerate faster after a bushfire. The report noted that the Eastern Grey had persisted in the urban area and fringe, but was treated as an unwanted 'pest' in the national capital despite being integral to the biodiversity of the region. And, unspoken, despite being Australia's most recognisable tourist icon.

The report included several case studies demonstrating these points and quoted NSW university research ecologist Dan Ramp, describing the role of kangaroos as so-called keystone species in grasslands and woodlands. Their grazing pattern maintained suitable habitat for other species, including threatened and endangered species. He suggested negative biodiversity consequences should the culls continue.[1]

COMMON NATIVE SPECIES STEP INTO THE BREACH

Ramp noted that common native species like the Eastern Grey kangaroo, or the wombat, played an increasingly important role in maintaining ecosystem functions as more vulnerable herbivores and other species had declined due to changes wrought by humans – broadscale clearing for stock and settlements being the most obvious example. For these reasons, the report questioned the snowballing ACT policy of culling kangaroos.

Robin Tennant-Wood had no context at the time that her little centre's report was challenging a local scientific theory and management program that came with employment and funds. But she was about to find out. It became apparent that opposing the ACT kangaroo cull assumptions with positive information about kangaroos was seen as heresy that needed to be quashed.

Tennant-Wood told me for an article: "The commissioner contacted me by phone the next morning, before I had had a chance to see the newspaper. She accused me of leaking the report to the media, admitted that she hadn't read the report and later indicated that she would be refuting the *Canberra Times* article."

That same day, emails went out to ACT politicians and department heads. Seemingly, the only aspect of a 40-page report of interest to everyone was the brief kangaroo biodiversity study. A similar briefing letter went to the *Canberra Times* and suggested for the first time that the report was done by a student in an unauthorised fashion and that it had not been peer-reviewed.

The term 'peer review' became central to this story. While it was used as a rod to publicly beat the Environment Centre, Dr Tennant-Wood, and the biodiversity report, normally it means that specialists in the same field review and comment on a piece of original research on its way into a scientific journal. This report didn't qualify for such strict treatment – it was not original research but rather a summary of what the small amount of baseline biodiversity research was suggesting.

KILLINGS INCREASE UNDER SCIENCE COVER

The Commissioner's letter to the rest of government highlighted the ACT's claim of scientific justification for taxpayer-funded agencies having killed some 10,000 kangaroos on public land up to 2009 – including on defence land, with more to come. In the years following, the ACT government's 2017 revised kangaroo management plan indicated, an average 2,000 kangaroos were killed annually bringing the total killed on the Canberra's nature reserves to 14,000 by 2016.

In addition, the ACT had for decades issued kill licenses to private landholders around the capital region and to neighbouring defence facilities: 97,070 kangaroos were killed between 1997 and 2016 under this system, mostly by private landholders.*[2]

---

* ACT public/private killing licenses increased dramatically after the 1990s. In 2015, 82 licenses were issued to kill up to 20,722 kangaroos in one year, mostly by private landholders. Ref: letter to Regional Friends of Wildlife from ACT Conservator, 17 August 2016

The day after the Commissioner's letter went out, Tennant-Wood was contacted by ACT Senior Ecologist Don Fletcher. Dr Fletcher's public pronouncements based on northern hemisphere hypotheses about population explosions among grazing mammals was then the public voice of the science underpinning the ACT's case for culling. I had heard him explain this theory at a local Landcare meeting.

According to this, the ACT was suffering a unique biological explosion of kangaroo numbers. Not mentioned were other factors bringing kangaroos onto grassland and woodland reserves and hopping around the city. Possible factors included inward migration from surrounding farms where shooting took place, presence on reserves due to habitat loss for new suburbs, and lack of wildlife corridors. Commissioner Maxine Cooper's position was that "independent experts" advised her that "overgrazing" was a problem at some sites, leading to the cull recommendations.

CONSPIRACY THEORIES

Email traffic shows the ACT Senior Ecologist charged that there was a campaign against the kangaroo cull and wondered whether the Environment Centre was in collaboration with the *Canberra Times* journalist on this campaign. Another email surmised they had been "suckered in" by someone, maybe the student author or others. "The CKC [Canberra Kangaroo Coalition] includes some very clever people and some have enormous time and motivation for this sort of thing," he wrote.

He also had a problem with anecdotal material about the kangaroo's role in the ecosystem. The sin here was "unscientific" observations from a farming couple who had observed kangaroos on their property for 20 years. They had seen how kangaroos are important for regenerating native grasses as they spread grass seed with their bodies and habits.

Anecdotal material is often all that can be called upon, given the almost complete lack of ecological research since settlement on the role of kangaroo species with the surrounding flora and fauna. (Lack of baseline research on common Australian species was highlighted again by a recent news story reporting that, for the first time, scientists had discovered that Australian bat species are highly migratory and travel across the continent.)

It was becoming apparent that members of the ACT conservation biology/applied ecology fraternity found the anecdotal material – and proffered evidence of the kangaroos' ecological role in grassland ecosystems – to be dangerous heresy.

Ecological defence of macropods in the environment came from ecologists Dror Ben-Ami and Daniel Ramp – both by that time at the University of Technology, Sydney, with published studies on macropods part of their resumes. They reviewed the offending report and sent a supporting letter to Tennant-Wood to pass on to the commissioner's office.

If publication numbers and peer review are the standard of scientific credibility, Dr Ramp was a greater expert than anyone in the ACT on kangaroo and wallaby population dynamics and interaction with urbanised land conditions and with humans in south eastern Australia. He had early in his career co-authored a study showing that kangaroo populations stay stable over time.[3]

In 2009, Ramp testified at an ACT Administrative Appeals Tribunal case that citizens had brought against the cull. He testified that the methods described by the government's witness, Dr Fletcher, on how government researchers drew conclusions about "overgrazing" – based on measuring grass mass or ground cover height – is not an accepted ecological method for judging kangaroo interactions with either grassland health or other creatures.

Plant scientists I asked about that issue noted that measuring vegetation height only tells you something in cropping systems.

Regardless, ACT city park rangers and associated ecologists continued to use measurement of "green herbage mass" (grass height and volume) as the major yardstick underpinning their case that kangaroos "overgraze" – that they damage ground cover.

Critics of the government pointed to a PhD thesis by one of the city's advising ecologists. That work looked at natural kangaroo densities in a nearby national park and found densities of 4.5 and 5 kangaroos per hectare could not be characterised as damaging to surrounding environments. There was no evidence that these densities of kangaroos reduce ground cover to levels where erosion can accelerate or predictably result in low levels of ground cover. Yet the city he advised was shooting for a head count of one kangaroo or less per hectare on reserves. I contacted that scientist who said the critics had "misunderstood".

PATH TO MASS KILLING

Five years before Robin Tennant-Wood was publicly pilloried for a report that agreed with the above thesis assessment – that is, no apparent negatives at typical kangaroo densities – emails obtained through freedom of information requests unveiled a further back-story. At that time, park rangers had been told by their advising ecologists that kangaroos are not the cause of ground cover damage. The ACT rangers were proposing the first mass killing of kangaroos on public reserves at the Googong water reservoir, citing protection of ground cover.

The 2004 correspondence showed ecologists advised rangers that killing kangaroos would do nothing to restore ground cover or grass mass, the weather being the significant factor. That correspondence also signalled that the main motivation for killing kangaroos was to please surrounding sheep farmers who were armed with traditional beliefs that kangaroos were pests who ate 'their' grass. The park rangers overrode the ecological advice and killed kangaroos.

Seemingly still in agreement with the farmers, by 2009 when the Environment Centre report was commissioned city officials had been persuaded to set a desktop target of reducing urban grassland reserve densities to one kangaroo per hectare (from an estimated natural population averaging two to four kangaroos per hectare). The target density of one per hectare reflected averages preferred in the agricultural sector.

Canberra residents meanwhile were treated to flexible narratives justifying annual culls to achieve these low densities – unless killed pre-emptively, kangaroos would starve, or maybe they would damage their ground cover/environment and damage endangered species. The narrative grew and flip-flopped over the years but the plan stayed the same. No wildlife corridors were contemplated. Submissions on ecotourism were batted away.

CANBERRA BUBBLE DEFIES NATIONAL FINDINGS

In 2006, a national review of scientific knowledge on kangaroos was produced by two senior public-sector ecologists for the NSW government. The Olsen and Low report stated that "damage is difficult to monitor, predict or even to prove empirically to be an issue".

The authors suggested that dropping 'damage' as a reason to kill kangaroos, removes the 'pest' mindset as well. Damage was precisely what the ACT was dog-whistling. It was notable that of 237 learned papers on kangaroos canvassed for this national review, none was written by an ACT researcher or government administrator appearing in this controversy.[4]

Undeterred, within the following decade Canberra researchers were unveiling a novel interpretation of pest and damage that spread to other wildlife managers and has since been used by the commercial kangaroo industry: kangaroos would be labelled as a threat to biodiversity, somehow outside Australian biodiversity.

In the previous chapter on Australian wildlife science I noted the international spread of these ideas by the same research cohort.

In 2009, defending the uproar over the Environment Centre report, ACT Environment Commissioner Cooper said her decision to green-light culling had been advised by an expert panel. On examination, the ACT scientists on that panel may well have trained and worked in traditional agricultural and wildlife sciences that positioned kangaroos as abundant pests causing damage to farmers. Committee members were Dr Lyn Hinds (from CSIRO, at the time in vertebrate pest animal research), parks and land management bureaucrat Dr David Shorthouse, and Dr Tony Peacock, former director CRC Invasive Animals and an agricultural scientist in pig research.

Later, Tony Peacock was appointed inaugural chair of the Mulligans Flat 450 hectare experiment bringing almost-exterminated small marsupials back to the ACT in a fenced enclosure, while healthy kangaroos were shot around the perimeter.[5]

Supporting the Environment Centre report, NSW ecologists Ben-Ami and Ramp wrote, "we know of no studies showing that Eastern Grey Kangaroo populations have diminished biodiversity (flora or fauna) due to overgrazing".

They might have saved their breath. In mid-2009, and again in 2013 and in 2014, administrative tribunal judges (lawyers and administrators on the payroll of the ACT), considered legal challenges to the culling, brought by citizen groups. Each time the tribunals rejected testimony from ecologists, animal welfare experts and peer-review experts not employed by the ACT government, who challenged the cull's purpose and methods.

PUBLIC HUMILIATION

Just how seriously the ACT parks bureaucracy took its kangaroo killing mission was about to be felt by Robin Tennant-Wood in that

October of 2009. A public relations agency had been engaged. Two scientists who did not specialise in kangaroo population dynamics or the animal's biodiversity role were asked to peer-review the Environment Centre report. They were Arthur Georges, reptile specialist and Dean of the Faculty of Applied Science and director of the Institute for Applied Ecology at the University of Canberra, and Lyn Hinds, the vertebrate pest group leader at CSIRO who had advised the commissioner on culling.

A meeting was arranged at which commissioner Cooper read to Dr Tennant-Wood from an unflattering review email, but did not offer the names of the reviewers or their full reviews. She received no feedback on what was allegedly missed or how to improve the report – standard peer review practice – and never saw the review. But what the reviewers had to say would be revealed to all in a newspaper article a week later. Public humiliation was next on the agenda.

'Peer reviews discredit kangaroo cull findings', headlined *The Canberra Times*. The story this time, by a different reporter, made much of the report being written by an undergraduate student, and described its finding in a way that sounded odd (for example, making direct links between culling and erosion and weed outbreaks, which the report does not say).

The city's newspaper reported that the money had been returned and Tennant-Wood had apologised for the report's leaking. It said eminent scientists had peer-reviewed the report and found it "at odds with most scientific research".[6]

The article quoted wholesale from the peer review that Tennant-Wood never saw. Lyn Hinds appeared to object to the suggestion that kangaroos were part of the local biodiversity, and not intruders. Dr Hinds was quoted as saying the report missed "a large body of relevant information with respect to the roles and impacts of kangaroos and other large stock on biodiversity". And management of "overabundant" species was ignored, she said.

Professor Georges didn't like the link between kangaroo culls and bushfire management, and said the report should not be considered for the next State of the Environment report. Commissioner Cooper indicated that she would not use any of the findings or suggestions.

She later told me for an article that once these strong objections were made known to Dr Tennant-Wood and her colleagues, they withdrew the report and refunded the money. Yes, under duress, said Tennant-Wood, since the centre as a whole received vital funding for its work from the ACT government.

Next, the ACT Labor Government's Urban Services Minister dismissed the report on a radio program, saying incorrectly that Tennant-Wood had "apologised" for it. Toeing the party line, he said that there is plenty of peer-reviewed science to support the government's position, but failed to name any.

Robin Tennant-Wood and others came to see this as an issue of academic freedom and freedom of speech, as much as a concerted effort to demonise kangaroos and quash any scientific or lay view that was different.

"What I found most extraordinary about the whole saga is the extent to which the commissioner sought to have the report, the Centre, and me, publicly discredited for questioning a piece of government policy. The scramble to have a minor part of a report removed from the public arena bordered on the hysterical," she told me.

Here in the nation's capital – that calls itself 'The Bush Capital' – was a startling example of the orthodoxy demanded by a sector of science on the right way to think about native animals, particularly kangaroos, in the Australian landscape. The preferred group think in the ACT was emerging from the University of Canberra, the Australian National University, and the CSIRO from applied ecology programs.

Photo: Supplied

Herding of kangaroos before the Belconnen Naval Station mass killing. Canberra parks put cattle and sheep on reserves after they killed the kangaroos.

A year before Robin Tennant-Wood's ordeal, kangaroo killing got underway in the suburbs of Canberra guided by the same applied ecology voices that had been asked to peer review the Environment Centre's report. They were credited with advising the government and the media on the herding and massacre of kangaroos at the Belconnen Naval Station. It caused an international outcry.

The reason as preserved in media reports, was that the defence-administered land was being "overgrazed" by kangaroos (who had lost their habitat to surrounding suburbia and had become confined) and they needed to be culled. Variations on this theme were repeated in regard to both defence land and urban reserves in the following years. The ACT government then and since has rejected translocation proposals for confined macropods.

Ideas cemented in tertiary education play a central role in this saga. Both the ACT's chief ecologist until 2018 and Daniel Iglesias, who in 2012 became the head of ACT Parks and Conservation, studied applied ecology at the territory-government supported University of Canberra. Iglesias thereafter spearheaded the government's cull, and was the voice of the city's propaganda to normalise killing kangaroos.

In the years following this drama, Robin Tennant-Wood was teaching environmental politics at the University of Canberra and receiving students from the science faculty. She said they often reported being taught the basic assumption that there are 'too many' kangaroos.

VOICES FROM THE CANBERRA SUBURBS

Being thus told how to think about things and what not to think, how were Canberra residents responding to this slaughter next to their backyards? Over the years I asked a few.

A 2010 newspaper article I wrote about the Environment Centre saga was accompanied with photos from an inner-city reserve, Mount Painter, showing a relaxed and inquisitive kangaroo and a field of healthy-looking grass. The opportunity to mix with unafraid wildlife on this small reserve was treasured by the neighbours who spoke to me.[7]

The site is bounded by a four-lane highway and leased sheep and cattle paddocks continued to monopolise the best lowland grass at the time. The grass on the mountainside where only kangaroos fed appeared lush but elsewhere the mountain was infested with weeds, which presumably was not the kangaroos' fault. (But yes, they have been occasionally blamed for that too.)

I had the pleasure on that day to walk amongst the mob lounging, unafraid, on the hill. Neither neighbours nor visitors would enjoy that experience again. Five years of shooting from 2010 onwards killed many hundreds – decimating the local mob numbers and structure. Ten or so urban reserves were targeted repeatedly in this way after 2010.

In 2016, a resident of the suburb of Isaacs gave me a moving account of the year that her kangaroo friends, as she called them, were slaughtered on a reserve that had not previously been shot on.

Her story connects a lot of dots on what else this program might be about, a question that has mystified many, including myself.

It was 11 June on a holiday long weekend as Canberrans were enjoying their barbecues and weekend sports. Christine Stevens was walking her dog on the ridge behind her home. What happened next: "I was just chased off by park rangers eight minutes to 5pm at the top. They were there with two park ranger tray trucks, a 4wd buggy, a truck and a yellow digger. They were 200 metres from the most magnificent roos. I had just been admiring them, the only ones remaining, the last cluster, maybe 20." She likened the experience to watching a shark circling swimmers and feeling helpless.

Stevens said she and her family have walked Isaacs Ridge for 30 years, and knew the families of kangaroos, and found no greater number of kangaroos now than at any other time in the past 30 years.

"We have had kangaroos coming into our suburb for all those years to graze on our lawns. They are the perfect lawnmower. Never eating too low, nor up-rooting grasses, and their soft feet never break the ground unlike horses, cattle, sheep. Those of us who have walked upon the ridge several times each week for 30 years can testify that kangaroos are not overpopulating Isaacs Ridge, nor causing stress to the grasslands nor to themselves."

She said she was too scared to photograph the shooters, as they were watching her and told her to go. "One truck drove after me with its lights on. Very intimidating. If I had been there five minutes later, I might have been shot."

On the same day the public broadcaster ABC reported that the ACT parks department admitted its contract shooters had probably been using illegal silencers in its recent reserve culls, most of which take place within a kilometre of residences and all within three kilometres of residences (said to be a proper yardstick of a shooting 'danger/safety' zone).[8]

"A cull is brutal to kangaroos who are herd creatures," said Stevens. "Many neighbours suffer every night of a cull at the thought of the trauma inflicted on these endearing creatures. They have interacted with them over a long time.

"The distress to sympathetic residents is not short-lived. It is protracted over two-and-a-half months. No one is directly informed and we do not know if the cull is executed over a matter of days by way of coordinated effort. Or whether it is like duck season and shooters can enter and cull any time over the two-and-a-half months. Nor do we know if the count includes joeys in the pouch [who are bashed to death]."

Stevens was aware of the yearly press releases and fact sheets, released by Parks Director Daniel Iglesias and posted on the government's website, that claimed killing kangaroos protects threatened species and ecosystems. But events at Isaacs Ridge in the months leading up to the cull convinced her and others that the cull has little to do with saving endangered species. Development and getting kangaroos out of the way appeared the driving force here, as it has been at other sites around the capital.

The ridge has been a popular recreational place for neighbouring residents and visitors who came to experience native plants, the wildlife, and the views. But it is also home to a large pine plantation, is infested with weeds, suffered a major fire in 2003 and back burning since, and finally became the site for Canberra's latest and extensive mountain bike competition course – none of which indicated that the ACT government thinks this is a site of sensitive flora and fauna in need of saving.

Stevens concluded there was no evidence of any habitat or species requiring protection on Isaacs Ridge. Otherwise, the commercial pine plantation, orienteering events, and the trail and outdoor adventure park would never have been established there. Instead, she and her neighbours came to believe the kangaroo killing was related to a high-handed intrusion on their neighbourhood: the Isaacs Ridge Trail Plan includes a mountain bike racing course, and expanded routes for cross country cyclists, equestrians, and walkers. (Can't have a racing cyclist colliding with a kangaroo.) Residents were not consulted or informed in advance of this plan.

Nor was there consultation about the dangers of high-powered ammunition use close to houses. Those were only flagged when residents found signs warning of stiff penalties (prosecution and fines up to $7,500) if they 'trespassed' on the closed walking paths across the ridge during the slaughter. That meant residents who used the area for exercise or walking dogs before and after work and after dark might be in danger of either being shot or getting a massive fine.

Remembering her family's 30 years of observing a stable kangaroo population on the ridge, Stevens is one of the many who understand that kangaroo lives and breeding are adapted to seasonal conditions.

"They have evolved though multiple-thousands of years in Australia, needing to preserve their grassland." Canberrans, she advised, need only open their eyes. "An observer will notice a vast difference in the grasslands of Isaacs Ridge and those of the horse agistment properties abutting the northern end of the ridge. The lands agisting horses can be quite denuded compared to the grasslands which are grazed by kangaroos only."

Stevens was unusual in speaking out. But in 2018 the cull appeared to have finally woken up some of the national capital's becalmed population, with a spate of letters to the city's daily paper lambasting the government for the cull and for ignoring much more positive opportunities, like wildlife tourism. But the authorities were not listening.

In 2019, as the ACT park bureaucrats announced an improbable, all-time-high cull of 4,000 animals on nature reserves (always well-timed to coincide with Mother's Day), a Canberra resident posted on the local public broadcaster's Facebook page. It was in response to a little poll questioning whether people support this cull. (The comment section was packed with people saying 'no'.) She wrote:

> "We've had a little mob of roos living on a vacant block in North Watson for the 22 years. I've enjoyed their company. Although the numbers have changed throughout the seasons, with the instinctive urge for males to leave, and in response to previously vacant land being developed, the fluctuations disappear over time leaving a mob of just a dozen or so there permanently.
>
> "This mob are a family, with 3 babies this year, and yesterday they were forcefully removed to Mt Majura to be culled. Just breaks my heart and the thought of unborn joeys being so inhumanely destroyed brings me to tears. They've been left alone for 22 years and managed to stay their population growth to a size the block can support without needing culling."

CRUELTY, AND A CODE FOR KILLING MOTHERS WITH BIODIVERSITY THREAT NARRATIVE

As I write these words, a newly-emerged kangaroo joey hopping after mum appears on the lawn outside my window. My desk chair scraping leads to a quick dive back into the pouch, now dragging near the ground with its toddler weight. Mother looks around, then bends to graze. An older sibling is not far away, the so-called 'at foot'. Daughters can stay with mum for years. Kangaroos seem emblematic of protective motherhood.

The cruelty of the cull has been an enduring theme for the handful of wildlife defenders who have borne witness, night after night for two cold months, when the Canberra slaughter starts. Environmental scientist and long-time animal defender Frankie Seymour told me: "Every year we see hundreds of orphaned at-foot joeys lining the roadsides where their mothers were shot. Every year we hear the popping of the 'euthanasia' shots hours after the last of the killing shot has been heard." A partially-weaned joey's future is very uncertain, facing stress, hunger, car strike, and canine predators.

The fact that kangaroo mothers, with joey on board, likely accompanied by a young at-foot joey, are indiscriminately shot, has been made possible by a manipulation of the already minimal national animal welfare code of conduct governing the shooting exercise. When 'management' and ecological safeguards are cited as the reason for culling, the code drops to an even lower bar, allowing shooting of mothering females, that is otherwise discouraged.

This may provide a vital clue to why the ACT found convenient – or encouraged – the 'kangaroo threat to biodiversity' theory and narrative. Seymour spent years on the Territory's Animal Welfare Advisory Committee. She witnessed the trajectory to wholesale slaughter with the help of a welfare code that was adopted by the ACT against the committee's recommendation.

The adopted code of practice now permits killing of females with young in pouch or at-foot, if environmental conservation (say involving endangered species) is cited. Its wording is vague, and difficult to enforce. Seymour says it has all the hallmarks of a code whose main function is to legally shield those engaged in the killing from prosecution for animal cruelty.

KANGAROOS PART OF BIODIVERSITY?
NEXT DOOR THINKS SO

The 'kangaroos are a threat to biodiversity' narrative was becoming more embedded by the 2017 cull. The ACT Parks statements assured the public it is all about "ensuring these sites are not overgrazed [while protecting] threatened species and ecosystems, habitat for creatures such as lizards and ground-feeding birds and preventing excessive soil loss and still maintaining sustainable numbers of kangaroo."[9]

To look more widely at the local ecosystems, I had been taken on a tour of Queanbeyan grasslands next door in NSW. I was told that some of the endangered species cited by ACT Parks, the Earless Dragon and the Golden Sun moth, were recovering very well after a 10-year drought despite free-living kangaroos being present. NSW researchers found higher Earless Dragon counts than in the ACT. They said the varied plant heights that accompany kangaroo grazing are natural and good for these ecosystems.[10]

COST TO THE TAXPAYER TO KILL KANGAROOS

There appears no end in sight to what started in 2008–09 as a "pilot" culling program. Early in 2020, the ACT government reportedly signed a five-year contract with a private firm which describes itself as dedicated to invasive wildlife removal from public lands, heavy on ex-military personnel and hunting prowess. They might do a cleaner job than the part-time shooter with a spotlight, or his successor.[11]

Conservation in the national capital marked itself further as a war zone against the government's enemy. Militarised hardware has become routine with night-vision headgear, silencers and high-powered ammunition for the hunt in the suburbs. The enemy: Australian kangaroo families on Canberra's nature reserves.

The government's 2017 revised kangaroo management plan made shooting the enemy even easier. Remaining legal protections were dropped along with the idea that kangaroos were protected native species. Further appeals to the administrative appeals tribunal were blocked. A four to one community dissent to this direction (as indicated by submission numbers) was brushed aside.

Whether the cost of the new shooting contract will extend further the taxpayer-funded annual kangaroo "management" budget was unclear. That budget already nudged a million dollars a year since 2015, according to FOI documents I requested. Estimates from 2014 translated to about $400 per animal killed or targeted in the quota. The costs are not going down.[12]

Shooting and managing kangaroos, now including immunocontraception research, has proven a nice jobs and budget cushion for the parks and applied ecology sections of the city government.

Program life revolves around a straightforward blame and desktop numbers game, much easier than dealing with the weeds that infest the grasslands, or with historic stock damage, or the damage inflicted by stock the parks authorities recently put on reserve grasslands after killing the natives – for fire control. The public message is that authorities are caring for the reserves, getting kangaroo hazards off the roads, and clearing away kangaroos from development sites.

A drive past the Belconnen Naval Station, site of the first Canberra kangaroo massacre in 2008, recently revealed a few sheep grazing amidst knee-high grass, with a new subdivision on the drawing board.

In the previous chapter I looked at the academic discipline of applied ecology as it developed in Australia as handmaiden to landscape conversion and agricultural development. The ACT case, and its demands for conformity of thinking that crashed down on Robin Tennant-Wood, shows how this idea-set is spreading to public lands – taken up by politicians, bureaucracy, and research cohort, all in lockstep.

HOW VALUES AND ASSUMPTIONS DOMINATE A CITY'S WILDLIFE MANAGEMENT

From the ACT case I learned how values become embedded in an academic discipline.

The revised 2017 management plan for kangaroos revealed language, traditions and assumptions familiar since colonial days. It starts by reminding today's citizens of historical and oral

accounts that kangaroos on ACT lands were "in plague proportions" in the latter 1800s "when kangaroo and wallaby drives were
carried out and states introduced bounties". Another way to read
this is that the early colonists found kangaroos were widespread
and plentiful.[13]

The plan says that natural densities could not be determined a
hundred years later because the kangaroo was widely shot by landholders "to reduce perceived competition with sheep, provide food
for dog packs, to reduce damage to fences and for recreation" and
therefore kangaroos were considered "relatively uncommon".[14]

By the mid-1990s, regional surveys (including in a number of
large national parks) indicated numbers averaged around two-to-
three animals per hectare. In reality, numbers would have fluctuated
with weather conditions and human development activity.[15]

The first ACT Kangaroo Management Plan, in 2010, compared
this regional average kangaroo population unfavourably with
the goal of one or half a kangaroo per hectare typical of culled
(shot) rural grazing properties. The point? To 'save grass' – a cry
heard since the 1800s. Around that time citizens started being fed
the narrative that the ACT was suffering uniquely high levels of
kangaroo numbers and something had to be done.[16]

If you consider that a hectare is about the size of an international
rugby football field, and mentally place a kangaroo or three on
that field, keeping in mind that these social animals like to mob
up from time to time just like humans watching a rugby match,
you start to see what the contemporary 'plague proportions' and
'overabundance' actually mean on the ground. The 2010 kangaroo
management plan did admit that 'overabundance' is a social and
political value judgement, and not a scientific concept.[17]

The ACT parks bureaucrats and their consultant researchers
were warned in 1997 by a senior CSIRO wildlife ecologist that it
was an error to treat wildlife populations like domestic stock in

determining fixed optimal numbers, since numbers invariably fluctuate with environmental conditions – to no avail.[18]

A favoured narrative for lessening kangaroo numbers oft-repeated by officials and members of the public, not only in the ACT, is the argument that killing kangaroos saves them from starvation. In nature, most adult kangaroos might eventually starve in old age because they run out of teeth. Less often acknowledged is that starvation is also the likely fate of unweaned juveniles whose mothers are shot or run over. Or that starvation of this nature is the long-term fate of all grass-dependent animals, including the domestic ones if they live long enough.

This argument is often coupled with one that says there are now less Indigenous human hunters and dingos (which the ACT has poisoned using kangaroo carcasses and 1080).

'TRUST US WE'RE SCIENTISTS' MUZZLES PUBLIC

With one argument or another, 'Trust us, it's based on our science,' has been the core of the message to the public, amplified by the mainstream media. Yet by 2017, eight years (or longer going back to the first 2004 cull at Googong) had passed without any actual evidence of benefits or impacts of the million-dollar kangaroo killing program. Under pressure from critics, and the occasional question from a politician, the ACT Department of Territory and Municipal Services belatedly posted eight academic papers, calling them the scientific backbone of their management of kangaroos. One merit of this approach was that most media reporting to the public might not have time to read or judge them individually, nor would the public itself, nor would politicians. [19]

David Brooks, emeritus Sydney University English professor and an author who has written on ethical relationships with animals, did take a good look in 2016 for accepted norms of academic papers and how they are presented to the public. He confirmed what a lay person could see: that these papers did not validate culling kangaroos. He concluded (without criticising the intent or work of the researchers involved), that the way the ACT government used these eight papers was an intellectual insult to the people of Canberra.

One paper is a widely-shared study that has been used to claim the macropods are eating reptiles out of house and home (discussed in the previous chapter). Two of the papers were co-authored by the government Senior Ecologist, closely associated with the ACT killing program's assumptions and design. The papers treat the government's 2010 kangaroo management plan as a scientific authority.

Brooks noted all eight papers were co-authored by a small cohort of ACT-based researchers, locating at the CSIRO, the University of Canberra's Institute of Applied Ecology, and the ANU's Fenner School of Environment and Society. All the institutions are partly funded in some manner (scholarships, research partnerships, etc.) by the ACT government, he noted. Some of the same names advised the ACT government from the start and some were consulted to voice outrage at Robin Tennant-Wood's Environment Centre report.

I asked Steve Garlick – who frequently published academic papers in his time as an economics professor and more recently papers on wildlife behaviour research – to apply his critical lens to the ACT's declared evidence that kangaroos do damage. In his reading, "if you analyse the research papers backing the cull you find that they range from the irrelevant to the unproven to the speculative in terms of the role of kangaroos. The research papers show the ACT is sponsoring research which either assumes kangaroos do damage to other creatures just by measuring grass height or they use the lives of kangaroos as experimental units: If we kill this many kangaroos, can we count more beetles or skinks or legless lizards?"

In fact, looking at the eight papers as a lay reader, it was not hard to see some methods and conclusions appeared irrelevant to the issue of kangaroos in an environment, while others didn't support the government's claims about what they demonstrated.

There is another problem. Saving the temperate grasslands and ecosystems is the rationale for these eight papers. Brooks said aloud what many observe privately: "Nothing destroys an area of natural temperate grassland like a new suburb."

You have to enter beliefs, values, and assumptions into the mix to get what is claimed to link these bits of research to kangaroos.

That assumptions are deeply embedded became transparent when in 2017 I filed a freedom of information request with the ACT government, asking for evidence of outcomes and impacts of the kangaroo management program. I asked also for evidence of sustainable kangaroo populations and the basis for the one-kangaroo-per-hectare goal. Several ACT research documents were released that reveal measuring grass height and mass remains the basis for data collection. The documents failed to show any benefits of the program other than taller grass.

A common thread of this batch of documents is the guiding assumptions about negative impacts on ground cover, also demonstrated by the eight papers. The in-house research, released under FOI, is everywhere prefaced with code phrases that kangaroos need to be "actively managed" to prevent "overgrazing." Paraphrased, the assumption is: everyone knows kangaroos damage the grass environment and we have to cut the density.

CANBERRA NARRATIVE DISMANTLED BY REVIEW
The released documents included a 2014 independent CSIRO analysis of ACT research data and sites. That document dismantled the government's position and assumptions. Unlike the government claims, the reviewers could not find any negative

impacts on reserve vegetation where kangaroos graze at (the natural) two-to-three kangaroos per hectare.

Nor could they identify an optimal density beyond which "vegetation richness, diversity and overall condition declines". In other words, they found no evidence to back the goal of one kangaroo or less per hectare to save the ground cover habitat for this or that species dependent on the existing ecosystem.[20,21]

Refreshingly, the CSIRO authors Robert Godfree and Lyndsey Vivian are experts in the fields they are commenting on: one a botanist and ecologist, the other a specialist in native vegetation ecosystems. Their brief was to review the government's data collection from 2009, 2012, and 2013.

They started by asking an assumption-free scientific question: whether relationships exist between kangaroo density and vegetation condition in the Canberra grasslands and grassy woodlands. The authors checked ACT-studied sites with densities up to three kangaroos per hectare, and could not say that vegetation indicators had declined on any front up to that number of animals.

They noted that the ACT's claims that endangered species welfare is negatively affected by unmanaged kangaroo numbers of two-to-three per hectare was not based on evidence from the official data – it was merely referred to as being monitored.

This review supported previous criticisms about the lack of variables studied by the ACT in-house ecology team, particularly the weather: "At the site level, changes in vegetation structure and composition varied more between years, which may be associated more with different prevailing climatic conditions, than with kangaroo densities." Other variables can also affect a site's vegetation structure. That includes grazing history, previous fire and drought, soil conditions, and nutrients. Godfree and Vivian stated all of this had more effect on site condition than did kangaroo density.

The sobering CSIRO review provides a rare counterweight to the narrative about kangaroos damaging biodiversity or the ecosystem that also justifies the killing of mothers and joeys, a narrative spreading out from the ACT.

Apparently disregarding this fact-checking review, in 2018 ACT government ecologists released another science-cloaked report doubling down on their goal of somehow achieving a uniform number of one kangaroo per hectare on their reserves.

That report admitted the program was aligned with land management goals for production properties on surrounding leased government land, some of which was being converted to new subdivisions. The 2018 document's language – including talking about a "rural cull calculator" – did nothing to dispel the impression that this is a desktop exercise – viewing the animals as units to be killed across the board for a predetermined outcome.[22]

The 2019 kill target of 4,000 Eastern Grey kangaroos was the largest ever since this program began. I wondered whether there were 400 kangaroos left on Canberra reserves, let alone 4,000. Soon there would be the announcement of locking in contract killers for another five years.

Again, the question: why have the ACT ecologists and rangers worked so hard to make kangaroo slaughter a normal feature of life in the national capital? I found no other reasons than that it a well-resourced program for the parks' and ecologists' budgets. Weed invasions or concrete may be the biggest threats to native grassland biodiversity, but killing kangaroos is a visible sign of doing something if you can overlook the bloodshed. Additionally, the public may also be witnessing a multi-year lethal experiment bound for a few journal articles and thesis opportunities in applied ecology and conservation biology.

All three political parties in ACT government – Liberal, Labor, and the ACT Greens – have defended the kangaroo slaughter for more than a decade. Labor, with Greens support, has presided over most of it.

The payoff for the politicians is not hidden: expansive new subdivisions, or intensive bike trails such as on Isaacs Ridge, will suffer no wildlife collisions; no need to bother with planning wildlife corridors or translocation; and motorists stop writing irate letters about car insurance claims. Sanitised narratives about "humane" killing, amplified by media, stymie debate – or at least create immobilising uncertainty.

With no end in sight, cloaked with science but dog-whistling 'pest', the Bush Capital politicians, parks bureaucrats and allied scientists, have destroyed the structure of local kangaroo mobs. They've hired gunmen who are obliged to shoot adults and decapitate or bash small joeys, and bury them all in pits while leaving at-foot siblings to starve or jump in front of cars. They have traumatised residents and gone to great lengths to silence some of those with a more sympathetic and informed view of the kangaroo's place in the environment.

In just a decade, the national emblem in the national capital has been ever more bloodstained and diminished, rather than being celebrated as a vital player in biodiversity and as the international icon of Australia that kangaroos are.

POSTSCRIPT

The shooting continues around Canberra suburbs, even when the official 'cull' has been closed. Leaseholders on surrounding pasture land get generous tag quotas to kill the wildlife, as the statistics make clear. The graziers and shooters can apply for silencer permits so few know how close the shots are coming to suburban houses.

On 6 July 2018, a woman from the Canberra suburb of Spence wrote this public Facebook post: "Shooting still tonight in Spence … another sleepless night listening to death. Mongrel bastards. It's not a nature reserve across the road from my house. I think it might be the CSIRO."

A night earlier she had written: "Shooting again tonight so close to my house I was able to film them. Environmental Protection Agency told me to call the police … police told me to get stuffed basically."

Photo: Maria Taylor

COUNTING VIRTUAL KANGAROOS

"You do realise there are 500,000,000 kangaroos in places in Australia that are not in cities? 3 times the number of cattle and sheep, so why not utilise the resource."

— ANONYMOUS FACEBOOK COMMENT ON A STORY ABOUT WELFARE
ORGANISATIONS SAYING 'STOP THE SLAUGHTER OF KANGAROOS'

"This could be the greatest wildlife swindle in scientific history ... In 2011, I reviewed government data finding that kangaroos are in serious long-term decline in New South Wales. I submitted exhaustive scientific evidence detailing critical errors in government population surveys, flaws in the harvest model, systematic inflation of kangaroo numbers and over-allocation of quotas. Government population estimates since then show increases that are biologically impossible, ensuring that millions of kangaroos continue to be shot annually from ever-shrinking populations. It's an industrial-scale slaughter of an international icon."

— RAY MJADWESCH, WRITING IN *THE SACRAMENTO BEE* NEWSPAPER AT
THE TIME THE AUSTRALIAN GOVERNMENT WAS TRYING TO CONVINCE
CALIFORNIA TO RESUME KANGAROO MEAT AND SKIN IMPORTS

HOW THEY GET THE NUMBERS AS NEW FRONT OPENS ON WILDLIFE WAR

It may be hard for Californians or Londoners to believe, but a casual comment like the one above about 500 million kangaroos is not beyond coming from an Australian. While researching this book, and daring to bring up an invariably fraught subject for many people, I heard 50 million (give or take a few million) figures repeated reassuringly by various acquaintances – and by media.

Australia has internalised a widely-repeated belief about kangaroos and their extravagant overabundance as they eternally bound through the Aussie landscape: in advertisements, on airplane tails, and on government publications. Many people trust almost any fantastic number without much looking around the wildlife-free landscape. The government statistics allow people to be relaxed and comfortable about whatever is meted out to kangaroos.

In policy terms, the treatment of 'common' species like kangaroos, wallabies, wombats, emus, cockatoos, or bats is always framed as one of abundance, as distinct from risk of endangered status – the message is simply not to worry. Environmental laws and government policies and budgets for funding research underpin this thinking. There is lots of money for endangered species research and conservation, but little to none for research on the rest of Australian native animals.

Conservation is defined narrowly as 'avoiding imminent endangerment and extinction.' The fate of common species (along with a poor understanding of their interplay with natural ecosystems) has been largely left to the intentions of private property owners or state reserve managers, as we've seen. And if possible, the situation by 2018 had gone backwards in the eastern states, with politicians eager to relieve rural landholders of any government regulation on their self-assessed activities.

For kangaroos, the most hunted and homeless, the so-called

national conservation status is simply counting numbers as the basis for harvesting and pest management policies. Since the question was first raised in the 1980s by overseas governments, there still is no conservation plan per se. The official stance is to confidently proclaim that kangaroos are plentiful and not endangered – just as governments did with now critically-endangered koalas in the 1920s.*

MEDIA AND POLITICIANS: DON'T ASK QUESTIONS, JUST REPEAT ABUNDANCE NARRATIVE

Ramping up a new assault on kangaroos in response to drought, in June 2018 in the NSW Parliament the state government's National Party Minister for Primary Industries, Regional Water, Trade and Industry Niall Blair gave a classic response, filled with the assumptions and prejudices that characterise official discussion of the national emblem on the ground, laying bare the link to farmers and always with the overabundance narrative in the background:

> "The Government and our agencies have a whole-of-government response for the management of kangaroos on behalf of our farmers," he said genially. "When all agencies work together and the Government has made the decision to adjust the way we administer kangaroo numbers, this is good government.
>
> "Anyone who has recently ventured outside the city limits and into regional New South Wales will tell us that there is an ·

---

* One research project looked at the whole framing of 'abundance' in regard to kangaroos and concluded: "If abundance is not only a taxonomic description of fecundity, but a normative adjective hiding the practices of a complex network, it is also a license to kill with wide public support. For this reason, consideration must be given to the spatial imaginary of abundance as it works in the popular imagination with respect to kangaroos." Lorraine Thorne, 1998 *Kangaroos the non-issue.* Society and Animals, Vol 6/2 pp 167 – 182. Whitehorse Press, Cambridge. Thorne led the Greenpeace kangaroo campaign in the late 1980s.

abundance of kangaroos," he asserted. "These kangaroos have a huge impact not just on pastures and native grasses but also on our roads. The number of collisions with kangaroos has increased hugely, and those conditions are not just with motor vehicles but also with cyclists. As we go into the colder months and this drought continues, unfortunately large numbers of kangaroos will probably starve to death. The answer to the member's question is that we have a whole-of-government response to the current plight of regional New South Wales."[1]

The whole of government response soon became transparent in August 2018 when the NSW government decreed what was essentially open killing season on kangaroos in NSW, dropping already minimal justification, supervision or detailed application requirements. The state environment department's National Parks and Wildlife Service, the legal guardians of a so-called protected native species, were put in charge of implementing the killing on the ground.

Was this Minister Blair's gift to the rural community in the run up to a tight state election? It seemed so. Putting National Parks on the front line gave arms-length deniability for any possible mishaps: accidental shootings of humans or other animals with high-powered bullets that can travel three kilometres or more; cruelty against the victims; ignoring quotas; or shooting any other 'protected native species'. Here was an unsupervised program set in motion without any wider community consultation but with media fanfare that it was benefitting farmers.

The new open-season approach flew in the fact of NSW's official stance since the early 2000s that damage mitigation should not be used as a reason for kangaroo killing. Damage could not be audited, according to a 2006 national review. "Indeed," wrote the authors, "there is little convincing evidence of substantial damage by kangaroos to crops, pastoral production or rangelands, except in a few localized areas."[2]

George Orwell's famous book *1984*, about government propaganda using 'doublespeak' – giving government offices a benign and meaningless name with the opposite intent – may have inspired the NSW government when it labelled the National Parks section tasked with administering the kangaroo killing program as the "Biodiversity Reform" team.

In October 2018 I learned more about what the Biodiversity Reform team was doing or not able to do under their instructions to implement a "non-commercial cull" in what the government decided would be a uniform fashion across the state.

That meant the NSW National Parks and Wildlife Service had been relieved of most discretion to say no to *any* landholder who asked for "consent to harm" this protected native species. In the cause of "uniformity," high-powered bullets could now fly across small blocks that might be at a village or town perimeter.

The spokesperson for the team told a Landcare workshop in my region that in little over a month after the government announced the relaxed rules, the number of "consents to harm" had doubled. Between June 2018 and 8 September, permission to kill had gone up 100 percent to 1,115,422 kangaroos – between both commercial and non-commercial permits. In the South East kangaroo harvest zone where I live, landholders had more than quadrupled their requests, and by September had been granted permission to kill 108,567 kangaroos.

The Landcare audience was told that unfortunately the government had no resources for monitoring any of this. Instead, National Parks, the nominal stewards of flora and fauna in the state, were responding to calls from landholder groups and the NSW Farmers Association.

WHO TALKS TO THE POLITICIANS?

NSW Farmers topped the list of lobbyists granted NSW ministerial meetings from 2014–18, with almost 100 meeting days counted. Environmentalists and animal welfare groups did not appear in a list of top 20 lobbyists, dominated by agriculture, mining, local governments, and development bodies.[3]

I also saw that the farmers' lobby had handed Primary Industries Minister Niall Blair a 'to do list' early in his tenure. The Biodiversity Reform team was eager to make harming kangaroos as painless as possible for the landholder to "get the grass back." Cutting red tape for the farming community was the team's mission. Wildlife protection had become 'red tape.'

Ironically, the renewed direction of mass culling to ease complaints of property damage was pitching the graziers' activities into competition with the commercial kangaroo industry, as was evident when I visited central Queensland, a visit I will come to later. In both states, as drought bit, the farmer mood had become more genocidal than commercial in regard to Australia's national emblem.

At the Landcare workshop, a spokesperson for the government department administering the commercial hunt (different office to the non-commercial culling) reported that drought had already dropped national kangaroo numbers by 10 million. This happens in every recurrent drought, soon be followed in 2019 by massive flooding in north-central Queensland that killed most of the wildlife. And then finally the apocalyptic wildfires at the end of that year. The disconnect with the favoured "plague-proportion" narrative was mounting.

At the time it was only a matter of drought casualties, the super-abundance narrative hanging off government counts stayed firm. The NSW National Parks biodiversity reform team said the government's "sustainable" limit for killing kangaroos is 15.8 percent of their assessed state population. According to their accounting, the 1.15 million permissions to harm granted by October 2018 was merely 7.4 percent of the assessed state population – so room for more killings to come.

How state governments count kangaroo populations – really for the commercial hunt – is what I wanted to examine more closely. But first, a look at how mainstream media played this story in 2018: the amplification of government and farmer claims that aids the destruction of the kangaroo.

MEDIA IGNORANCE COMPOUNDS FANTASTIC CLAIMS

As the NSW government followed Queensland by announcing 'blame the kangaroo and shoot it' as drought relief, the NSW Primary Industries Minister was quoted as saying that commercial quotas were just not cutting those kangaroo plagues.[4]

How the national broadcaster, the ABC, framed that drought relief beggared belief. But, in fact, it was typical of uncritical repetition of politician and farmer claims in Australian media, without balancing points of view.

"As a result of the drought," stated an article, "kangaroo numbers have soared, creating more problems for farmers." The reporter then cut to the National Party Deputy Premier of NSW, John Barilaro. He announced that the government was dealing with "the explosion in kangaroo numbers" by extending more culling privileges to farmers and extending the commercial harvest zones. These zones already cover most of the state, barring a few pockets in the south east, which happened to be in the Deputy Premier's electorate.[5]

The National Party is faithfully accepted by media as representing the thinking of country people, even though it has been polling less than 7 percent of the electorate in federal elections and less than 10 percent in NSW elections. The party wields power from rural electorates that enjoy a traditional high number of parliamentary seats compared to voter numbers. (In perspective, in state and federal elections the National Party poll numbers fall in the same arena as the Greens, but the Nationals will get 10 seats and the Greens one). Worse, the Nationals are given control of the natural resource portfolios, covering land, water, forest, and soil, when allied with the Liberal party in state and federal governing coalitions.

Reading newspaper quotes about kangaroo numbers soaring as a *result of* the drought, I had to ask: what kind of thinking inhabits a reporter and editor who, without further query, tell readers that a native grazing animal reliant on rain-fed ground cover, subject to widespread hunting and harassment, not only prospers in a drought, but "soars" and "explodes" its population numbers under such circumstances?

A month later, the rural press and the ABC were continuing with tales of desperate graziers dealing with the fifth or sixth or seventh year of drought in south-western Queensland and in northern NSW. Nobody was quoted about the possible influence of man-made climate change in worsening the drought phases. Nor was there discussion about the economic viability of some marginal grazing lands or the impacts of overstocking for the conditions. But, standing around now bare paddocks, there was talk about blaming the wildlife, kangaroos specifically, to the point of absurdity.

Reporters scribed grazier assertions that kangaroo plagues "caused" the drought, backed by eye-popping government population figures. Perhaps crafted at a desk in Sydney or Melbourne, the articles missed balancing issues: that kangaroos die in large numbers in droughts, or that wildlife might also be entitled to feed and water – and where should they go in a sea of private property?

A property owner north-west of Broken Hill told a reporter for News Corps' *The Weekly Times* that kangaroos are "putting the area into a drought situation," and that it will last longer because of their presence. He said the extraordinary drought conditions had seen the surface water options disappear, and that emus and kangaroos were drinking day and night from a bore water trough raised for stock. This was not acceptable. In his view, the underground water belongs to the landholder and his stock, not to be shared with native animals.[6]

The Broken Hill article quoted record numbers of kangaroos said to be present in NSW in 2016: 17.4 million. (A year later in 2017 the count was three million less. Just seven years earlier the NSW population officially sat at seven million.)

In late 2018, newspaper articles were reporting similar stories from another state, South Australia – accusing the kangaroos of bringing on early supplement-feeding costs to farmers, and calling for damage culling. Always the economic argument is reported as the only one – except on social media where animal-friendly stories often garner massive interest.

Documentary filmmaker Kate Clere spent five years on and off travelling the country to gather material. She told me that whenever farmers spoke to them about plague-proportion kangaroos on the property, the filmmakers would ask to come and see them. Not a single visit was offered to verify those claims. Co-director Mick MacIntyre did many media interviews after the release of their film *Kangaroo: A Love-Hate Story* in 2018, and told an online discussion about the biased state of Australian reporting he encountered, particularly with the national broadcaster. He reported: "Most of our ABC interviews (including morning TV) were aggressive towards us. We did over 20 ABC radio interviews and some were pretty shabby – they were so biased against us."

In 2020, as they brought the documentary back to Australia after informing overseas audiences, I saw a *Sunrise* breakfast show interview with them. It was not friendly or open to new information. Host Samantha Armytage argued with 'facts' about kangaroo competition with stock – things that had been debunked in the 1960s.[7]

VICIOUS CYCLE AND A POSSIBLE SOLUTION

Apart from questioning the wisdom of farming semi-desert country, I can understand some points made by hard-pressed graziers from personal lessons about land management. Once land is degraded by overstocking hard-hooved animals, leading to soil and water erosion and native vegetation removal, it is difficult to restore and combat weed invasions. At that point native grazers pruning green shoots do not speed recovery. In my case it was overstock of horses on a native pasture paddock which has not recovered, although with rain, valiant efforts are underway. Is this the wildlife's fault or a matter of human land management?

In their national review of the existing research, Olsen and Low wrote: "The issue of land degradation will never be redressed by simple reduction in kangaroo numbers when there is no concomitant control of sheep and other introduced herbivore grazing impacts." They concluded that kangaroo management and commercial harvesting need to be integrated with whole of property grazing management to address land degradation.

They cited studies showing that closing watering points or removing the kangaroos did *not* result in a rapid return of previous vegetation. It might take years. Introduced weeds don't help either. Once the ground cover is destroyed, there is no quick fix.[8] Instead they pointed to on-ground experience that maintaining taller perennial grasses would discourage kangaroo presence.[9] The benefit of maintaining constant healthy ground cover, innovative stocking practices, and working with the natural flora and fauna is being demonstrated by regenerative farmers as I recount in the chapter 'Sharing'. The kangaroo 'problem' tends to disappear.

POPULATION NUMBERS: HOW THEY ARRIVE AT THEIR COUNTS

How do government authorities count the millions of kangaroos on the ground? It's a good question. How it's done appears rather like creative accounting, as I first learned from a field ecologist working in the pastoral lands of eastern NSW.

I first met Ray Mjadwesch in 2012 when he had finalised submissions to the NSW Scientific Committee, an advisory body to the state government. He warned that all was far from well with the counting methodology and interpretation of kangaroo populations, and also with the popular notion that kangaroo populations can explode to those well-worn 'plague-proportions'.[10]

The committee took its time, but ultimately refused to review Mjadwesch's evidence that kangaroos were threatened by current practices – stating that the government's kangaroo management and counting methods are rigorous and scientific. Puzzling too – given the consistent history of population plunges during drought, which was increasing at the time – that the committee cited kangaroo population increases to back its refusal to consider a threatened species nomination.

Based in Bathurst, Ray Mjadwesch started looking at the NSW picture after very publicly questioning the Bathurst city council about the shooting of the resident kangaroo population on Mount Panorama to facilitate a car race in 2009. "There were hardly any kangaroos left in the Bathurst basin," he says.

He spent the next two years delving into the statistics, population trends, and published science of kangaroos. His findings were sobering, and led him to file state and federal threatened species nominations for the four harvested macropod species in NSW – Red and Eastern Grey kangaroos, Wallaroos/Euros and Western Greys kangaroos – in a submission to the Scientific Committee.[11]

Mjadwesch hoped this might stem further decline and possible collapse of populations. Instead, he was essentially ignored. It had happened before in Australia, from koalas to fisheries, when commercial 'harvesting' is at stake.

His analysis of massive data sets from government agencies found declining population trend lines in every NSW kangaroo management zone. "It's a mess," he told me flatly. "Everyone has accepted the state department data as valid and has not really looked at it on a zone-by-zone basis." Nor had many questioned the counting methods and population explosion assumptions.

FROM SAMPLE TO ALGORITHM

Kangaroo numbers are sampled out of fixed-wing planes or helicopters. Observers fly in transects and count kangaroos within a fixed distance of their flight path (in cases where there are few kangaroos to be seen, that distance is sometimes extended – one type of correction factor). It has been noted that flyovers were developed for counting Red kangaroos on open country – but the Greys and Wallaroos/Euros are in cover much of the day. Such species that are seldom sighted have their numbers boosted by desktop correction.

When Mjadwesch was looking, the samples were thus multiplied by another correction factor: the vegetation type where animals could be spotted – a substitute for habitat. A desktop study then supplies kangaroo numbers based on theoretical densities, starting from these flight counts. Those were numbers multiplied across the whole potential habitat of the species throughout the commercial zones, which in turn cover the whole state.

"They often apply their density calculation to landscapes which are completely devoid of kangaroos," noted Mjadwesch. "Often kangaroos only persist in isolated pockets in farming or grazing landscapes, a tiny fraction of their potential range. For example, kangaroo counters allocated high densities to the Bathurst basin, an area of 450 square kilometres where there are nearly no kangaroos.

This has inflated figures in the Central Tablelands [a new harvest zone] by tens of thousands of animals."

National parks and reserves are excluded from sampling. But Mjadwesch's enquiries indicated the likelihood of some national park flyovers, inflating population figures from a different angle. Other states' counting policies have followed similar formats to NSW.

LANDSCAPE OF VIRTUAL KANGAROOS, ADD EVERY SQUARE KILOMETRE

Despite shifts in methodology since 2012, the basic desktop nature of the exercise has stayed intact and may be even more simplified. The counting methods continue to cover vast tracts with paper or virtual kangaroos.

In NSW by 2018, corrected sample densities, without talk of habitat, were simply multiplied by the total square kilometres of each management (or harvest) zone. That produced zone population totals. Then the 14 zones that cover more than 90 percent of the state are added up to yield the state total. It took me a while to accept it was this simplistic.

It appears the formula does not subtract most square kilometres of towns and villages outside the Sydney metropolitan area – nor intensive agricultural areas – that include cropping, horticulture, or forestry or other unsuitable habitat. The desktop conclusions also do not adjust for private grazing properties that conduct extensive pest management.[12]

In Queensland, with its three harvest zones, two of which are dedicated to cotton and other cropping or mining – areas that are not in any way kangaroo habitat anymore – the government is said to rely on densities gleaned by flyovers in the central pastoral zones (also the zone that has been most heavily pest-eradicated while struck by drought). The authorities then average the sampled densities across the three zones, and, as in NSW, apply that figure to almost every square kilometre of the state for their virtual kangaroo numbers.[13]

As well as seemingly inflated numbers, big fluctuations are par for the course with kangaroo counting. Mjadwesch's trend analyses for NSW leading up to 2012 showed counts fluctuated wildly from one year to the next, with 100 percent and even 300 percent increases suddenly popping up from year to year. Biologically that is impossible for a kangaroo population. Even pigs with litters of 10 piglets only attain an average population growth rate of 86 percent.

SINGLE BIRTHS, HIGH INFANT MORTALITY, LONG MOTHERING

As Mjadwesch and other zoologists and ecologists who studied the kangaroo in the 20th century have pointed out, and been ignored: annual net natural kangaroo population increases are no higher than 3–10 percent. That reflects births, natural deaths, and high juvenile mortality rates, before acts of God and man. With drought, adult mortality can rise to 25 percent a year and epidemic disease, as I learn, has not been factored in.

Unlike pigs, goats, and domestic pets, kangaroo females, like humans (most of the time), can give birth to just one joey in a year, and may also be raising an older dependent joey for a year or longer. Kangaroos have been observed to slow breeding in hard times.

Starting at three to four years of age, on average, a fertile female may birth about eight joeys in her lifetime. But infant mortality is considered high (this might include pouch death, as in the joey never emerges viable; juvenile disease; foxes; dogs; now cars). With Red kangaroos, CSIRO zoologist Harry Frith had noted juvenile mortality can be more than 80 percent in dry times and other research has supported such numbers.

Out of eight joeys that are born, two may survive to independence, and only one might be female. "Simply put," Mjadwesch tells me, "kangaroo populations cannot 'explode' or naturally increase to 'plague proportions' – this is a biological impossibility; however, they can crash, and that is what we are seeing now."[14]

PENDING REGIONAL EXTINCTION: REDS, WALLAROOS ALREADY FLAGGED IN 2008

A 2008 report to the federal government by Nikki Sutterby of the Australian Society for Kangaroos included some science understanding and government figures related to 'quasi extinction'. This is where natural population densities drop below a threshold considered an extinction warning sign – in this case five kangaroos per square kilometre (or 100 hectares). At two per square kilometre they are called quasi extinct, according to government assessments.[15]

On this basis, in 2008 in Queensland Red kangaroos would have been flagged as in danger of quasi extinction, with fewer than five per square kilometre counted across 70 percent of the state, and were at densities of less than 1.6 per square kilometre across 40 percent of the state. Wallaroos/Euros were quasi extinct in 86 percent of the state. Sutterby obtained her population density figures from the Macropod Management Unit at the Queensland Environment Protection Agency.

Based on these same criteria, in 2008 South Australian populations of Red and Western Grey kangaroos, and Wallaroos/Euros, were equally or more extremely absent from the landscape.

Similarly, in NSW, where commercial kangaroo zones cover 93 percent of the state, as in Queensland and South Australia, Red kangaroo populations were down by 75 percent from earlier years in some areas and as much as 90 percent in other areas – across 70 percent of the state. Sutterby calculated that, as a result, in 2008 Red kangaroos were 'quasi extinct' at less than 3.3 per square kilometre across 68 percent of the state. Grey kangaroos were quasi extinct across 36 percent of the state according to these measures, and Wallaroos/Euros across the whole state. The NSW figures were taken from the *NSW Kangaroo Management Program – Quota Report for 2008*, compiled by the NSW Department of Environment and Conservation. The same department, with a different name, remains the harvest or cull licensing authority through its National Parks division.

Regardless of such troubling data, political leaders in Queensland and NSW responded to drought and complaints from the rural sector after 2013 by maintaining historically high commercial killing quotas, based on those questionable counting methods plus also opening the non-commercial unrestricted shooting programs because there were "too many kangaroos." To help out, between 2010 and 2016 official counts and quotas appearing in national figures showed improbably high kangaroo numbers, mainly Greys, notably in Queensland.[16]

Yet, by 2019 the Queensland government would quietly close the commercial season for Grey kangaroos and Wallaroos/Euros for the following year, citing extinction risk thresholds. What was going on?

Just two years earlier, in 2017, and despite drought, official national counts of the four hunted kangaroo species were hovering around 46 million – a count that had almost doubled in drought years since 2010, when it was 25 million. Along the way, totals hit a highpoint in 2013 of 53 million – more than doubling in just three years – and staying high through the succeeding drought years until 2018. Prior to 2010, there had been a steady count of around 25 million since 2004.

In NSW the official counts had the kangaroo population, similarly to Queensland, booming upward from seven million after 2009. Here were population increases of 100 percent and 150 percent in three to five years – begging big questions for an animal that biologically only increases its population by 3–10 percent annually.*[17]

STATES OFFER SIX MILLION PLUS KANGAROOS TO KILL AFTER 2013

For the commercial industry, whose shooting zones blanket whole states, high kangaroo counts are an advantage both for the abundance narrative and because the kill quota is set at a standard percentage – around 15–17 percent, regardless of environmental conditions.

Federal government records show six (or more often eight) million animals were made available to 'harvest' across all states annually between 2013 and 2018, compared with quotas of about three million on average for the decade previously, when weather conditions were more benign. These numbers do not include the non-commercial and illegal numbers killed in the recent upsurge of grazier-initiated destruction.[18]

REALITY BITES KILL QUOTAS: DIFFERENT STORY ON THE GROUND

Animals actually taken on the ground tell another story, more in keeping with the quasi-extinction figures. Consistently low harvest figures (they have to find the animals before they can kill them) are seconded by the testimony of shooters that the kangaroos are not there as they were 20–30 years ago, regardless of record counts and quotas. Industry diligence in killing kangaroos may also have been affected by the success of welfare groups' campaigns to curb overseas demand.

---

* Comparative statistics: a 2017 comparison of sheep, cattle, and kangaroo numbers arrived at almost 73 million sheep, almost 27 million cattle, five-and-a-half million feral goats, and half-a-million wild horses and donkeys. (Source: www.kangaroosatrisk.net)

For example, based on 2015 statistics, with a national count of almost 50 million kangaroos, the state governments between them offered a kill quota of seven-and-a-half million kangaroos. But the actual take was six million shy of that: 1,632,095, or 21.6 percent of the quota. About one million of that killing activity took place in Queensland after the first years of drought.

NSW's statistics too had a red flag suggesting inflated numbers. From the 2017 NSW government quota report I learned that low harvest rates of all species in all zones in 2015 were equivalent to less than 2.1 percent of the quota the government had offered based on their population claims.[19]

The following year, 2016, Queensland, like NSW, was again claiming record numbers – 22.5 million kangaroos for the northern state. That led to another historically high quota of 3,285,600 animals for the three commercially harvested species, Red, Grey and Wallaroo/Euro, in Queensland alone. Again, the actual commercial kill was just 3.8 percent of that quota.[20]

Despite the reality of what was to be found or taken on the ground, despite biology and drought and the quasi-extinction calculations, despite the government's own warnings about low Red and Grey kangaroo population numbers and closure of hunts in western NSW in 2019 (soon to be followed by Queensland), the official population totals for a decade encouraged the conclusion that the macropods were multiplying alarmingly. The story became that the commercial hunters were not making enough of a dent. In this way, the super-abundance narrative also enabled the no-holds-barred non-commercial killing program that then took hold, under the banner of property damage.

Another incentive to keep quotas high is the paying of public servants. The government's commercial license-to-kill operation – in NSW the Kangaroo Management Team of the Parks and Wildlife Service – supports itself by selling harvest licenses and tags. A user-pays cost recovery model recently supported about four employees and a handful of contractors. NSW in 2018 had 413 licensed shooters, down from 900 before 2012. A similar cost-recovery model applies in Queensland.[21]

The smoke and mirrors surrounding kangaroo numbers still leave enough clear air to see that federal government statistics between 2010 and 2016 claimed the four hunted species of kangaroo doubled in population in five dry years. While populations may recover following a respite in shooting, mortalities because of drought, flood, and disease were also taking millions. Significant Red and Grey kangaroo mortality has occurred after floods in the past decades – a big medical mystery ignored by state officials that I get to shortly. Meanwhile, widespread non-commercial and illegal shooting added to the death toll.

Some arguments for official booms in population numbers may add to fluctuations, but would not overcome the statistical impossibilities. Periods of male bias shooting that destroy the normal mob hierarchy can increase compensatory birth rates. Migration from new NSW cropping areas may account for some greater numbers of Grey kangaroos counted in Queensland. Research has confirmed that Eastern Grey kangaroos have relatively recently moved into the hotter, dryer parts of the continent, west and north, and that Red kangaroos will travel long distances to follow rainfall events.

For both species, human changes to the environment – native vegetation clearing, sheep overgrazing, and perhaps changed rainfall patterns due to climate change – can push populations around, but the national total would not change therefore.

LOOK AROUND: WHERE ARE THEY?

Whether a field ecologist like Ray Mjadwesch, or a local driver, or a tourist, or a long-time kangaroo shooter – all have told me they hardly see a living kangaroo where private agricultural properties are dominant from coast to coast. Roadkill does not signal a bigger population somewhere else. Often roadsides are the only place that native grazers can find feed and are not shot. The lack of live animal sighting simply flies in the face of what the NSW Minister for Primary Industries liked to tell the city folk: Where are all the millions hiding?

In south-central and south-east Queensland, former shooter Lyn Gynther, who now cares for rescued joeys, makes it her business to know what is happening with her region's kangaroo populations. She can compare with how things were in earlier decades – she says that compared with the 1980s and 1990s, when shooters like herself were regularly bringing in 100 carcases, now on a good night a shooter may bring down nine kangaroos on a 40,000-acre block.

"If they bring in 60 or 70 the suspicion is that they have entered national parks," she says. "When you have long-haul truckers saying from their dash cam, 'We have found nothing [no wildlife] from Sydney to Brisbane to Mount Isa,' you know you've got big problems. Tourists say the same." Lyn told me she believes there are no wild kangaroos left in her region around Warwick, and that I and my neighbours are lucky to still have the wildlife around.

AS POPULATIONS DECLINE, KILL YOUNGER ANIMALS AND OPEN NEW ZONES

Veteran kangaroo shooter Michael Charman, from Barcaldine in central Queensland, who tried for years to alert authorities to the mystery post-flood die-off syndrome claiming millions of kangaroo lives, also warned about the prevalence of shooting the next generation of young animals before they reached sexual maturity – a trend that has been noted by observers like zoologist Jock Marshall since the 1960s. Charman said that starvation is not a problem for most kangaroos because they don't live long enough to age and thus starve due to tooth loss. He noted in correspondence to authorities in 1998 that most younger shooters would not know what a big kangaroo looks like. Instead, the overshooting of young wildlife to make equivalent skin or meat loads has escalated.

Once the kangaroos are no longer there to easily pick off for a commercial load, shooters work longer hours; they travel further. And in addition to condoning the shooting of younger animals, state governments open new harvest zones for the industry that create an impression of stable numbers. In NSW since 2004, the Northern Tablelands, Hunter, Central Tablelands, and South-East kangaroo harvest zones were brought online.

A renewed focus on the pet food market extends commercial opportunities without anyone worrying about animal size, age, or coat quality. Such was the successful drive in recent years to reopen the state of Victoria to commercial shooting for pet food while helping out graziers complaining of problem wildlife.

To do this, the Victorian government pushed aside a 2017 departmental evaluation of a five-year trial of the renewed slaughter. The evaluation made transparent the basic fallacies of a commercial kangaroo industry; it is unsustainable. Regardless of the high official counts and abundance narrative laid on for public and overseas markets, a commercial industry turning kangaroo mums and joeys into pet food needs a steady body count. And that is unlikely, given weather, disease, private property whims, and the overshooting due to dishonest claims and the dollar incentive, all noted by the department.

The Victorian report also identified that monitoring and compliance are hard to establish and enforce, and attempting to do so may cost the taxpayer more money than the industry makes – all issues experienced elsewhere and denied by authorities over the years.[22]

The commercial industry would have pushed hard to reopen Victoria and expand in South Australia because older NSW and

Queensland zones have in fact been commercially shot-out: the 2019 closure of western NSW zones Cobar and Tibooburra (north of Broken Hill) cited quasi extinction fears as did Queensland for Greys and Wallaroos/Euros.

"You can shoot a lot of kangaroos for a long time, but soon enough they are not there to shoot," Ray Mjadwesch told me seven years ago. "You move on to the next property, and maybe come back to mop up survivors next year, however this cycle eventually creates a landscape where kangaroos are few and far between." No authority has been connecting the dots focused as it is on the lobbying of graziers and the commercial industry.

ABUNDANCE AND EXTINCTION NARRATIVES

Localised perceptions of abundance drive what people believe to be true. It may be a small country town that experiences an influx of kangaroos at the caravan park or the sports oval as animals seek some green pick in a drought, or it is the grazier who reports a 'plague' on his block, or peri-urban people who see lots of kangaroos that have moved in from the farmland shooting gallery or from the new subdivision – what people see in urban or developed areas rarely reflect a regional population. Kangaroos will mob up on one rural property when they are "all getting blasted" nearby, as kangaroo industry veteran Tom King told me. Or if there is a rainstorm and green pick appears somewhere else, they hop over the fences. Following the rain is how they evolved.

Visions of endless abundance, supported by government numbers, is one side of a public narrative. Arguments about extinction are the other side. In the public square, the lethal management proponents are comfortable with the view that people only care about species that have been officially labelled endangered. Many discussions about the treatment of common species devolve to the argument: 'Well, they are not endangered so who cares?'

An article in *The Australian* newspaper when the film *Kangaroo* was released domestically, and it received a lot of angry public comments, showed how the numbers game is played to bat away evidence of injustice, persecution, or decline. The spokesperson for a national farmer's organisation voiced a common refrain: far from being on the verge of extinction (which was not the thesis of the film, which was about the culture of persecuting kangaroos), kangaroo numbers had grown to "crisis" proportions and needed sound, humane management. This argument often comes, as here, with a "humane" veneer: that if not shot in a "pain-free and instant" way, as this article noted, kangaroos will suffer a miserable demise some other way.[23]

With the article, the newspaper printed a graphic, credited to a federal government department, to hammer home just how un-endangered kangaroos are.

In the graphic, the two chosen comparison years of population figures for kangaroos (2002 and 2014) just happened to have about the same official count – about 44 million – supporting the notion of a static and stable population. Neither the reporter for *The Australian* nor the readers would know from this graphic the true picture of dramatic changes in counts from year to year, or any of the caveats about the count.

BIOLOGICAL COLLAPSE PREDICTED

Twenty years ago, in the 1999 edition of the AWPC book *The Kangaroo Betrayed*, animal genetics specialist and veterinarian Ian Gunn from Monash Medical Centre foreshadowed what was likely to happen. He wrote that continued culling and related practices on behalf of rural production did indeed have the potential to precipitate extinctions. He offered three good reasons.

Firstly, the practices of eliminating the largest, healthiest, kangaroos from the selected population, which also affects the populations immune response to disease. Secondly, the unreliable and largely estimated density figures presented to justify and secure culling permits. Thirdly (and this may reflect the sudden spikes in Queensland Grey kangaroo numbers that could not be biological) the transfer of species habitat. "Since 1940–50, competition for grazing, clearing and culling have significantly altered the species habitat range and the population densities ... In NSW there has been a continuing shift of the population concentration further and further west, into areas which are extremely sensitive to climatic variation and increasing grazing pressure."

"The evidence is indisputable," he wrote. "If left to continue [it] has potential to result in reduced genetic variability, lower reproductive efficiency and a radical reduction in population density below sustainable levels in certain regions of the country when associated with ... seasonal conditions such as drought."

Gunn wrote this sobering prediction with pessimism about what modern civilisation has achieved in maintaining natural systems. "Civilisation seems hell-bent on a course of self-destruction; destruction of our environment, resources, wildlife and humanity itself."[24]

MYSTERY DISEASE PANDEMIC: NO ANSWERS, LESS INTEREST

In March 2011, Lynda Staker wrote to Prime Minister Julia Gillard. Staker, from North Queensland, had a long history of citizen care and understanding for wild kangaroos, having set up a sanctuary and animal recovery centre. Later she began teaching about macropods and their care. In her possession was a trove of correspondence that long-time Queensland kangaroo shooter Michael Charman had sent to authorities. He detailed a history of epidemic and little-understood kangaroo die-offs known since the 1960s. That the epidemics followed flood was understood, but little else was.

The number of deaths were staggering, matched by the seeming disinterest from wildlife management decision-makers, environment departments, and politicians to whom Charman had written over the years. Charman and Staker were concerned that on top of relentless shooting, drought, flood, and habitat loss, kangaroo populations were under even greater pressure due to the epidemics, and no one was taking them into account. It was mentioned that the kangaroo meat industry might be passing on unidentified pathogen to humans or pets when kangaroos were shot during flood die-offs.

So, Staker told the whole story to the Prime Minister. Here is some of what she wrote.

There is a recent past history of a massive mortality rate of Eastern Greys, Western Greys, Wallaroos/Euros, and Red kangaroos throughout Queensland and New South Wales, and also Western Greys, Wallaroos/Euros and Reds in South Australia. This is well known as the 'post flood die-off'.

The cause of these deaths is unknown, but is thought to be due to an influx of post-flood insects, likely bringing a deadly virus.

Deaths occurred over a short period of time in localised areas. The syndrome is fatal to all macropods in affected areas. No sick animals survive longer than a few days. Red kangaroo and Wallaroo/Euro carcasses had been generally found in small groups of up to 17 individuals, under cover, and with no evidence of a death struggle. Paralysis appears to be associated with the disease. Most animals show significant bites received from sand flies. Assessed dead animals were regarded as in good body condition, and don't bloat up like road kills or normal death.

No signs of blindness or any abnormality of the eyes was observed, indicating that this disease was not Wallal virus (*Chorioretinitis*), of which there were massive outbreaks in kangaroos from 1964 to 1996.

The outbreaks occurred following substantial rainfall or floods throughout the affected areas.

There was a die-off in 1961 but it was not investigated. A 1990 outbreak did spark a detailed report, compiled by Professor Richard Speare, Graduate School of Tropical Veterinary Science at James Cook University, and two Queensland National Parks and Wildlife Service officers, Peter Johnson and Timothy Pulsford. The report, titled 'Epidemic Mortality in Large Macropods of Central Queensland During May 1990,' was inconclusive, but suggested that pathological changes indicated a virus as the most likely cause.

A request for further research funding was not forthcoming from the government.

Staker continued, quoting a Charman letter to National Party state environment minister Brian Littleproud in November 1997. Opinion from the kangaroo industry at the time was that the meat processors wouldn't want any negative results coming out of such research. It is on record, she wrote, that a departmental officer said at the time of the report that if the pathology report hit the media it would put the industry backwards for four or five years. A proper scientific evaluation in order to ensure the industry's safety would have been appropriate.

She reported that in May 1997, tens of thousands more Red kangaroos died of the mystery disease in northern Queensland in the Boulia/Dajarra/Cloncurry and Mount Isa areas, covering approximately 40,000 square kilometres. Most of the dead kangaroos were on the western side of gidgee trees, and died as if at rest. Station (property) owners commented on how quickly the animals died, without lingering or any sign of struggle. They also stated that nearly all – if not *all* – Red kangaroos had died on a number of other regional stations.

Staker told the Prime Minister that there was significant concern within the kangaroo industry at the time regarding possible implications for livestock and the potential impact on kangaroo meat for the human consumption market. A ranger from the NPWS in Broken Hill stopped the human consumption kill for two months. When the fuss died down, he opened the industry up again.

A year later there was another big Queensland post-flood die-off that covered a bigger area than ever before. In NSW in October 1998, a detailed report of post-flood die-off titled 'Investigations-Major Epidemic Mortality of Macropods in the Northern Part of Far Western NSW in October 1998', by Greg Curran from NSW Agriculture, Emilie Gay of the French National Veterinary School, and Joshua Gilroy of NSW National Parks and Wildlife Service Broken Hill, was sent to government agencies.

The NSW summary reported initial estimates that around 250,000 Red kangaroos and about 50,000 Grey kangaroos may have died in that epidemic, over a period of about two weeks in an area of about 30,000 square kilometres. A 42 percent decline in Red and Grey kangaroo populations was found between surveys in 1998 and 1999 in the affected area– centered around the Bulloo River Overflow. In 1999 an outbreak was reported in Currawinga National Park, south-west QLD and at Tibooburra in north-west NSW.

DROUGHT AND FLOOD IN A CLIMATE CHANGE WORLD. RED KANGAROOS AGAIN MOST AT RISK

Staker noted that in 2002 Red kangaroo populations plummeted in South Australia due to drought. (This is relevant to both the stable abundance narrative and also the 2020 situation where South Australia was shaping up as a renewed go-to region for the commercial meat industry headquartered in Adelaide.) The 2002 drought drove the state's Red kangaroo population to a 25-year low.

Staker then moved on to the weather conditions of 2010, where the impacts of ongoing drought were interspersed with severe flooding in some regions. Staker sent the Prime Minister scientific references showing that: during drought, mortality is high, especially among adult males and juveniles; more kangaroos are killed on the road, as they increasingly seek green pick to graze on the verges; and they are more vulnerable to dingo, feral dog, or human predation when they congregate around water.

In 2011, far north Queensland was again in flood. Surely, she wrote, the eventual outcome of these disasters will affect macropod numbers significantly. Staker asked for a moratorium on the commercial killing and culling permits until a scientific investigation could determine the disease and its impacts.

"Our large kangaroos' future survival," she wrote, "now depends upon our duty as Australians to ensure our national icon does not become extinct in our lifetime. If steps are taken, and they do survive, it will take at least five years for their numbers to recuperate."

The letter to the Prime Minister also raised Charman's and Staker's knowledge and concerns about the biological degradation of the mobs, echoing genetics expert Ian Gunn and others over the years. They too testified that the industry was killing predominantly half-grown – sometimes unweaned – animals, and often females with joeys. The larger adult males were always shot-out first for the size of their skins and for their meat.

I asked Lynda Staker, when we discussed this correspondence, what the response was from the Prime Minister's office. "Oh, the usual," she said. "It's always the same. 'We are confident the industry is sustainable' and so forth."

In 2019, I spoke to Greg Curran from Broken Hill, who was a co-author, while working for NSW Agriculture, of the 1998 outbreak analysis. Curran, as veterinarian and pathologist, was still trying to piece the puzzle together. He said the disease agent remained unidentified, but agreed with the weather relationship and the odd symptoms. It is his belief that the pathogen possibly crosses the species barrier – with goats he has seen similarly affected in his opinion.

Despite having been inside the tent as a former government veterinarian, Curran has received little interest from state authorities in pursuing the matter. It has been noted that if the epidemic was striking cattle or sheep, the uproar would be deafening.

IN THESE TIMES, THE BASIC QUESTION

At the end of July 2018, the ongoing drought in NSW and Queensland was compared with the epic Federation drought of

1902. As if in an apocalyptic fable, the ecological catastrophe on the NSW Darling River that I related earlier, partly brought on by drought, was followed by more deadly signs of climate disruption.

In February 2019, north Queensland experienced cyclonic-style storms and floods that, along with causing urban mayhem, quite unexpectedly destroyed the grazing country north and west of Townsville, claiming the lives of half a million cattle as well as killing the wildlife across that country.

A year later, at the end of 2019, eastern Australia was in the grip of its worst bushfires in modern times. When they were finally tamed, they had destroyed an estimated three billion native animals, including frogs, bats, and a huge number of birds and reptiles. The coastal forests and escarpment woodlands and grasslands were indeed silenced.[1]

These times, that will not get easier, that will boost the disease and natural disaster casualties, are the backdrop to the virtual numbers game supporting the industrial and amateur killing of the remaining kangaroos and other 'common' wildlife. That slaughter, with state approval, has continued everywhere post-fires, despite the staggering losses.

Fundamentally, ethically, whether we are talking about 50, 500 or 50 million kangaroo lives, or those of other Australian so-called 'common' species, should we be treating our wildlife as an industrial product or throwaway object the way we do?

END GAME, US AND THEM

"I rang the federal member for Roma the other day and said: have you been into parliament to tell them to change the coat of arms for Australia? She says why? I said because you've shot the kangaroo and emu out. She slammed the phone down on me ... Between the drought and the cluster fencing, the poisoning (of waterholes) and the shooting, the kangaroo is wiped out in western Queensland."

— TOM KING SR, CUNNAMULLA

"We've been driving through [Central Queensland] for seven years. Except for one very wet year we have seen (and smelt) lots of dead animals. One year we saw the bodies of kangaroos and other wildlife every five metres around Longreach. We've seen dingos killed and scalped and hung from posts and large poison bait [1080] signs. The region has an all-out assault on wildlife. These ways of treating wildlife are very traditional; but what about the desire in these areas to increase tourism?"

— DR ARIAN WALLACH, UNIVERSITY OF TECHNOLOGY SYDNEY, CONDUCTING DINGO RESEARCH IN CENTRAL QUEENSLAND

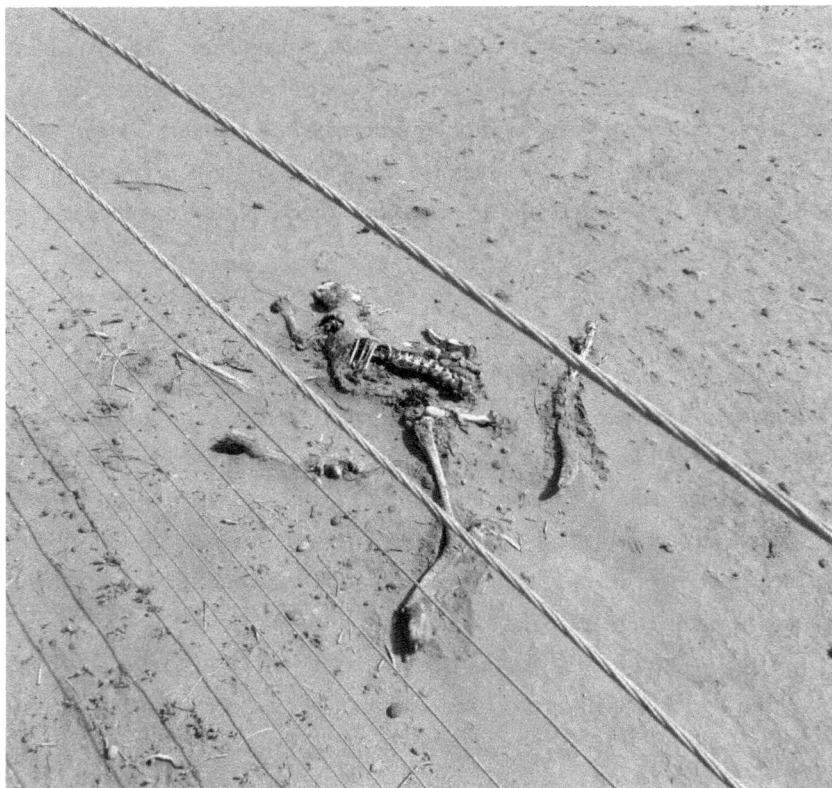

I n March 2018, a truck driver from southern NSW who had been delivering loads of hay to central Queensland graziers recounted similar experiences to those quoted above. He said he was seeing dead kangaroos and emus everywhere along the outback roads he travelled.

Lyn Gynther lives next door to an abattoir. She tells me of a recent experience with a load of cattle: they had been left there by the owner over the weekend, with no feed, and as much water as a dog would drink in a day. She got on the phone to the owner and told him that if he didn't come around with some feed and water, she'd do it and bill him. He came.

I had gone to central Queensland to interview Lyn Gynther and Tom King Sr about their first-hand experiences. Lyn, from around Warwick, is a fighter for animals, but she was also a killer of animals as a former roo shooter. Tom King lives in Cunnamulla. He is also outspoken for wildlife these days, while still a licensed and until recently practicing roo shooter in an arena the kangaroo industry and state and national governments insist is sustainable wildlife management.

Given his unusual candour, Tom's also been pushed off properties and called crazy or lying for breaking the tradition that demands conformity and silence towards outsiders in rural communities.

But with an intractable drought pitting domestic stock graziers against the commercial kangaroo 'harvesting' business, and attracting wildlife welfare advocates, things have been breaking out into the news. From the kangaroo industry's perspective, the wildlife 'resource' is being wiped out by the graziers.

Tom had interested local journalists by fingering as a major culprit the kilometres of 'cluster fencing' – so called because they spread around and through multiple properties, nominally aimed at stopping wild dogs that maul sheep. The fences also cut across remaining wildlife corridors, paths to water and to opportunistic forage, and both emus and kangaroos die as a result.

Photo: Maria Taylor

The fences are just one weapon. Both Lyn and Tom told me about the direct destruction of kangaroos and wallabies, and, more quietly, emus, by a Queensland state government program to help graziers newly excited by the wool market. This entailed basically open season permits to shoot macropods for three years, 2017–20. It costs no more than $158.80 to the state coffers to obtain a shooter's license.

In central Queensland, the renewed war on the wildlife (spreading down into NSW) was happening on cleared and endangered brigalow (*Acacia harpophylla*) native tree and grass ecosystems. Further south are the mulga, brigalow, and gidgee woodland associations that have also been extensively cleared. On this country since the mid-1990s there had been conversion of land-use from sheep to frequently opportunistic cattle grazing. But by 2018 it was going back to sheep with the help of cluster fencing.

LATEST SAVIOURS FOR INLAND PASTORALISM
Local officials hailed the move back to sheep, to lamb production, as the newest saviour for outback communities like Cunnamulla. Wool prices had also rocketed back upward thanks to the China trade.[1]

Exclusion fencing is the latest weapon in this attempted rural revival. The fencing is also accepted by an increasing number of corporate investors who are taking taxpayer money paid as carbon credits for letting their vegetation grow. I saw two-metre (six-foot) high shiny new fencing down to ground level, running for many kilometres in this direction and that, around and between neighbouring properties, forming an impenetrable maze of fencing across wildlife pathways.

Driving south, I saw cluster fencing running for some 120 kilometres (70 miles) from Cunnamulla to the NSW border. Land behind much of that fencing belongs to an overseas investment company. I learned that there are at least eight large properties in Paroo Shire now owned by overseas hedge or pension funds, investing in cattle or government carbon credits, or both.

A 2017 ABC media report quoted the Labor Premier of Queensland visiting the cluster fencing outside Longreach and saying that this was money well spent to save the sheep industry. That report cited cluster fencing by then encompassed 300 rural properties and 4.3 million hectares, at a cost to the taxpayer of $27 million, the rest of the cost being picked up by producers.[2]

By 2019, another round of government-funded fencing was announced, extending around St George and throughout Balonne Shire, north from the Paroo Shire around Cunnamulla that Tom and Lyn were observing.

Balonne is the area around Terri Irwin's family property Mourachan, managed for conservation, research, and ecotourism, as well as some production. The proliferation of fencing, as she told me, is a big concern for the regional wildlife, not least due to the total lack of environmental impact studies that accompanies this trend.

Cluster fencing is being promoted not only in central Queensland, but around Australia's semi-arid grazing regions more generally, particularly for sheep graziers – against dingos, but also against kangaroo, wallaby, emu, and feral animals like wild pigs and goats. This looks like tacit admission that the business is either so marginal or so greedy that keeping out kangaroos, wallabies, or emus that might share some grass and water over many thousands of hectares, is a make-or-break situation. The official reason is 'wild dogs,' but the collateral impact is killing all the wildlife.

A Kondinin sheep industry report promoting exclusion fencing confirmed that as of early 2016 "it is not uncommon" for fences to stretch to 200 kilometres, enclosing 100,000 hectares or more.[3]

Pastoralists have also called for a $25-million rebuild (utilising taxpayer funds) of the deteriorating dingo fence that stretches between the north and south of Australia, protecting sheep flocks in the southern part of the country from the more numerous dingos surviving in the north. A news report had a grazier saying this was essential for survival of the industry in semi-arid South Australia.[4] Veteran kangaroo shooters say the landscape scale fencing bails up macropods and other wildlife and they die along its expanse.

Along with the disappearing animals, the fencing trend is signalling further demise for the commercial kangaroo industry inland. However you turn it, the outcome spells doom for kangaroos in central Queensland.

POVERTY IN THE BUSH, LYN'S STORY

Lyn Gynther says she was a wildlife carer, always caring for something, before she started shooting (aged 17) in the early 1980s. She worked along with her ex-husband. "We got ourselves into a situation where there was no work out home, we had nowhere to live, we went to the local council at Barcaldine and enquired about Centrelink payments, denied, they said move back with your parents." The young couple got a loan from family to set up a truck, the spotlights, the guns, the racks, and went shooting.

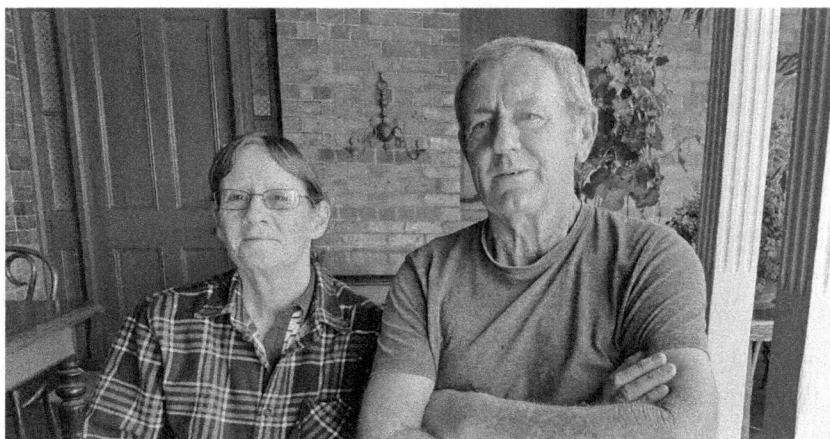

Photo: Maria Taylor

Lyn Gynther and Tom King.

As someone who cared for animals, how did she cope? "I had to switch off. It desensitises you. Every normal person has to desensitise when you have to do this killing every night." We are having a cuppa and a chat with Tom as Lyn tells me this, and he agrees. There was a time in the late '80s when it got to him and he just didn't want to do it. Both say they had to do this because it was the only possible income.

"It's hard, dirty, filthy work, that's desensitising," says Lyn. "Your brain's dead. When you get home, then you've got to salt your skins, unload your roos, do your knives, reload your bullets, then you get a few hours' sleep and then you're up and at it again."

She did it full-time for three years, and then part-time for a total of five years. She had two children in that time. Her ex-husband was in it a lot longer. She went and managed a motel and he was still shooting. "We left Barcaldine when the kids were five and seven and he did it until then."

"We used to also go pigging – not like these people do with dogs, we never had dogs that were allowed to touch pigs. Or we'd take 'em home and sty them, clean them out. My job was to shoot a roo every second day to feed the pigs. If there was a joey on board, grass was high couldn't always see the pouch, if I hit a doe instead of a buck, I had another joey to rear."

She stopped shooting finally, sick of the heavy work, and of being tired and exhausted: "My parents were looking after the kids while I was trying to shoot at night, trying to sleep through the day, and mum didn't want kids all day and all night." In the end, her husband employed an offsider for $50 a night.

AFTERSHOCK: REALISING FAMILY AND MOB STRUCTURE MATTER

"I struggle now," says Lyn. "Get quite depressed, since I have educated myself on the biology and the mob structure and that sort of thing.

Because I know now how many macropod families I've blown apart and completely destroyed and caused chaos within those animals."

While it is soothing to view 'game' or 'pest' animals not as families but as mechanical units that managers can count and kill, destroying the group structure, the natural behaviours and interactions, has consequences.

We talk about the dingo. Wild dog predation on sheep is the official reason for cluster fencing across contiguous properties. People say the years of cattle farming encouraged the dingos to breed up because cattle producers aren't particularly threatened by wild dogs. Or that graziers, out of desperation at the dingo predation, went out of sheep into cattle. Terri Irwin tells me on a different occasion, that in their experience, a lot of the 'wild dogs' are just that: domestic dogs that have been abandoned, have run away, or been lost by pig hunters.

Indiscriminate killing of the apex predator, the dingo, makes matters worse for producers, as they struggle to maintain domestic animals in a pre-existing ecosystem that had some stability and predictable patterns of behaviour between, for example, dingos and kangaroos.

Work at the University of NSW confirmed that where dingos are culled there is more kangaroo activity, and conversely there is more grass where dingos are not culled. The whole system is correlated with irregular rainfall events. Solutions by graziers and governments, of fencing out and killing both the predators and the natural prey, is an expensive destruction of an existing ecological pattern with no promise that it has any effect on mitigating the real threat: the drought.[5]

Less well known is that killing wild dog packs indiscriminately, particularly removing the dominant males, creates chaotic family structures where the surviving young, uneducated dogs are likely to be the ones preying the most on an easy target, sheep, and also causing higher birth rates. It becomes a vicious circle that has also been observed in North America with persecuted wolf populations.

FIRST TARGET: THE ALPHA MALE

A population-stabilising mob structure applies also to kangaroos. Unmolested, a mob is led by an alpha male, the prime target for shooters. Not only are they big and easily seen, but they stand and face the threat – including against guns – as the mob disperses.

Lyn Gynther is one more ex-shooter who says that, in Queensland grazing lands, after years of 'harvesting' and pest management, most people now hardly know what a big kangaroo is. "The [male] roos we were shooting back then were massive animals. They used to keep all the young males in line. And all that's gone now. So you have young stuff raping immature females, causing problems like prolapses, infections ... It just goes on."

Tom King chimes in to say that as early as 1984, shooters meeting at his place agreed the roos were not as big as the old fellas used to be. Since then they had to shoot more and more for the same amount of money for skins and meat. From their on-ground observations, Lyn and Tom agree that one reason for the vicious cycle is that the gene pool is changing (Lyn says she also sees the weaknesses as a carer of joeys) with kangaroos that are continually hunted, producing smaller offspring.

Pest management, whether it is by graziers or the city of Canberra, perpetuates the biological imbalance. They call it 'culling,' which in nature takes out the weak, but here it's the strongest males that go first.

The roo shooting system has been an agreement between a professional shooter and a number of property owners. Massive outback acreages are involved – tens of thousands of hectares, or twice as many acres. Says Lyn: "We used to take a trailer as well as back of ute. A normal nights shooting was 60–70 roos, five, six nights a week in those three properties [where they had a deal to shoot]. A really good night's shooting was 100-plus. The animals were there all the time." Until the animals weren't there any more, in any predictable way.

Nowadays, says Tom, "One bloke said he reckoned he had 10,000 kangaroos on his country. I went out and shot 10 kangaroos for the night and I wouldn't have seen 100." Lyn mentions the suspicion that a larger haul now involves national parks kangaroos.

Faithful media repetition of producer claims that kangaroos are nevertheless on central Queensland properties (and elsewhere inland) in "plague proportions" may partly be a function of perception. As one sheep grazier told me, in the drought the only reasonable patches of grass come up as a result of fleeting rainstorms. Then all the kangaroos in the region are likely to descend and be seen as a plague. Research shows that sheep and kangaroos are only in competition for grass during a drought on degraded country.[6]

The fencing and freelance 'mitigation' shooting that has characterised central Queensland in past years has also disrupted previous animal home-range patterns. When one grazier puts a mitigation license or fence into effect, it's likely that the neighbouring property may suddenly see hundreds of fleeing animals not seen previously.

JOBS FRONT

A standard government claim has been that 4,000 jobs are at stake with the commercial kangaroo industry, a situation not seen since the early 2000s. Lyn and Tom say most shooters are not full-time, just weekend part-time shooters. Many are leaving the industry because they cannot make even a part-time income for their trouble.

Yet government figures suggest kangaroos should be thick on the ground with national totals of 40 to 50 million in recent years. Lyn is one of the sceptics who says the government counts cannot be believed, and points to the anomaly between the government's allocated quota and actual take as an indication that the animals are not there.

In Queensland, shooters have not taken more than one quarter to one third of the quota, even in their best years of the past decade, before the loss of the major Russian market in 2012 and again in 2014 thanks to the hygiene issue. The take has since dropped further thanks to drought, disease, fencing, and related pest management.

It doesn't take an advanced degree to look around. Like other observant Australian citizens and also disappointed visitors, Tom and Lyn have said repeatedly they rarely see a kangaroo these days. Tom tells me: "We had a bloke come out with a machine on the bottom of a helicopter doing the grid for minerals. Flew all over the country. I said how many roos do you reckon you see flying all over like that? He said, I might count 10 a day if I'm lucky. They were flying millions of acres and they weren't finding any. That country used to have tens of thousands of roos."

TOM'S STORY

Tom King, 61 when we talked, has been hunting kangaroos since he was 12 years old. He drove trucks for his main living in recent years, and more recently has been caretaker and manager for a couple of carbon farming properties. As a youngster he shot roos for pocket money around school hours, bagging five or six a day for skins. Later with a motorbike, while working on the land, he shot kangaroos on a Friday afternoon and sold them in town. He says it bought him a café meal, movie, and cigarettes, so he could save his wages.

As is commonly the case, it runs in the family. "Dad done it when he wasn't fencing, droving. Dad always shot kangaroos to make more money." Tom King's son Tom Jr also has worked as a roo shooter.

When he was selling lots of carcases in the 1980s (he named Warrego Wool and Skins, Hilton O'Dare, Jack Fish, and Wattle Glen Rendering as buyers) skins dominated the overseas market. He found the demand started drying up in the late 1980s. That was when conservation groups and zoologist Peter Rawlinson convinced the Americans and the odd celebrity to do without kangaroo leather – by showing that an Australian government public relations campaign, brandishing kangaroo population numbers, proved to be misleading.

I ask Tom and Lyn about allegations that the kangaroo trade had operated with organised crime links and official corruption, as unpacked by Raymond Hoser and journalist Fia Cumming in books and newspaper reports up to 1996. They say this was certainly suspected. As they put it: everyone knew in the '80s and '90s of organised crime elements (with some recurring names). It was commonly alleged these led to more than one murder. Everyone on the bottom rung of field shooting, relying on making a few dollars as the sun rose and the carcasses were handed over, was cautious of talking about the industry heavyweights and who they should sell to.

I ask Tom what the turning point was for him to start speaking out, and he tells me a story that shows how myths grow, a story that illustrates the renewed showdown between the wildlife and what people decide to produce – because they can on their private property.

It happened seven or eight years ago, as everyone continued going into cattle, when everyone was "hating sheep and hating kangaroos". At the time, a major local land owner started growing cotton around Cunnamulla. Kangaroos don't eat cotton. "But they'll eat every blade of green grass between the rows. So as soon as they started watering the cotton, kangaroos for miles started swarming in." That family owns property all around Cunnamulla.

"So then they said they had kangaroos in plague proportions, gotta do something. So they got a mitigation permit and wiped them out."

By 2018, Tom King was telling anyone who would listen (and he says that did not include the authorities he tried to talk to) about what he'd seen and heard of conditions in central Queensland during the recent dry and drought years, on top of the grazier stocking changes.

In 2015, he told the Australian Society for Kangaroos, which passed it on to the media, about a slaughter he came across where 30 kangaroos had been herded against a fence, riddled with bullets and left to die. The *Daily Mail* reported it, with photos.

> "Professional kangaroo shooter Tom King uncovered the blood bath on a property near Cunnamulla in south west Queensland when he was driving through earlier this week.
>
> "The herd of kangaroos had been mustered, possibly by vehicles, into a corner near an electrical fence and had been shot multiple times in the stomach, neck and back.
>
> "You can clearly see the bullet shots in the kangaroos and their broken legs. Some of the roos have even hit the electric fence … At least six had hit the fence when I saw the carnage … Mr King said he felt powerless to act as the Department of Environment and Heritage and the RSPCA had failed to act before when he made similar reports of cruelty to kangaroos in the area."[7]

Australia's premier animal protection organisation, the RSPCA, in Queensland (and elsewhere) contends wildlife and its treatment is not its problem or remit.

Photo: Tom King

WEEKEND WARRIORS: BRING FRIENDS, KILL EVERYTHING

Lyn shows me a damage mitigation permit issued in Queensland in 2017–18 by a Labor state government. It's for killing unlimited numbers of wallabies over three years. She notes there is no such thing as a relocation permit.

On one property, says Tom: "He's got a mitigation permit, so invited shooters – 'got a job to wipe them out whatever they are.' There were six cars in that convoy all had buggies on the back. Gunracks and cases on every one. They were there for three weeks. When the commercial roo shooter went out there, all he could find was roos laid out everywhere." Lyn adds: "Professional shooters can now add 50 roos at a time for 'recreational' personal use. That all has to go."

Tom believes fewer Red kangaroos are migrating to central Queensland from further west to feed. "Weekend warriors [or the odd enterprising professional] go way out west shooting them out there," he says. Technology has made this possible with new roads and four-wheel drives able to carry much more fuel than earlier.

They agree that policing is hard to do in big, remote country. And almost no one will talk. The code of rural conformity is strong, meaning often no one wants to hear, either.

But, insists Tom, the ammunition sold tells the story. Like when 27 part-time commercial shooters around Cunnamulla shot 4,700 kangaroos in a five-week period. At the same time the local gun shop sold 25,000 rounds. "None of those were sold to us, not one professional roo shooter. That was all sold in big boxes of ammunition to the graziers for getting rid of kangaroos. A man goes out and buys 10,000 22 magnums a month. Why? What's he shooting? That's a terrorist act as far as I'm concerned."

Tom talks about a page he has seen on Facebook aimed at recreational shooters. It's all about filling your car with big old dead kangaroos. A page that sells four-wheel drives and guns. He cites another Facebook page for a regional firearms dealer that boasted of selling 30,000 rounds in four hours for mitigation work.

Bringing in the "weekend warriors" to have fun and destroy the wildlife theoretically still requires a mitigation permit, held by the landholder. That is different than a test of accurate shooting by the helpers. The Sporting Shooters Association claims it is regulated to a professional standard. However, a quick check of police fact sheets on requirements for sporting shooters on rural properties and "game/vermin" control mentions nothing about shooting accuracy or professional standards. Landholder permission is the big issue. On-ground evidence, as shown in the *Daily Mail* and related reports, raises further questions.

Tom and Lyn are also disgusted that no authority checks anything either before or after permits are handed out. Says Tom: "No one goes out and counts the kangaroos to see if he's got a roo problem; no one goes out to check if the joey's killed humanely, no one does it." Lyn claims that the government attitude since 2014 has been that while a drought is on, its job is to expedite issuing mitigation permits without inspections required.

They agree the whole scene looks a lot like genocide.

DEADLY MAZE

On top of all the gun carnage, the cluster fencing subsidies – for which even town businesses were applying as kangaroos sought food and water in human settlements – were ensuring widespread wildlife death in the years up to 2020, and beyond.

It's affecting every species, says Tom. "Emus, echidna, every wildlife that is caught." The animals can't migrate to water, can't get to rivers because these are also fenced off. "They have all these little corridors going in where kangaroos think they can go through and they can't get back out or get water or food. There's nothing – they die. It's happening all around, Charleville, Mitchell, Morgan, St George."

Lyn notes there are laws against fencing all the way down to the water, yet this is what's happened. And public stock routes are being fenced. "In Paroo Shire you go to the Lands Department and they'll say they're all open stock routes, but now they're full of stock, the gates are locked, and the cockies got a big cluster fence going across."

I learned later that exclusion fencing was actually an old colonial idea that 19th century large-scale pastoral holdings in the north had used to exclude the wildlife from its previous habitat, water, and movement corridors.

EFFECT OF STOCKING DECISIONS

We talk about what they have observed of the land management challenges in these boom and bust lands. Changing stock to cattle and to Dorper sheep possibly worsened the on-ground effects of the drought. Many of the stocking changes were opportunistic.

Some involved absentee landholders who were moving cattle in and out. A long-time sheep grazier told me that they weren't neighbours in the traditional sense.

But the hard environment is not easy cattle country, and everywhere stocking rates are paramount. The move to Dorper sheep – a meat sheep that is said to eat more like a goat: everything and often – did not help. Tens of thousands of feral goats saved a lot of graziers from going broke but did serious damage before they were mostly mustered for the halal market.

The severe land degradation brought on by such landholder decisions is seldom appreciated by the passing motorist, who may see kangaroos and wallabies eating road-side grass. There are likely no animals on the other side of the fence.

Tom King has not made himself any more popular with local critics by speaking up further for the voiceless and telling people that, in his opinion, stocking decisions and treatment are in some cases as ignorant as the treatment of the wildlife, and that modern technology has put theory ahead of understanding.

He'll say things like: "Fellow told me one day you gotta keep up with technology. I told him take that phone out of your pocket and tell that old ewe with her tongue hanging out there, she's gotta walk another three kilometres to the yard." Or he'll tell you about the fellow who caused stock deaths by turning off watering points that cattle had become used to, over a period of 18 months, while opening others. And then blame the wildlife. "Sheep and cattle haven't changed. They can't read a computer, and a kangaroo can't read a computer either."

CORRIDORS SHUT DOWN AS SOME WITHHOLD WATER AND SOME ADD POISON

"Yet," says Tom, "everyone is blaming the kangaroo for everything, (even) for the drought, and nothing is true … This day and age everyone hates kangaroos out in the western area, they hate 'em. So some people when they have no stock, they turn all their waters off. There's no kangaroo on that country now." Or emus.

Even on public land, I learned from ex park rangers, closure of man-made watering points in inland parks has become an article of faith for some who are striving for an idealised return to an era considered more natural. It has been pointed out this is an unnecessary cruelty, not only to the demonised macropods, but to every other wildlife that had become used to the water – particularly birds.

Poisoning of water sources has also been reported in this renewed war on wildlife. According to a 2017 report by the national broadcaster, the ABC, Surat-based kangaroo shooter Geoff Moore said landholders were using poison to kill kangaroos inside a cluster fence.

"They close it off to their livestock and just put urea in the water trough and the roos go there for a drink because they can't access rivers and creeks or waterholes and it just decimates them," he said. "They [kangaroos] get a horrible pain in the guts [from the poison] and go away and die – it's barbaric practices really."

The same 2017 article by journalist Elly Bradfield that unveiled Tom King's story about the cluster fence massacre, with pictures, and the poisoning of water troughs report, also checked with a regional kangaroo processing plant on whether the 'harvested' numbers were down in areas with cluster fencing, and was told: yes.

CLUSTER FENCES WILL CRIPPLE RURAL COMMUNITIES, CLASH BETWEEN GRAZIERS AND COMMERCIAL KILLING

Warroo Game Meats employs about 25 to 30 people in Surat. The company's spokeswoman Betty Mickleborough said the number of kangaroos it processed had halved since the introduction of cluster fencing. "Without us here there's a lot of these people in this little town would have to leave and move because of the mining industry shutting down – there's not a lot of jobs in these outback towns," she said.

Mickleborough said she has raised her concerns about the diminishing supply with the state government, but it had fallen on deaf ears. "I don't want to see them be totally destroyed because they are a lovely animal," she said.[8] The clash between the kangaroo industry and the grazing industry in central Queensland, which either way results in dead kangaroos, has been bemoaned as poor government policy by the kangaroo industry. It highlights the binary choice of the Australian status quo: is the national icon a pest or a product (or something else entirely)?

Out of self-interest, the kangaroo industry is now the spokesperson for wildlife protection in this environment. The president of the Kangaroo Industry Association of Australia, Ray Borda (managing director of South Australian kangaroo meat manufacturer Macro Meats that produces K-Roo), has criticised the lack of a holistic policy approach to land management in Queensland, saying measures as simple as protecting some wildlife corridors have been ignored. He told a reporter for a regional paper: "The government keeps on telling us to market our product better, but we already are putting so much money and research into this, but then the government turns around and calls our product a pest, so it makes it hard to convince an overseas buyer that kangaroo is a product worth them buying."

The same article, looking at all sides, quoted at length from a grazing industry (AgForce) spokesperson defending current mitigation and fencing. He said graziers rely on government counts that purport to show that, despite drought and destruction, there are more kangaroos than at any time since 1992; that they feel confident with the claim by recreational shooters from the Sporting Shooters Association of Australia's Farmer Assist program that they adhere to professional shooting standards, and that the aim is to rebuild the sheep industry in the area.[9]

HOW ABOUT SHARING?

Nikki Sutterby for the Australian Society for Kangaroos gave the same reporter a different perspective: "The kangaroos were here first, so why can't you give up 10 per cent of your land for your native animals? The research shows that when you graze kangaroos with stock it can actually increase production.

"The kangaroos are struggling too, but no one has any sympathy for them, everyone just wants them out of their property. We know that when the rains come, they'll head back out west and won't be in everybody's way, so why can't we feed them just like we do with other livestock and animals? Just chuck them some hay, chuck them a bit of horse feed.

"Especially if it's a tourist destination and you have tourists and travellers going through, I imagine they'd love seeing the kangaroos."

Photo: Maria Taylor

Kangaroos on Cunnamulla football field at dusk.

Cunnamulla townsfolk testify that the kangaroos are coming in, hungry because of the lack of feed in the paddocks or at times to escape the shooting. Such scenes are not uncommon in rural communities throughout Australia. When we were in Cunnamulla, the kangaroos were on the football field. I made a show with the camera, and passing locals smiled and waved.

Lyn Gynther had a parting thought to city-dwellers who still sometimes see hemmed-in kangaroos in urban spaces: "These people need to remember that all these cities that now take up so much space (or for that matter grazing or cropping areas) used to be the 10 square kilometre home range of these animals. So they've just been pushed and pushed."

2019: EMUS ALSO EXECUTED, SHOT-OUT

I caught up with Tom King again in May 2019 after he had spent a year caretaking five central Queensland properties, ranging in size from 90,000 acres to 270,000 acres, that are being managed for carbon credits. I caught Tom on a Sunday afternoon as he was on his way to perform at Music in the Mulga – a welcome break from the ceaseless driving that the caretaker role entails. This was a break too from his worries about some of the agisted cattle grazing activities that are putting pressure on the ground cover. He was not too happy about some people allowed onto the properties thanks to the cattle managers.

I asked him what he had observed of kangaroos and emus. The answer was not good. "On 90,000 acres I might see one Wallaroo. Not an emu on the place, they've all been shot out." He told me that he found emu bones everywhere. The shearers' quarters were full of hunting gear when the carbon farming people bought the place two years earlier. Tom said he might be able to auction off these things and give the proceeds to a wildlife care group.

On the day after a federal election that jolted the country with its 'business as usual, it's all about money' vote, Tom King repeated his fears that rural Australia was in deep trouble – with drought compounded by greed and traditional thinking. As for the wildlife, he saw no law safeguarding it. People did whatever they wanted. He spoke of graziers who had killed thousands of kangaroos in recent years without even bothering with a mitigation permit.

The deadly cluster fencing that continued to be funded by the state government was in 2019 openly and more honestly being called roo fencing. But in Paroo Shire, he said, there's no kangaroo left. They've all been shot out – reputedly some by officers of the law, who used kangaroos and emus on the roadsides as target practice.

Photo: Maria Taylor

HIGH ON THE SHEEP'S BACK

As the drought became more apparent down south, the kangaroo blame game ramped up on the neighbourhood electronic notice-board as well. There are still some sheep and cattle graziers on the periphery of this rural residential area near the national capital, and they were showing the stress of dried-out paddocks. They attracted sympathisers, with strong traditional opinions about "plague-proportion" wildlife presented as fact. There were also people chiming in who were trying to feed horses on 10–20 acres with some grass on thin soils – not enough to sustain three, four, five horses through good times and bad.

The argument raged on. It see-sawed between those who seemed to believe that blaming and shooting kangaroos will counteract the impacts of the weather, or, another favoured theme, the risks of country roads, and those who believe that kangaroos have taken up shelter in rural residential districts to escape being shot elsewhere. Many said they valued the opportunity to co-exist.

Simultaneously appearing on the noticeboard were well-intentioned drought relief food and supply appeals. In this environment, I was talking with a neighbour who told me her sister called and they discussed the drought. It's bad, they agreed. But you know, said her sister (herself on a grazing property), the sheep 'cockies' in the region are still buying new four-wheel drives every year, their children still go to elite private schools in Sydney, and they have their hand out for extended drought relief while still enjoying a lot of tax benefits that other citizens don't.

I had heard similar observations from Tom and Lyn in Queensland, where the opportunistic return to sheep farming in the midst of a drought stoked the move to cluster fencing and the war on wildlife. I had filed these stories under 'maybe,' but they were piling up.

Postscript: In late 2019, the Queensland government suspended the 2020 commercial harvest for Grey kangaroos and Wallaroos/Euros in central Queensland, suddenly claiming populations had dropped by 10 million animals between 2013 and 2018, triggering population warning flags due to drought. The indignant outcry from the grazier community and its politicians, who had been doing their utmost to kill off the resource with gun and fence, was immediate and fierce, and studded with the usual super-abundance rhetoric.[10]

A COUNTRY DRIVE, A TROUBLED LANDSCAPE, AND A GLIMPSE OF SOMETHING ELSE

I saw on a 2018 drive through drought-stricken south-central Queensland that people who manage kilometre after kilometre of variable quality private land continue to clear bush for new paddocks. Some then seemingly overstock for the land's capacity. The contrast was stark between the stony red ground (it's hard to call it soil) on some land – once optimistically cleared for sheep or cattle – with uncleared brigalow, mulga and ironbark woodlands on a neighbouring block. Yet elsewhere, conservative stocking and partial tree cover had left ground cover intact despite seven years of drought.

Photo: Maria Taylor

I saw what looked like bewildered emus and kangaroos running along miles of fences, shut out of their former home ranges or pathways to food and water. By then I'd heard how both species were eliminated by graziers and weekend warriors.

I heard the Red kangaroo casually derided as an invading pest. It was possible that Red kangaroos – escaping commercial hunting and grazier 'culling' to the north and west, as well as the dry – were on the move, seeking respite and food in the drought.

Photo: Maria Taylor

On better soils in the coastal hinterlands, I had seen brolgas and a few returning bustards, as well as more emus. Protected platypus live in the Broken River, west of Mackay. Their reserve is promoted as a major draw. (As if to prove just this, a tourist stopped us in the middle of nowhere to get directions to the nearest platypus colony.) Large lizards, kangaroos, and wallabies might still be seen with a break in the hunting. Birdwatching is a proven tourist magnet on public or private conservation land.

Hard-hit graziers – the actual and spiritual descendants of the pioneering settlers – many of whom are not now running a viable business given the state of the soils and the impacts of gathering climate disruption, could add wildlife tourism or encourage government conservation payments to trade-off destocking or less cropping, as pioneered in Europe.

As it is, most city people – and that includes media reporters – have never seen a wild emu, kangaroo, wallaby, wombat, platypus, dingo, or koala, or many of Australia's fabulous birds – other than in a zoo. There is hope, and I will soon meet some pioneers who say that this failure to respect and live with our wildlife and natural ecosystems is not destiny.

But before I get there, I detour to meet whistleblowers, activists and scientists who have taken the fight overseas with more compelling reasons to live and let live with kangaroos.

WHISTLEBLOWERS, BUSHMEAT, AND INTERNATIONAL PUSHBACK

"Adelaide-based Macro Meats is the world's biggest distributor of wild game kangaroo meat and is planning to rollout even more products, including a range of ready-made meals ..."

— 'THE PLAN TO TAKE OUT READY-MADE ROO MEAT TO THE WORLD',

THE DAILY TELEGRAPH, 21 SEPTEMBER 2018

Shooters reap $1000 a night as Russian sausage makers demand a slice of our emblem

Picture: Lee Griffith

Marksmen hit jackpot: Kangaroo shooters such as Barry Chambers are earning up to $1000 a night as roo meat becomes a multi-million-dollar a year market thanks to European gourmands, Russian sausage makers and changed tastes in WA. West Australian Newspapers Ltd, 7 March 2007.

" **E**xporters now have access to more than 60 overseas markets, where they deliver high quality fresh meat cuts to restaurants and dinner tables across the globe." In 2017, one could find these words on a federal government information file about the kangaroo meat and skin trade.

By now I have no doubt that the Australian federal and state governments consider kangaroos an export commodity, like coal and iron ore (or live sheep and cattle), and lobby foreign governments to buy these commodities. The federal Department of Agriculture and Water Resources regulates the export of kangaroo meat, registering processing facilities, and claiming to oversee production ensuring food safety.

Australian governments also provide public relations, research funding, and a supportive narrative for the kangaroo industry. The federal information sheet tells me the commercial kangaroo industry began in 1959 and is considered "one of the world's best wild harvest operations," and claims "quotas are scientifically set and regularly monitored."

If one relied on federal government information, for instance in 2017, one would believe that the country has what sounds like a static 50 million kangaroos, of which three percent are "harvested" and used for meat production each year. Red and Grey kangaroos and the common Wallaroo/Euro are said to be widespread and abundant, according to this narrative. Everything is seemingly okay because none are listed as endangered or threatened with extinction.[1]

As I found out, and detailed in a previous chapter, there are significant problems with the national statistics and actual 15 percent kill quotas that underlie this rosy picture. The method yields theoretical kangaroos, alleged to populate the length and breadth of states in never-ending abundance, which are not reflected on the ground.

WHISTLEBLOWING ON STATES OF MYTH

Pushback over the decades from concerned citizens is still frustratingly slow for many activists. But there have been significant impacts on the kangaroo export trade, thanks to what overseas communities have learned about the Australian "harvest."

Much of that was thanks to whistleblowers from within the industry, and other direct observers, including independent scientists, journalists and politicians with open minds, and overseas activists. Some wrote in a series of books published in the 1990s by the Australian Wildlife Protection Council (AWPC) under the stewardship of Maryland Wilson and her colleagues who followed in the footsteps of Arthur Queripel.[2]

FROM WITHIN THE INDUSTRY A DARK PICTURE EMERGES

Amongst the writers for AWPC-published *Kangaroos Myths and Realities* is former kangaroo shooter David Nicholls, who also spoke to me for this investigation. He says kangaroo shooting is inherently cruel, and he has no doubt that if the public could actually see an unsanitised version of what goes on under cover of darkness in the kangaroo killing fields, the trade would stop overnight.

Nicholls told me that his hunting memories still haunt him every day. Nowadays we call this post-traumatic stress. Shooting is not an exact science because of the many variables, and the result causes horrific non-fatal injuries:

> "You cannot shoot an animal from 300 metres away and not stuff it. You can be an Olympic marksman, and most roo shooters are not, and still not hit the head which is a very small target. [At that distance] You can't tell males from females. The shooter could be tired, sick, pissed ... Difficulties include nervous roos that have been continually shot at, weather conditions, telescopic sights,

butchering on site. There only has to be slight error in aim for wounding to occur.

"The mouth of a kangaroo can be blown off and the kangaroo can escape to die of shock or starvation. Forearms can be blown off, as can ears, eyes and noses. Stomachs can be hit expelling the contents with the kangaroo still alive. Backbones can be pulverised ... Hind legs can be shattered with the kangaroo desperately trying to get away on the other or without the use of either. To deny that this goes on is just an exercise in attempting to fool the public.

"Another form of cruelty is straight out of the annals of our brutish past and is a blight on all that we hold to be decent and fair ... young joeys are unceremoniously dragged out of their previously secure world [the pouch] and swung against a hard object. One swing may be followed by another and yet another if the prior does not complete the kill ... even hardened kangaroo shooters are often sickened by this never-ending process.

"It was not understood that the joey-at-foot would also die in a state of terror by psychological deprivation, predation and starvation. Many kangaroo shooters now convince themselves that the joey escapes and lives happily ever after. Delusions of this sort are not uncommon in the industry and in governments and their acting agents. Self-delusion played a large part in my experience as a kangaroo shooter ..."[3]

The problem is compounded by the tradition and lack of legal restraint allowing people on rural properties to feel entitled to 'manage' the wildlife however they wish. In Nicholls' view, things have not changed much from the colonial days. He calls it a total disregard for law and order when you step outside the cities.

WORD OF AN INDUSTRY OUT OF CONTROL, HYGIENE EVIDENCE AND A TRADE PUSHBACK

In the mid-2000s (25 years after Peter Rawlinson and conservationists slowed the trade in the US), a small band of determined kangaroo defenders utilised insider information to again throw spanners into the gears of Australia's international kangaroo meat and skin export operation. They continued to counter the bland official narratives and added a new concern: the human and pet health risks from consuming kangaroo meat.

In 2005, Mark Pearson, one-time opera singer, then psychiatric nurse, and more recently a NSW state senator for the Animal Justice Party, was the head of Animal Liberation in that state. He says he was contacted by first one and in subsequent years by five or six shooters, who all told similar stories to David Nicholls. They told Pearson "the industry was out of control", and they were worried kangaroo populations could not survive the amount of slaughter taking place.

Pearson's informants said it was no longer just professional shooters out there (long before Queensland and then NSW generous cull permits opened the door further from 2013 on). Weekend and recreational shooters were becoming involved as this outback industry tried to boost competition amongst suppliers (as in, the shooters) and gain lower prices for themselves. That meant a lot of extra people were going into zones that had previously been shot, leaving no time for populations to re-establish.

Pearson's industry whistleblowers also testified about the systematic animal cruelty outlined by Nicholls, observed by neighbours like the Keightleys, and documented by the film *Goodbye Joey* followed by outrage from UK and US animal rights groups amongst other overseas critics. One shooter said to Pearson: "You know, we are almost seeing a genocide." While the world remained aghast at the clubbing of baby seals in Canada, the brutal bashing and slow death of unweaned, lost, and bewildered Australia joeys was estimated to have claimed around 800,000 lives a year on a 30-year average.[4]

Pearson told me that in addition to industrial hunting, the casual, unregulated shooting of kangaroos by volunteer pest-eradicators was brought home to him by none other than leading kangaroo industry figure Ray Borda. He recounted how Borda showed up in his office with a bag of bullet fragments that processors found in kangaroo meat.[5]

The whistleblowers were also bringing Pearson more evidence on an issue that he quickly realised could blow up the long-standing export trade: hygiene.

FIRST 12 HOURS ON A RUSTY HOOK IN A TRAVELLING UTE

"Here's an animal that was shot at say 7 o'clock at night," Pearson told me, "then was bouncing around in the back of a truck in very hot temperatures in summer, reaching a chiller maybe 12 hours later – that would not be acceptable in an abattoir. If you can imagine sheep or cattle shot 12 hours before and then spending 12 hours on the back of a truck, not refrigerated. Kangaroos carcases might then sit in a chiller for a further two weeks or so."

"I went out bush with the first shooter who contacted me," he continued. "I said, 'Show me what actually happens on the ground' and he agreed to do that. My interest at first was of course the welfare of the joeys and the kangaroos. But when I got to the area and saw the condition of the chillers – old broken- down shipping containers, with all the seals broken, maggots crawling all over the place, the animals hung there on rusty hooks – I just looked at him and said 'Are you telling me this is for human consumption?' And he said yes."

There are many hundreds of carcass-holding chillers on private properties across Australia. In NSW in 2018, 413 commercial shooters were still registered (nationwide an estimated 1,400 professional shooters had registered a year earlier –short of the 4,000 claimed by the federal government). The fall in numbers was telling, and Australian activists abroad may have played a significant part.

International unease and disgust had led to decline in demand for kangaroo meat and skins since the early 2000s, even though the kill numbers in the mid-2000s were still staggering. International welfare groups, including Viva! in the UK and the Humane Society International in the US, led the charge, free from the Australian government, industry, and media perspectives that had left most Australians in comfortable ignorance, or confused and apathetic.

At home, Pearson and others had not been idle: they'd been assembling evidence, particularly on the health and hygiene front, and presenting it to overseas buyers.

FOLLOWING THE HYGIENE TRAIL TO MARKET

After his first encounter with the whistleblower, Pearson contacted a reputable pathology lab and got instructions on what has to be done to take proper tests for contaminants on the carcasses in the chillers. "We went to chillers and swabbed the inside of the carcasses that had been gutted; put that sponge with the blood and other material into a container and headed off to the laboratory and the result was worse than we thought. They found high levels of E. coli, many salmonella readings, faecal matter.

"So then I realised what's going to bring this industry to its knees," he told me. "We'd been trying to get welfare to do that, but hygiene and public alarm by say the Russian and European people [major markets] would become a major issue." At the time, Russia was the largest importer, receiving 70 percent of the kangaroo meat exports.

In 2007, Pearson and a colleague, Angela Stephenson, went first to China. At that time federal Labor minister Tony Burke was trying to open up markets into China. The duo then planned to go to Russia, and on to Europe. China had just experienced a major hygiene issue with dairy, so was sensitive to food health. Pearson and Stephenson showed their Chinese government hosts the results of the hygiene tests, hoping to stop the trade before it started.

A 2016/17 trip to China attempted a follow-up. China has not said anything (and still had not by the time this book went to publication) and Pearson has remained hopeful. He reported that a European Commission contact assured him that when China says nothing, that means 'no.'

In Russia, they set up meetings with the Russian meat authority, the umbrella body for veterinary services, and the body that oversaw the hygiene status of food. "We weren't particularly well received, initially," Pearson continued. "There was a lot of suspicion. The Russians said: Why should we be talking to non-government organisations? We trust the government of Australia to do this properly. And we said, well here are our results, and we're alarmed out of concern for the Russian people and also the welfare of the kangaroos, that's why we bring this to your attention.[6]

"They did their own test at the end of 2007, early 2008, with some shipments that had come into Vladivostok from Australia, and they found the same as us, plus faecal matter and antibiotic spray. They announced a ban of 75 percent of the imports into Russia in 2008, and in 2009 they banned 100 percent of the imports. That ban, despite it lifting a little bit in 2011–2012 is now back in place since 2014."

How did the Australian government react to all this? According to Pearson they didn't say much other than 'we don't agree there are any hygiene issues, our tests are not showing anything so we don't know what you are talking about'. The Australian government's ongoing promotional material about a sustainable and safe industry supports that rejection of independent evidence.

Zoologist Dror Ben-Ami was soon to join the effort. He told me the industry response was to say the Russians were just using the wrong tests. In 2014 there were charges that it was a political move by Russia against Australia. This was made easier due to Russian bans against agricultural imports from Western countries in response to Western sanctions following Russian political activities in Ukraine.[7]

When Pearson's 2007 mission got to the European Union, the Australians were told 'we need an independent scientific report and then we will analyse your concerns.' Russia was also agitating for an independent report. That brought in Dr Ben-Ami, who was researching marsupials at the University of NSW at the time. He produced a report, 'A Shot in the Dark,' detailing the dark side of the industry.[8]

FOOD INSPECTOR FINDS PLENTY WRONG WITH KANGAROO FIELD STORAGE

A NSW food hygiene inspector, Des Sibraa, supplied testimony to this report on what he saw in photographs supplied by Pearson, of 420 carcasses stored in northern NSW chillers between 2005 and 2008. In about half that sample, where he could see, he noticed the head was removed from the vertebra at a point lower than the neck, which indicated that there was likely not a clean headshot as legally required for human consumption.

He described that carcasses were stacked too closely together, not allowing cool air and adequate chilling to circulate as required by the food standard; kangaroo legs were penetrating the gut cavity of another animal or legs and paws were sweeping the unclean floor; general hygiene was not good with old and new bloodstains covering surfaces and animal parts coming in contact with those surfaces; wild pig carcasses, covered in mud stored nearby and sometimes touching, threatened cross contamination – all against the rules.

He concluded it was clear the requirements of the Australian Standard for Game Meat for Human Consumption were not being met.[9] In 2020, images (that I saw) were being passed around Facebook by animal defenders. It showed a chiller containing a very similar layout of closely stacked kangaroos with wild pig bodies nearby.

More supermarket meat sampling was done between 2009 and 2012 by Pearson's group, and again in 2015, and compared with lamb. Hundreds of samples from major supermarkets were taken in Sydney, Melbourne, Brisbane, and Adelaide.

The first three years reportedly continued to yield unacceptable levels of E. coli and salmonella in kangaroo meat, while lamb from the same outlets was clean. The results were presented to Australian, Russian, and European food safety authorities. While the Australian and European authorities (trusting the Australians) did not react, the Russians again banned kangaroo meat imports after conducting their own tests.

ADD ACETIC ACID AND A 2015 REPORT

By August 2014, the then federal agriculture minister Barnaby Joyce was telling the media that extending the trade to China was vital for survival of this industry.[10]

In 2015, on the heels of a renewed federal government marketing push, Pearson, Ben-Ami, and colleagues were planning another China trip – but first they did another round of meat sampling. This time they found only a few low levels samples of E. coli and salmonella. However, they also found evidence of the use of acetic acid to sanitise the meat in production, with unknown nutritional consequences – an industry move confirmed by questions in federal parliament.[11]

Five years after Sibraa's testimony, unhygienic conditions continued in a largely unregulated industry, according to a March 2015 article in *The Sydney Morning Herald* by Health Editor Amy Corderoy. She examined documents obtained under freedom of information laws by a NSW Greens member of parliament. She wrote that investigations by the NSW Food Authority found kangaroo 'harvesters' were not adhering to the most basic hygiene standards. What was sold to consumers as the healthy red meat alternative could be riddled with pathogens, due to the practices still observed in the field.[12]

Investigations showed carcases were still found hung on rusty hooks, initially processed over a tray with old dried blood, and exposed to live animals (mostly cattle) roaming around, with the danger of faecal and other contamination. Compliance breaches also found dirty floors, walls and ceilings in chillers, and lack of washing facilities.

The NSW testing found 16 breaches of this nature in required annual inspections of chillers. The Kangaroo Industries Association of Australia responded to such reports by saying that kangaroo meat operations are subject to more stringent testing than any other meat products. Another 140 chillers did pass inspection.

However, kangaroo shooter Tom King told me that where he operated in Cunnamulla, in south-west Queensland, while the chiller box operators were good, shooters sometimes have too many carcases in a hot truck, sometimes for up to 12 hours. In his lengthy experience, there has been no independent hygiene oversight at any level. Government inspectors are never seen "unless there's a big problem overseas".

And if there is an inspection, here's what he's seen happen: "If Safe Food comes out to check our vehicles, we get word a week or fortnight before. All these roo shooters take everything off their car, they paint their rack, paint their floor, it's all nice and spic and span, no spare tyres, toolboxes, jacks and all that. If they came back the next morning, they'd find tools, skins and butts boned out for dogs on the back of the car in blood that thick."

NUMEROUS PARASITES AND PATHOGENS IN KANGAROO MEAT

The critics who have taken their case to overseas markets point out that kangaroos can carry numerous parasites and zoonotic (species crossing) pathogens that may threaten human health if consumed. Applying similar knowledge, country people generally don't eat kangaroo in rural areas and on properties where kangaroos are shot, citing 'worms.'[13]

In 2016, Pearson, Ben-Ami, and Aboriginal Elder from Yuin Country, Max Dulumunmum Harrison, set off for China once again, armed with hygiene, cruelty, and unsustainability evidence and arguments. They met with the Animal Welfare office and informed them about the hygiene and welfare issues.

The Chinese were very interested in the animal welfare issue and the Indigenous issues in particular, Ben-Ami told me. "Uncle Max showed them Indigenous people care about the kangaroos and many are not happy that kangaroos are killed in an industry context and then shipped overseas. He told them something to the effect of, 'you don't eat my kangaroo and I won't eat your panda.'"

That comment may have gone up the chain to the trade officials. Ben-Ami noted wryly that what followed has been mystifying Australian bureaucrats trying to get kangaroo meat into China. "The Chinese won't import the meat and they keep talking about pandas."

A FIRST AUSTRALIAN VIEW OF THE KANGAROO INDUSTRY

Uncle Max's Indigenous perspective is unsolicited by Australian state authorities, but impressed the Chinese.

The Malu, or kangaroo, he says, is a totem of the Yuin people, but was also a food source that was traditionally cooked immediately, which matters with the hygiene argument. His concerns (outlined in a 2008 open letter)[14] relate to the manner in which the kangaroos are killed for consumption: "Killed and then transported long distances to processing factories during which time the build-up of harmful bacteria is likely to occur resulting in unhygienic meat which has lost most of its nutritional value."

He also says that using most kangaroo meat for pet food, as is the practice in Australia, disrespects both the animal and the Indigenous cultural beliefs and traditions of totem animals.

The Malu plays a significant role in country through the Dreaming, sustaining songlines and tracks across the continent – "the lines and centres of energy upon which our culture and all humanity is dependent for sustaining its balance and centredness". This is a traditional cultural view of landscape ecology and the web of life that also serves conservation. Kangaroo slaughter and the loss of habitat can only be detrimental to the wellbeing of both Aboriginal and other cultures, wrote Uncle Max.

Indigenous kangaroo activist Aunty Ro Mudyin Godwin, who lives in the Blue Mountains near Sydney, has fought long and hard for the totem kangaroo in mainstream Australia's public arena. She is scathing in her criticisms of modern Australia's disrespect for its national emblem. And she says aloud that she has no time for any present-day Aboriginal people who try to express culture by matching the white man in animal brutality.

"There is nothing cultural about barbaric practices," she told me. "It's not about mass killing. There is nothing traditional about driving through the bush gunning down whole mobs, or trying to buy into the commercial industry. Culture is about taking as you need, and giving back and conserving wildlife."

Just how little has changed in the thinking of some influential pastoralists, scientists, and media organisations is clear from her voluminous correspondence. Recently, she wrote a letter to a grazier outside Braidwood NSW after he was profiled by the national broad-caster, the ABC, on his clever way of turning a hopping "invader on his land" into a desirable dinner item. The same article quoted one of the Australian National University Fenner School scientists who have lent their academic credentials to justifying large-scale kangaroo slaughters. Aunty Ro wrote to her as well. And to the ABC.

To the pastoralist she wrote: "You are forcibly eradicating a Sacred Totem Animal from their ancestral home via mass indiscriminate slaughter, fuelled by an ideology that has seen irreversible destruction continue on country for over 200 years."

OVERSEAS VIEWS AND A STANDOUT CAMPAIGN FOR KANGAROOS

Australia's hypocrisy is more notable on the world stage. Says Dror Ben-Ami, who now lives and works in Israel: "Australia has taken on this knight in shining armour position against Japan on whaling. The government has taken Japan to the international court of justice, funding the lawyers. Yet, Australia is killing kangaroos by the millions. The hypocrisy is unbelievable. How blind do we have to be to our own folly?"

Critical overseas views on Australia's treatment of its wildlife (and that includes the well-loved koala) continue to shine a spotlight that hardly penetrates domestically. Australia is not alone in believing its cultural myths and values are civilised while other cultures are barbaric (whale and seal hunts being exhibit A). But overseas critics looking at Australia see an economic narrative steeped in colonial myth, and a casual attitude to native animal suffering.

One of the most successful efforts on behalf of Australia's kangaroos was led by Viva!, the British vegan animal welfare organisation. Their campaign started in the 1990s and continued for two decades. Viva! Director Juliet Gellatley visited Australia on several occasions, and achieved a deluge of media attention as she argued with reporters and kangaroo shooters, taking no prisoners.

Here's a summary of that campaign, as told to me. (The full Viva! campaign as described can be found in the Appendix.)

"In 1994, shortly after the launch of Viva!, our attention was drawn to a new 'product' range in Tesco's meat chillers, simply labelled 'kangaroo steaks'. We discovered that this so-called delicacy was the product of the largest slaughter of land-based wildlife in history – hunted at night in the vast outback, with powerful four-track vehicles and mesmerising search lights, the startled animals are shot, supposedly in the head.

"We obtained video footage of a kangaroo shooter in action exposing a cruel and barbaric blood bath. The footage showed animals being shot in the throat, their legs slashed open, a hook inserted and they were hauled on to the back of the vehicle, still gasping in agony. Large, still-conscious males were dragged up by their testicles.

"Determined to stop this cruelty we targeted Tesco – persistently campaigning for two years to show the truth of the matter to consumers. We printed specific materials for their customers, organising hundreds of local groups outside their stores to distribute it, and supplied information to the media. The culmination was a double-page spread in the *News of the World* on kangaroo killing; Tesco dropped the trade four days later. That was 26 September 1997. As a result Somerfield also dropped sales, cancelling an entire frozen food range."

Following that success in the UK, in 1998, Gellatley was invited to Australia by various wildlife groups and created a storm of controversy – doing about 50 media interviews and a press conference at Canberra's Parliament House, filmed live on national and regional TV news. She returned to the UK to reinvigorate the campaign – including a demonstration outside Sainsbury's supermarket's headquarters in London on 24 July 1998.

Juliet Gellatley returned to Australia again in 2002. She appeared on the popular *60 Minutes*, exposing key issues with the kangaroo slaughter. She visited the home of a kangaroo shooter to debate the industry. The hope was to build a collaborative network across countries. To some extent that has succeeded.

Kangaroo skin football boots made the headlines in 2011, after it was discovered that large manufacturers (such as Adidas) were moving away from using the leather due to pressure from Viva! and other groups. A quick check in 2019 indicated the big four (Adidas, Nike, Umbro and Puma) still used some kangaroo leather for sports shoes.

Kangaroo meat began making a resurgence in British supermarkets around 2013 when budget chain Lidl introduced a promotional burger range. Viva! re-energised its campaign again with consumer protests and press coverage and soon Lidl and others responded positively.

This model campaign, carried out over two decades, showed how persistent the Australian kangaroo industry has been but also that persistence in return paid off.

A EUROPEAN FILM SHOW AND AUSTRALIAN FURY

According to the Eurogroup for Animals (the welfare alliance that advises the European Union), it is continental Europe (mainly Belgium, Germany and the Netherlands) that is Australia's biggest market for kangaroo meat and skins. The EU had been buying upward of 1000 tonnes of kangaroo meat per year – the carcases of more than one million kangaroos.[15]

Eurogroup, wanting to change this with bans, in March 2018 screened the film Kangaroo: A Love-Hate Story to the EU representatives and invited a panel featuring the team of Pearson, Ben-Ami and Uncle Max. They were joined by the filmmakers, Mick McIntyre and Kate McIntyre Clere, and then Australian Greens federal Senator Lee Rhiannon. They testified about the unmonitored killing fields, and the cruelty, unsustainability, and food hygiene issues relating to an unchanged trade.

At the time, the EU was in trade negotiations with Australia. The film was part of a Europe-wide campaign – testing kangaroo meat in different countries with hopes of consumer campaigns and a ban by the European Commission if enough evidence warranted it. Ben-Ami said that early testing in the Netherlands showed all fresh meat samples were washed with acetic acid and lactic acid, and many still showed E. coli contamination.

Until she retired, Lee Rhiannon was one of very few Australian politicians, including from her own Greens party federally (and in the national capital, where Greens in coalition with Labor managed the kangaroo slaughter), to stand up publicly for the 'common' wildlife. She went to Europe, because, she said at the time: "Myths about kangaroos are uncritically repeated as facts in Australia and abroad which provides social and political license to keep shooting these animals beyond their reproductive capacity. Most people still aren't aware that government management of kangaroos is not from a framework of conservation, but from an intent to bolster commercial shooting."

The European trip was either unreported or damned back home. A closer look at some domestic political and media reaction shows the neo-colonial mentality of delivering wildlife units for export sale has hardly abated. Strong pressure to conform had not gone away, either.

National Party federal Agriculture Minister David Littleproud – who was soon to be engulfed in a major scandal involving Australia's live sheep export trade after reports of tens of thousands of ship-board deaths and calls to end the trade for unavoidable animal cruelty – called the action of Australians talking to the EU about the cruel kangaroo trade "treason." He said this to the right-wing Murdoch press in March 2018. (Littleproud also quickly dismissed the reports of sheep deaths at sea as activist exaggerations threatening a good Australian industry.)

I looked around, and found that the treason talk resonated well with, for example, a regional columnist in the Wagga Wagga *Daily Advertiser*, a Fairfax paper in an agricultural community. (For context, columnist Keith Wheeler had also fulminated against gay marriage and climate science in those pages.) He reminded his readers that Australia is first and forever a raw resource exporter. On show was a tendency to call anyone opposing the export meat trade socialists, communists, or worse, unpatriotic Greens. He didn't get to evil vegetarians, but others have. Rhiannon matched at least two of these criteria.

"[Federal Senator from NSW] Lee Rhiannon's trip overseas with the Greens-led delegation to help launch the new *Kangaroo* movie has a much more sinister edge," wrote Wheeler. "Suspicion should be aroused when the tourists include ratbags like NSW Animal Justice Party MP Mark Pearson." He called the documentary an attack on Australia's kangaroo meat trade and economy with subversive intent. He quoted Murdoch media on Rhiannon's parents' post-war left-wing political activism, and noted darkly that the senator as a teenager had attracted an impressive government file herself for protesting.

In Wheeler's view, Senator Rhiannon's hidden agenda still is to end capitalism, which is playing out in her treacherous efforts to undermine Australian exports. Attempts to frame kangaroos as anything other than a cog in Australian export production are part of this anti-capitalist crusade.

He wrote: "It's worth looking at Australia's exports and how protests, led or condoned by The Greens are threatening our export industries, and our standard of living. Food and other primary products account for a total of 13.9 per cent of our exports. An unchecked kangaroo plague could threaten all our food industries."

Whether it is about animal welfare, vegetation management, or rejecting coal mines, those who disagree with the viewpoint that Australia's forever destiny is as an export quarry, are seen as a threat. "Losing our exports would crash the Australian economy ... Humane culling when the meat is sold for export is a great rural opportunity," he insisted.[16]

UNITED STATES: SKINS AND FOOTBALL SHOES

Following the 1980s success by Peter Rawlinson and Australian mainstream conservation groups in convincing US authorities not to import kangaroo products, the situation slowly reverted to a less secure tenure by 1995. In March of that year, Red and Grey kangaroos that had benefitted from being listed under the United States Endangered Species Act as threatened were delisted from the Act. Thereafter the United States Fish and Wildlife service had options to list, delist, or keep the species under review.

As I found out earlier, listing Red and Grey kangaroos as an endangered species was a required US technicality, due to Australia's ongoing lack of an actual conservation plan for those traded species. That detail dropped off the radar as people argued about total numbers and whether kangaroos are endangered or not.

Although mainstream Australian conservation groups dropped kangaroos as an issue by the mid-1990s, in the 1980s Greenpeace was still in the frontline of the international trade pushback, running a successful campaign targeted at brand-name sports and football shoes that used kangaroo skins.

The Christian Science Monitor reported in 1987 that "the environmental lobbying group wrote to firms in Britain, showing them an advertisement that they planned to produce naming shoe companies that use kangaroo. '[The firms] had an opportunity to stop their name from being associated with kangaroo skin, and they took it,' says Ms. [Lorraine] Thorne. Indeed, four of the companies – including Nike and New Balance – have vowed to make their products kangaroo-free worldwide." A similar trade-focused campaign was mounted domestically in the US, naming companies that used kangaroo skins in their products.[17]

Skins have been the main trading item internationally from the beginning. They were used for everything from handbags to baseball gloves, as well as sports shoes. In 1987, it was a trade worth $10 million. It was reported in 1987 that Australia had 19 million kangaroos.[18] But the counts then were already labelled misleading, earning US mistrust, as highlighted in Rawlinson's 1983 campaign aided by the conservation groups.

Fast forward 30 years. Despite the commercial harvest, pest shooting, droughts and floods, disease epidemics, and incremental loss of habitat, the federal government by 2015 claimed domestically and internationally that kangaroos had boomed to a population of about 50 million, twice as many as the human population – which is much more visible. This would play out interestingly in the US in that same year.

CALIFORNIA HOLDS FAST, ALMOST
The US state of California, with the eighth largest economy in the world, and populous enough to outrank many a European country, had held fast with a kangaroo product ban – keeping up a tradition set since 1971, when then Governor Ronald Reagan signed legislation to keep the trade out. The ban was temporarily lifted around 2007, and sports shoe manufacturers rushed in.[19]

The issue came to a head in 2015, when the ban was about to be reinstated. California leads the United States in environmental and animal welfare progress, and kangaroo advocates were hoping that a ban in this massive economy would encourage sports shoe makers to move away from kangaroo leather entirely.

In the ensuing battle for the hearts and minds of California legislators, the Australian government was accused of paying US public relations firms to covertly lobby for the ban to be dropped entirely, encouraging a bill amendment to that end. Kangaroo defenders came together from Australia, the UK, and elsewhere to support the Humane Society of the United States in acquainting California legislators with the real facts of kangaroo 'harvesting'.

It was reported at the time that to lobby in California (with the assistance of then Australian ambassador to the US, Kim Beazley), the Australian Department of Agriculture funnelled $143,000 to the Kangaroo Industries Association of Australia in an effort to "retain market access to California." Some of the money went to hiring the lobbying firm Manatt, Phelps & Phillips.[20]

As a result, a complaint was filed with the California Fair Political Practices Commission, accusing the Australian government of sidestepping regulation by failing to register as a lobbyist employer.

The Humane Society of the United States' then CEO Wayne Pacelle told the media: "Californians want nothing to do with Australia's massive commercial slaughter of millions of these wonderful creatures every year. Companies using kangaroo skins for shoes and meat for pet food have alternatives and we call on them to stop making products from Australia's iconic kangaroos."[21]

The campaigners brought a cute Red kangaroo with joey in pouch to the California House of Assembly in Sacramento. The assemblyman who was being lobbied to secretly switch a gambling industry amendment for an Australian-drafted amendment to continue kangaroo imports was photographed beaming with the animals.

The Australian government's hands – in tandem with the commercial Kangaroo Industry Association of Australia (KIAA) – were all over this California push for the skins trade. Sacramento's daily newspaper, *The Sacramento Bee*, described the attempted legislative switch as the swamp of influence peddling by a foreign government.[22]

Following a Senate Estimates hearing in the Australian parliament, it was revealed by Lee Rhiannon's office that the KIAA had represented itself to the Californians as "representing wildlife management services in coordination with the Australian Government" and representing government-licensed kangaroo harvesters. The impression they hoped for was that they were a government body involved in wildlife conservation, said Senator Rhiannon.[23]

ENTER AGAIN SCIENCE

Hard-to-repel narratives of abundance and sustainability are purchased from the offices of the Rural Industries Research and Development Corporation (RIRDC) – a semi-autonomous, publicly-funded research and development agency. Like much of Australia's rural research, its work has a strong focus on exploitation of natural resources for export. RIRDC has a 'new and emerging industries' portfolio that includes monetising native animals for the export trade – kangaroo species chief amongst. That section is directed and partially funded by the KIAA.

RIRDC reports are paid consultant products, not government documents or independent scientific papers. But they may carry a persuasive university logo through the consultant researcher. Ecologist Ray Mjadwesch and his partner former Greens political adviser Helen Bergen have examined how RIRDC is used to support the commercial kangaroo industry. "Every one of its 72 reports on kangaroos is part of a sophisticated decades-old communication strategy. The purpose of every report is to grow the market," they wrote in late 2013.[24]

The expert-looking publications are then used by embassies and trade commissions and handed out to media under the banner of RIRDC. The goal is to convince domestic and overseas markets that consumption of kangaroo skins and meat should increase, and is a sustainable, good idea.

A parallel goal is to allay fears that are realistic but might hinder trade. Reports were produced to counter concerns – the ones that convinced the Russians, UK supermarkets, and possibly the Chinese – about health risks from pathogens in kangaroo carcasses – essentially wildlife bushmeat that is dismembered and often handled in unhygienic field conditions.

Beyond fears about unsanitary storage, in 2020 bushmeat was very much on the global radar with the risks of zoonotic viruses that can come along with consuming wildlife. Concerns about cruelty and sustainability troubling some potential client countries also needed dealing with.

In 2015, armed with RIRDC and KIAA reports, the abundance and sustainability narratives were deployed by the Australian Ambassador and the PR firm the government hired to lobby California legislators.

At the end of that campaign, in a celebrated win for Australia's kangaroos and international activist cooperation, the suspended ban on importing skins and meat was reintroduced at the end of 2015.

Then, in 2020, news emerged that some major sporting shoe companies were flouting the ban by supplying sales of kangaroo leather soccer and other sports shoes in California. The state's hard-pressed wildlife law-enforcement agency had not pursued them for it. Wayne Pacelle moved from Humane Society International to a new non-profit established to act as a change agent in the commercial world, starting with doing something about this breach. The new campaign has been joined by Olympic athletes and former Los Angeles prosecutor Robert Ferber who was outraged on learning that California law was so disregarded.

Under the title 'Kangaroos are not Shoes,' the Center for a Humane Economy is following in the footsteps of Greenpeace and Viva! with an international consumer campaign discouraging the use of kangaroo skins. Australia's apocalyptic wildfires and wild-life loss feature as the context, as does the decision by some state governments, notably NSW and Victoria, to continue shooting the surviving kangaroos as if nothing happened.

The Center's goal is to convince major sport shoe brands to not only abide by the law and stop selling kangaroo leather sports shoes in California, but to step away from this bloody wildlife trade altogether and embrace more ethically-sourced alternatives.

In a letter to the CEO of Nike, Wayne Pacelle reminded the shoemaker of its pioneering in the use of alternative synthetic materials. Even more interesting recycled and plant-based leathers were coming on line, including from corn, pineapple fibre, orange peel, and algae, joining cotton and hemp as key source ingredients, he wrote. Readers, watch that space.[25]

SHARING

Sharing with wildlife on author's property during drought of 2019–20.

Photo: Maria Taylor

After 30 years of living in the bush I know a bit about living with wildlife, but I did not know anything about building soil, regenerating the overgrazed, water-eroded, and sun-bleached sections of the property. I was about to find out more, visiting with some big landholders who were sharing the land with indigenous animals and encouraging the indigenous plants, with an appreciation of biodiversity and resilience. They had been learning in the past decades to live with the nature of Australia, rather than fight it.

A good anecdote about how to learn from indigenous inhabitants was told by zoologist Hugh Tyndale-Biscoe based on his field trips to western NSW where he and students stayed on a property near Booligal. The owner did not kill kangaroos but rather observed them as indicators of the health of his paddocks.

When the kangaroos left it was time to shift the sheep and spell the paddock. This happened through dry years and wet throughout the '60s and early '70s, reported Tyndale-Biscoe. The property retained good saltbush and much native grass and good sheep production at times when neighbours were destocking.[1]

Listen again to British-trained biologist and ecologist Francis Ratcliffe, who was hired by the Council for Scientific and Industrial Research (CSIR, later CSIRO) in 1935 to look into the severe soil erosion of central Australia, following less than 100 years of sheep pastoralism. He came to the unpopular conclusion that overhauling the previous ecology of native animals and plants was not the main solution.

Ratcliffe was a product of the imperial science that shaped Australian thinking. But he concluded that putting sheep or cattle on the boom and bust landscapes of Australia was based on some serious miscalculations and incompatible premises.

He concluded that "the only thing that would preserve the country would be 'consciously to plan a decrease in the density of pastoral population of the inland' ... to fit the social and economic order to the natural one".[2]

Today, there are farmers and other landholders taking up Radcliffe's advice and striving to become part of a more natural order while still successfully running a business on the land. In the past decades, there has been much successful experimentation with land regeneration to revive soil, water, and vegetation natural systems. Some without embarrassment call it farming in greater harmony with nature – they mean the nature of Australian land-forms and weather.

Others have turned land into private conservation reserves, while still feeding sheep or cattle or growing some crops. There are also attempts to learn more from traditional Aboriginal land management practices and ecological understandings as part of an abiding relationship to this unique land and its unique animals and plants.

I set out to learn more from some of these innovators and self-taught researchers – people who have taken a different path from the traditional mixed grazing and cropping model. I wanted to learn how they included the natural fauna in these new farming systems. Most concentrate on building and sheltering soil as the basic ecology of their enterprises, bringing back the natural grasses, unlocking long dormant seeds, and keeping ground cover.

I wanted to know whether graziers committed to regenerating Australian natural systems continue to calculate that they have to shoot macropods to 'save the grass'? Alternately, does sharing the land with the wildlife bring land-care benefits? And what benefits, financial and otherwise, accrue to those who are forging the way with wildlife ecotourism?

Jock Marshall noted in the mid-1960s: "A considerable number of Victorian sheep farmers, living as they do in a State where kangaroos were long ago almost exterminated would be glad to see a few roos hopping around their paddocks. A few intelligent and cultivated sheep farmers in southern New South Wales have already made their properties a sanctuary. They believe that it is worth running a few sheep less for the privilege of having a few wild marsupials on the place. Such people are rare, but it is hoped that their practice will spread."[3]

In 2019, I met people who think like that.

En-route to learning more about ecotourist potential, I came across this humorous endorsement for the value of wildlife tourism to Australia. Said a ranger on Tasmania's Maria Island, which is a wombat haven: "The tourists are in love with the wombats; so in love that we need to give them some education about how to interact with them." That led to asking for this promise: "I pledge, I will not chase you with my selfie stick."

Tasmania's Maria Island is a national park, and as well as wombats, it is home to Cape Barren geese, Forester (Grey) kangaroos, Bennett's Red-necked wallabies and Tasmanian devils. Tourists on Maria Island have doubled in number in the past decade – to 31,000 annually and climbing. Enthused one in an Instagram post: "This place is like the Galapagos of Australia!"[4]

WILDLIFE TOURISM ON TRADITIONAL GRAZING PROPERTY

Terri Irwin, along with her late husband Steve, did much to popularise and say it's okay to love Australian wildlife – notably the slithery and snappy variety. Terri is still doing this work. These days, much of her time is spent filming segments for a television program called *Crikey! It's the Irwins*, along with her children Bindi and Robert, while working alongside some 500 staff at the family-owned Australia Zoo. The zoo now houses more than 1,200 animals on about 1,000 acres of Sunshine Coast bushland. There is also a wildlife rescue hospital. Terri tells me that the goal with every animal species in captivity is to also help the wild populations. It is very much her goal to increase the appreciation and conservation of Australia's unique wildlife.

"When Steve and I married in 1992," she tells me, "we spent the first six years of our marriage filming, studying, and doing conservation work throughout Australia. I have seen a lot of Australia that has given me personal insight ... and more recently I've seen thousands of animals that have come through the wildlife hospital that we opened in 2004 [at Australia Zoo]." The hospital has treated the whole range of Aussie native animals – including rescued sea snakes and turtles, flying foxes and other bats, koalas in need of chlamydia vaccination.

This is all good. But Terri wants to talk about the still unresolved and unequal relationship between humans on production properties and the common wildlife, particularly kangaroos. We talk about her family's conservation grazing properties in central Queensland and in the Queensland gulf country. Both properties are living experiments, in that they allow the natural wildlife – from dingo to emu to kangaroo – to co-exist and live peacefully.

In central Queensland, between St George and Roma, neighbours may still be shooting kangaroos, poisoning dingos, or fencing emus from their path to food and water, but not on Mourachan. Steve and Terri allowed the property to revegetate naturally after they acquired it in the early 2000s. An unsuccessful attempt at establishing young river red gums indicated that regrowth was the easiest path. It proved too difficult to keep the water up to planted trees during drought. Terri tells me that the plan now is to consult with an ecologist about habitat management by increasing the diversity of the plant life. The property continues to commercially run some cattle.

Mourachan lies in the brigalow (acacia woodland) belt – a landscape that has suffered extensive clearing. Their holding expanded from an original block of 25,000 acres to now managing 118,000 acres (47,753 hectares) plus a neighbouring block recently added. (Terri's American heritage and Australian bush experience shows, with the preference for talking about acres rather than hectares.) "The intent was to manage it so things weren't being culled or killed on the property."

Steve and Terri started out with a project engaging the neighbours to document the presence of the rare Woma python. That worked out wonderfully, but what was disheartening was how much kangaroo shooting was going on. That's when they learned about Australia's industrial-scale kangaroo meat and skin industry, and how extremely poorly regulated it is. "I've seen really sad things with kangaroos," she tells me. "Probably 15 years ago, one of the first things we'd have to do when we go out to the property would be to humanely euthanise all of the injured kangaroos.

"Nobody is following these people around to see how they are killing the animals. There is also a sense if you are a landowner that you can treat wildlife in any way that you see fit without requesting permission or a permit. And, the manner in which the kangaroos are being killed was really eye-opening. It is essentially just a bush-meat trade."

REBALANCE TO NATURE WITH WILDLIFE-FRIENDLY FENCING, TREES, LONGER GRASS

Rebalancing the property with nature required removing some of the property's features, and expanding others. For wildlife, that included removing kilometres of old fencing, or modifying it to wildlife-friendly fencing – a project that Steve Irwin started and convinced the neighbours would be okay. "So we did it, and all these little animals, fruit bats, and gliders were no longer getting caught on the top strand," Terri told me. "And the bottom strand is not hurting animals ducking under the fence that kangaroos prefer to do. It's been working for nearly two decades. I'm really excited about things like that."

Commercial kangaroo and sports shooters, who, it was observed, shot anything that moved, and who had been coming freely onto the property, were denied access. It was a lengthy process. After years, Steve and Terri got the last roo shooters off their land – although not before being told by the police in St George that some people with roo shooting licenses were ex-felons and dangerous people, with guns, and to stay clear.

Wildlife and flora studies and fauna counts took their place. A longer-term aim has been to establish endangered species breeding areas for bilbies and Northern Hairy-nosed wombats, Woma pythons and Yakka skinks, common to the area before European settlement.

Regeneration of trees and shrubs was a key factor in retaining good ground cover, and went hand in hand with habitat restoration. It also helped move on the kangaroo shooters. That was when the vegetation reached a point that the shooters could no longer see the kangaroos as they would on a cleared paddock, said Terri.

Glancing back at settlement history, it is not hard to see that the European radical tree clearing to gain more grass invited the native grazers to congregate in the first years after clearing. With more clearing and set-stocking keeping grass height low, the cycle would encourage constant new growth. Terri still sees it in the neighbourhood: "One of the ironies is people who clear-fell to get more grass. Then it actually attracts kangaroos, because essentially you are building a golf course. 'Wow, we'll come to your house!'

"On our property, we have different vegetation areas, some grassed areas, some treed areas. Less of a monoculture still allows good beef yields while inviting less roos." Along with creating other biodiverse habitat.

The property has a complete live-and-let-live policy for native animals, while also running 300 head of cattle that bring in comparable income per head to other traditionally-run properties. Terri tells me they always have adequate grass, partly thanks to the vege-tation cover they re-established. The contrast is most noticeable when neighbouring properties have suffered badly in dry years. Terri says the wildlife populations all now have stable numbers. The birdlife is fantastic.

ADVENTURE TOURISM

The next step with the help of online marketing was to introduce wildlife tourism, billed as outback adventures or photography expeditions, with food and accommodation laid on. The venture showed that ecotourism brings in good money that can be rein-vested in the land. Websites and social media have made marketing much easier for country people.

"People will spend thousands of dollars for an outback experience where they can see this wildlife. Seventy percent of international tourists want to see our wildlife. We know in Africa it really works – people protect the wildlife and have livestock and when people come on your property to see the wildlife, they pay a token fee. And we're doing it so that we preserve the emus and the kangaroos and the goannas.

"Where we are the emus are so sweet, they don't even protect the chicks from you. They're just really cruisy. You can go out and see the emus and kangaroos and dingos. Because we don't shoot them, you'll see them. Others could do that in a very short amount of time. Many people want to participate – whether they're bird watchers or photographers or artists – all walks of life."

Portrait of Kirra the dingo.

"Let our dingo be. Look after the dingo, don't destroy him. The dingos would say: 'Let's share the country'."

AUNTY MARIE WILKINSON, BUTCHULLA ELDER, FRASER ISLAND (K'GARI).

Terri Irwin knows other landholders that are proactive with conservation, and adds: "The thing is, Australians are ahead of the game, because they figured out farm-stay a long time ago. People want to share the country life, the farm experience. It's been very successful for us and we can reinvest what we are earning back into conservation."

The immediate worry is the cluster fences that segment the wider landscape: deadly hazards blocking wildlife corridors and access to water. As a large property, Mourachan can manage the wildlife presence, but the problems being created are regional. "You'll have these tiny little distorted gene pools and you won't have a healthy ecosystem," Terri notes. Disease risk mounts as populations become genetically less diverse.

The African experience has shown that where game farms tried to fence in particular species, it doesn't work. They learned to have wildlife corridors and to cooperate with neighbours. Beyond Mourachan, continued clearing, overstocking, and salination of the soil are ecosystem issues besetting the area's habitats and ability to regenerate – or indeed for graziers' ability to farm profitably over the long haul.

When we spoke, Terri was alarmed that Balonne Shire local government was promoting a taxpayer-funding cluster fencing exercise to extend across the whole shire, on behalf of a resurgent sheep industry that claims to be beset by wild dogs, most of which are likely to be feral dogs escaped from humans, not dingos. Terri tells me there has been no attempt at any environmental impact assessment of the cluster fencing. She'll be asking about it.

Never one to shrink from a challenge – although this one is proving harder than snake-handling – Terri was also intent on convincing the Queensland government about the economic value of linking tourism and conservation for remote areas. She notes that for a small government investment, another 100 (doubling the current number in the whole state) Indigenous Land and Sea Rangers could be employed for remote tourism opportunities. That is still a modest goal. In comparison, the Irwin family's Australia Zoo alone employs up to 500 staff.

The ecotourism at Mourachan blends Australiana, like making damper and enjoying "an Aussie classic cup of tea," with wildlife encounters and nature walk-and-talks. River and wetland exploration are options. There are opportunities to photograph landscapes, relics, and old buildings on farm and in nearby town, backgrounded by the red earth – the picturesque iconography of inland Australia.

Iconic wildlife in this brigalow environment includes the emu and Eastern Grey kangaroos, Wallaroos/Euros and the Black/Swamp wallabies; bats and gliders; The Lace monitor and two other goanna species; skinks, geckos and lizards; and a lucky person may spot the rare Woma python. Also rare and present is the Warty Waterholding frog. Birds include the well-known kookaburra, Hooded robin, tawny frogmouth, cuckoo, currawong, choughs and more. Many more birds fly along the Balonne River outside St George. Dingos are allowed to live at Mourachan. And there are introduced wildlife species as everywhere in Australia.

When we spoke, Terri said the grass had remained sustainable despite the decade of dry conditions: "In my experience where we have left the kangaroos and the dingos, if you fly over it, it looks like an island. Everything around it has been decimated but our property is always healthy and we have roos, dingos and also cattle. Neighbours have come and asked to agist cattle on our property.

"I find it ironic because if their methods of extermination of certain types of wildlife and their husbandry are all working: why are they asking the person with kangaroos and dingos and conservation methods to agist? The grass is always greener on my side of the fence, literally."

While the Mourachan managers cull feral domestic dogs, dingos
are not proving a problem. "We have dingos and now that they are
realising that they're not getting shot we can see them. And they
are quite calm, they don't thrill-kill. We haven't lost a single calf,
although they might go more for lambs." The bonus, she said, is
that the dingos are really knocking the cats and the foxes. "I'm just
not seeing the problem, other than we humans are propagating the
problem with domestic dogs.

"And the kangaroos, I just don't get it. Why people hate these
beautiful animals. But we don't want to surrender one blade of grass
that isn't for livestock earning us money. In reality, you really can
achieve balance. We have to find a way for people to earn a living
without destroying everything."

What has she learned? "If you leave nature alone, your land
flourishes more than if you're trying to play God and manage every
aspect."

RETURN TO NATURE AND REGENERATIVE FARMING

There's a promising sign on the gate to Severn Park, where Charles
and Fiona Massy have accomplished a radical farming makeover
to a more natural way of grazing their Merino sheep. 'Land for
Wildlife' says the sign. I have one of these on my own gate – it lets
visitors or passers-by know that people who live there protect and
promote wildlife habitat.

On the road to the house, I can see on either side how the
Monaro grassland is regenerating, with poa tussocks, stipa (cork-
screw grass), and other natives, including danthonia, nine-awned
grass, and native legumes.

Charles Massy is the author of *Call of the Reed Warbler*. Published
in 2017, it is an acclaimed and comprehensive exploration of what
has gone wrong with European farming and grazing methods, with
case studies of alternative ways of doing things. The big picture is

that the traditional colonial methods are speeding the process of desertification in Australian landscapes. They also increase the risk of financial ruin to graziers and family cropping operations faced with the high costs of annual fertilisers, chemicals, and machinery to plough up and 'improve' the soils.

Elsewhere, family farming has ceded to corporate conglomerates that often double down with European traditional thinking about the land and its inhabitants as a resource quarry, establishing the latest wave of land and water exploitation for export products. Ultimately, these farming methods are not good for human health, he writes, extracting a cost from chemical exposure and lowered food and fibre quality due to the microbiology missing from the soil.

In Massy's book, I read a series of landholder stories told by farmers and graziers who are regenerating their land. Here was a path for my questions about integrating wildlife. Massy talked to more than 80 producers for his research, and recommended some I could fruitfully chat with, starting with himself. I have built on those regeneration case studies with thanks to the author.

I wanted to learn how sheep and cattle producers can make a living without killing off the native fauna and flora – the tradition since settlement. Along the way I started learning how working with nature turns out to be good economics – saving a lot of money that isn't spent on a shopping list of chemicals, superphosphate, and other artificial inputs for soil.

Charlie Massy started our conversation with an anecdote from a senior Ngarigo law man, elder Rob Mason who has been advising him on some land management approaches. Rob Mason has cultural memories that came through his grandfather: that somewhere in the 1860s his great grandfather speared a Jabiru stork on nearby Lake Bundawindirri, now a dry bed, just up the road towards Berridale from the property. The lake then was full of bird life, including Magpie geese, Blue and Yellow budgerigars, and brolgas. Early surveyors mentioned seeing frequent fogs until midday in that valley, attesting to the transpiration water cycle function. "Within decades of overgrazing and clearing, we destroyed all that."

GROUND COVER: KEY TO SOIL HEALTH, BIODIVERSITY, AND LIVING WITH WILDLIFE

Massy reflects on what land regeneration has done for Severn Park's 2,000 once-degraded hectares. The healing started with a major tree-planting effort and tree regeneration, keeping in mind natural contours and creek lines. Maintaining year-round healthy grass cover with plant diversity is another key feature of regenerative farming and natural soil management.

That is accomplished by strict rotational grazing and conservative stock management. A more natural landscape that is not grazed down to ground level, and therefore seldom exhibits the golf-course-greens attraction of new pick for grazing marsupials, is a tool that comes with this management method.

On one early morning survey across the countryside, he said he marvelled at myriad spiderwebs, still wet with dew and glistening between the grass clumps. The spiders catch flies, grasshoppers, and other insects. They tell this landholder that the biodiversity on the property is returning to healthy landscape functions above and below the soil line. "The fact we no longer get regular devastating wingless grasshopper plagues is another indicator of increasing health," he says.

Adding tree and ground cover aids moisture retention, even if just from dew and encourages soil organisms to get busy. They are an essential part of biodiversity, creating "a different, living absorbent soil structure" as he describes it.[5]

He tells himself that it is not necessary to catalogue everything, but just knowing the biodiversity is coming back is good enough.

He can see the wildlife returning. Not only birds and invertebrates, but the marsupials as well. In his book, he writes fondly about the wallabies that are now fairly tame around the place.

"As a kid we had no swamp wallabies or wallaroos. Now there are scores of them. With their cute little anvil faces and little paws and ears, the wallabies placidly examine me each morning. Only the other day, we had the excitement of discovering a dunnart (a small hopping marsupial mouse), a native bush rat, three new frog species, and two previously unrecorded woodland birds."

On regular walks around the property, getting to know plants and identifying animal tracks, Charlie Massy and his grandchildren often came across a quiet, solid, and large Wallaroo who spent his time on the green grass in the woolshed yards. They named him Mr Kev. His naming, wrote Massy, somehow made him a recognisable personality, with habits and extended family. Too bad, he lamented, few children today have the opportunity.

WHOLESOME FOOD AND A TOP WOOL CLIP
Equally gratifying is the knowledge that the land regeneration and changed farming methods mean they are growing nutrient-rich food and achieve top class fibre with the wool clip. With holistic grazing management, he tells me, the sheep get a more balanced diet. The animals are continuously rotated every few days into fresh paddocks with greater plant diversity. This means better body weights and higher lambing percentages.

"Last year, due to this more even nutrition, we topped the Sydney wool market because ours was the only clip, in that drought year, that had high tensile strength: a key parameter for elite wool processing. We also have to drench far less, because the rotation breaks the intestinal worm cycle."

Charlie tells me his conversion to being an "enabler" (his description) of the land, rather than a person wedded to domination, came with the realisation that his innate love of nature could now be given full reign. He sees this as including aesthetic as well as intellectual, emotional, even spiritual connections to the land around us, rather than viewing the land as an inanimate block waiting to be cleared of previous life, improved and exploited for profit.

His thinking was helped by developing a friendship with some Aboriginal people. "This allowed me to gain some understanding of their organic approach to and nurturing of country" – their ever-present connections to and responsibility for the land and what it holds. He wrote in his book that "until we acknowledge Indigenous people's dispossession and collaborate with them to jointly regenerate and care for country, we can never achieve proper recon-ciliation between people and country".[6] As one example, Rod Mason taught the Massys and others in the district about cool burning to clean up and encourage grass growth, and the complexity of the decision-making required.

Physical and mental ill health in rural areas, he ventures, may well be related to traditional European farming methods and divorce from nature. Chemical farming doesn't help, with some properties being encouraged to pour dozens of chemicals on their crops for the season.

LONG-STANDING WILDLIFE SANCTUARY AND MANAGING THE ECOLOGY

From the New England tablelands of northern NSW, Tim Wright tells me in 2019 they're experiencing the worst drought since records started in 1850 – when his extended family started sheep grazing in the district. Some of the more shallow-rooted eucalypts are dying, he says sadly. Still, he has grass for his sheep, and he tolerates maybe 500 kangaroos (Greys and Wallaroos/Euros) sharing that grass (the numbers can be a problem, as the animals come in from neigh-bouring grassless properties).

The 3,350 hectares of the family property, Lana – with about five percent in hills and rocky country – are well-treed, both old-growth and planted. There is water: creeks, springs and bores on the property. But the key to having grass on the ground while the neighbours are buying in feed is a still-evolving system of rotational (or cell) grazing, that never lets the ground cover get close to being eaten out in any of the smallish paddocks.

After a near fatal end to his farming, brought on by the early 1980s drought, Tim made a radical sideways turn. It took four years financially, and longer for the land to recover. "I started to question everything," he told Charlie Massy for his book. "What I had learned in ag college; some of the scientific stuff in journals; I thought, 'there's got to be another way' or I won't survive here."

The answer arrived in 1989, with the work of Queensland agricultural scientist Terry McCosker channelling the work of Zimbabweans Allan Savory and Stan Parsons. They taught Australians about holistic planned grazing – that involved rotational grazing as a basic concept, together with rest and recovery of paddocks.

The secret, he realised, is not in having more land, but how you use what you have in your environment, on your land. He now sees himself as a holistic manager of his farm's ecology. The wildlife he may cherish the most are the soil microbes and insects, like parasitic wasps, bees, and beetles, that keep the system turning over and functioning healthily. The methods are completely strange to traditional broad acre graziers focused on pasture improvement, annual ploughing, sub clover, legumes, and improved varietals and aerial application of superphosphates.

Massy in his book describes the regenerative approach as maximising solar energy function through grazing management and grass utilisation, avoiding overgrazing any paddock. Tim Wright now has 300 paddocks averaging 20 acres, divided from 50 larger paddocks when he started down this road.[7]

It's not just about the insect life. Diverse ground cover is the most important aspect, he tells me, because of its capacity to store carbon and add organic matter. The secret is also in having a good water cycle. "We work our ground cover on kilograms per hectare with a range of plant species. What we've forgotten is that the monoculture society and monoculture farming is the worst thing we can do because it upsets the balance."

VALUE OF NATIVE PASTURES WITH VARIETY OF GRASSES

"We have our native grasses, including cool season perennials," Tim says. "They're coming and going all the time, and we refer to this as a 'state transition model.' The 'state' meaning that grass is from seedling through to seed stage. It is in transition because you're going from cool season to warm season growth. Our native grasses are still in the warm season phase, and the cool season perennials are all sitting there, though you wouldn't know it. They start growing in June and they'll always be green no matter the frost.

"You have different grasses which grow up on the ridge, grasses that grow down lower and they've all evolved over millions of years. [Traditionally] we go along and spray it all and say we have to improve pasture. But economically it's one of the worst things you can do, because it's short-lived and during a drought you have to re-sow most of what you've already sown."

Retaining ground cover by resting paddocks, while rotating large numbers of herbivores who leave their manure, also means less added fertiliser – or even that none need be applied. The activity of herbivores is intrinsic to the success of this system, whether it is returning organic matter through manure, or assisting with their hooves over a short period to loosen the soil crust so seed can more easily come to the surface.

Native herbivores also assist with the fertilising and in spreading seed through their droppings. Tim has largely stopped ploughing.

Whilst this is counterintuitive, stocking rates can be high, as Tim is showing, as long as the sheep are not set in one place, but are in constant rotation.

WORKING WITH ALL THE WILDLIFE, RETAIN TREES

Related to the famous Australian poet and environmental writer Judith Wright, Tim and his family have a history in education, agricultural innovation, and appreciating the native fauna. Tim's father declared the property a wildlife reserve back in the '60s, and today koalas live here as well as macropods including Wallaroos/Euros, Pademelons and other wallabies, along with the Eastern Grey kangaroos. Echidnas and platypus are other cared-for residents.

Some get a helping hand in the drought. "Only last week we fed koalas," Tim told me. "This time of year is mating time, so you can hear them calling out near our house." The trees on the property support eight endangered bird species according to a recent survey. "I put that down to our diversity of trees," he says.

Does Tim see benefits for the farm by integrating native animals? Big benefits, he says, and kangaroos are part of that – acknowledging my interest in them. He had already told me that he understood the mob structure with the role of the alpha males, saying that shooters should not take them out because it can lead to greater populations as well as genetic weakness.

Balance is the key. "If you haven't got the balance with the birdlife, the water, the turtles, the insects, and the grasses then things will be out of balance. That's when you get things dying back, like trees for example. The landscape suffers. I work with the wildlife. I don't have an issue with them at all."

I ask him where someone would start, and how long would it take to emulate what he has done on Lana. It won't take long, he says. "The first step is awareness. If they accept that tomorrow is another day, they can move toward a better frame of mind and start accepting alternatives – which I did 30 years ago. I started to question what I was doing and why I had to borrow money to survive."

Continuing education is a theme for all regenerative farmers I engaged with. Tim Wright is no exception. "Holistic management isn't just about agriculture. It's a way of thinking and decision-making. You ask why – why do I have bare ground? You then address this by looking at what you can do to change your management practices and treat the cause rather than the symptom."

The surge of tree clearing in NSW, including for cattle production, is mentioned. Simply from a farming standpoint, particular with a drought and the water needs of cattle, tree clearing is no answer and worse. "I'd rather see education aligned with regulation so that farmers learn the benefits of the trees. It's not there. If we want to point the finger, it's the government being totally oblivious to it."

And he adds: "We've got to take more note in terms of Australia's ancestors, the Aboriginal culture. How did they survive? What did they do? We're very different in that sense in that we are more industrialised. But they had the ability to manage the land in a way that survived the intense droughts."

SOUTHERN NSW GRAZIERS: THE BENEFITS OF NATURAL FARMING, ECOTOURISM

Grazing stock naturally, and merging biodiversity protection with production and a tourism business didn't come as a matter of course to the Butt family, third- and fourth-generation farmers in the capital region outside Canberra. But since 2008, when they visited Tim Wright's New England property on a Landcare-awards field trip, they haven't looked back.

These days, the Butts hardly drench their sheep. They haven't used fertiliser in 20 years on their 3,500 acres (1,300 hectares) of grazing land. The animals, feeding on a more diverse plant mix, in rotated, conservatively-stocked paddocks, are in better health and the wool results are stronger and more consistent. 2,500 acres (1000 hectares) additional woodland has been fenced off as a reserve.

I met Debra Butt, who manages the farm day to day, at a Landcare meeting in the region. This meeting was focused on how to encourage and protect biodiversity while making a living off the land. She told the story of her own and her parents' journey from conventional to regenerative farming. Later I was given a tour of the property, marvelling at a cluster of six-foot healthy grass trees (Xanthorrhoea) in their Picaree Hill reserve, and we talked further.

"Until the 1990s the property was conventionally-managed," she told me. "I'd go out to hand-feed the sheep. There were bare paddocks. I felt like I was pouring money on the ground and thought 'if this is what farming is all about, I don't think I want to do it.'"

Now they manage for 100 percent ground cover at all times. Debra is not the first grazier to tell me they have discovered that with higher ground cover the place is less of a magnet for kangaroos that like new green pick. This pushes the lethal management approach down or off the radar.

And there may be a growing awareness that the kangaroos, wallabies, wombats, and birds add value to this family's long-standing trail-riding business. The trails wind through their reserved land. Enjoying a glimpse of native wildlife, along with the trees and understory, like those grass trees that caught my eye, adds aesthetic value.

Debra's obvious satisfaction with preserving the habitat of less obvious native animals, including the Wedge-tailed eagle, or a shy marsupial, the mouse-like dunnart that is making a comeback on the property, is part of the lure of managing for biodiversity. Koalas used to live in this area. There might be a comeback.

"The exciting part is to do both conservation and production," she says. The added economic benefits of diversification to tourism benefits equally from conservation. In some years, the income from the trail-riding matches the wool cheque.

Unlike some regenerative farmers, the Butts don't use mathematics so much as observation to assess when stock should go on or off a paddock. "We won't put the stock back on until the plants are fully recovered," says Debra. Their 1,200 fine-wool Merinos are at their lowest number compared to the family's previous stocking rates. Those Merinos are now matched to carrying capacity, rather than pushing the numbers envelope. Quality has trumped quantity.

Managing the threat of predators has called on some additional lateral thinking. The family has deployed three alpacas for guard duty. They chase off canines. Her father was sceptical, admitted Debra. But that ended when an alpaca stayed guarding a sick sheep while a human went for extra help.

Debra and her partner Paul Foster also keep an eye on the growing sustainability market, which calls for both a greener approach to farming and responding to animal welfare issues, like an end to mulesing. (Mulesing is a painful skin removal process aimed at preventing rear-end wool growth and fly strike.) Ten years ago, the family took the step to end mulesing and use alternative methods. I mention that two major Australian retailers recently announced their woollen products would no longer be sourced from sheep that have suffered mulesing. Premium prices are a promising horizon.

REDISCOVERING THE NATURAL BALANCE

The need to maintain the land and its flora and fauna in 'balance' is a shared understanding between the regenerative farmer and Indigenous Australians.

Bwgcolman elder and artist Billy Doolan was born on Palm Island after his parents were separately relocated there. He is now a resident of Townsville, and a citizen of the world – having been invited to places like Italy and Hong Kong to share his intricate painting style born from a north Queensland tradition. His totem is the brolga, the graceful indigenous bird that often features in his work, and also the owl from the other parental side. Queensland post-colonial authorities threw people from 51 different Indigenous groups together on Palm Island. That brought together many totems – animals that cannot be hunted, harmed, or eaten.

Traditionally, totems balanced conservation between different Indigenous groups and their country. Eating another clan's totem gives him pause, said Billy Doolan. Offence and disrespect might be signalled.

Art, he says, is the only clear way he can now express himself. Traditionally, his people and other First Nation groups told their stories, their history, and understanding of living with the land and its creatures through art, song, and dance. One thing he wants to express is the understanding that things in modern culture are out of balance, and that there needs to be more compassion for his people and for the environment.

As a saltwater man, he is keenly attuned to the marine wildlife. The balance there has been lost, he told another interviewer. Too many turtles are taken as by-catch with the help of modern fishing machinery.

Without being prompted by questions, he tells me some things about the natural world – things that seem to have escaped many conventionally-trained managers of Australia's wildlife as they apply lethal methods of wildlife control on behalf of economic interests.

"Animals have their own laws. You take the alpha male – they keep everything in order from mating to feeding. Population is controlled by the alpha. Without them you see things going unbalanced. Animals of all types also depend on each other. They live by their laws too. Nature is truly magical. I've heard the old people say that and it's true. One only has to look."

Billy couldn't agree more with regenerative farmers in 2019. "You need more native grass cover," he says. Also, trees. Why cut all those trees? He has been told by cattle graziers in Queensland that trees are removed so the landholders can to keep an eye on the animals and make them easier to round up. "Then comes the rain, erosion, wind blows all the topsoil away."

We touch on ecotourism, and he tells me his own northern country has beautiful highly spiritual spaces and landforms. Visitors to Australia find the oldest landforms on the planet, he says. There is money to be made through ecotours, encouraging painting, fishing, walking untouched areas, and story-telling around a campfire.

In the old ways, he says, "we danced the trails, waterholes, animals. We were part of nature." Not separate as a dominator, I understand from this statement. "We walked with the animals. We are true children of the earth; it provided what we need. This place was virtually untouched when Captain Cook came. Animals were the ones that did all this," he tells me. He mentions the soil-enriching worms, insects that pollinate, eels that clean the rivers, and marsupial grazers with their soft feet unlike the hard-hooved animals that came with the invasion. "That's why we had the beautiful grasslands."

This man is an artist, not a university-trained agronomist or conservation biologist. But from traditional knowledge of what the land needs, he knows. "It's the native animals, they keep the system going."

I am reminded of this statement on a recent bushwalk in a national park near me in the foothills of the Snowy Mountains. The valley where we walked had abundant macropods, Red-necked wallabies, and Eastern Grey kangaroos. The healthy grassland, dotted with native trees and picturesque rocky outcrops, and bisected by chain-of-ponds watercourses, made me think of the park-like environment described by early settlers.

This was no artefact of Aboriginal burning. It was a balance between the plants and animals that existed here. Drought conditions in this part of NSW, as elsewhere, were much more evident as we approached the park in the grazed-off sheep paddocks dotted with undernourished stock.

"I'm a great-grandfather now," Billy told me. "I want my grand-kids to see the brolgas dancing. There is hope if people make changes to heal the land and live with the native species. Mother Earth can heal herself if we help. Don't overharvest, overfish, let them live, eat something else." He's speaking of prawns now. "Let them breed. If people keep doing what they do, things are going to be very bad. No water is going to be the end of us.

"Everybody is responsible to look after this beautiful country. It's just common sense."

Brush-tailed Rock-wallabies.

CHAPTER NOTES

1   'An open letter to the Prime Minister from 248 concerned scientists' – https://www.envirolawsopenletter.com.au/

CHAPTER ONE: DATELINE 2018–19: THE LEGACY

1   https://www.smh.com.au/environment/conservation/nsw-koalas-on-course-to-be-extinct-in-the-wild-by-2050-inquiry-finds-20200630-p557j2.html

2   https://www.pnas.org/content/112/15/4531

3   https://www.environment.gov.au/system/files/resources/d947f8ec-dd8b-4e7f-bd3b-8246e0702547/files/plants.pdf

4   https://www.smh.com.au/politics/federal/why-is-australia-a-global-leader-in-wildlife-extinctions-20200717-p55cyd.html

5   https://www.brisbanetimes.com.au/politics/federal/deficient-and-doomed-to-fail-experts-roast-threatened-species-plan-20180608-p4zkc3.html

6   https://www.theguardian.com/environment/2018/feb/13/a-national-disgrace-australias-extinction-crisis-is-unfolding-in-plain-sight

7   https://soe.environment.gov.au/

8   https://www.theguardian.com/environment/2018/jun/27/senate-inquiry-threatened-species-crisis?CMP=share_btn_link, https://www.theguardian.com/environment/2019/mar/30/record-numbers-of-australias-wildlife-species-face-imminent-extinction?CMP=share_btn_link

9   https://www.smh.com.au/politics/federal/morrison-government-resurrects-abbott-s-one-stop-shop-environment-laws-20200827-p55ptw.html
    https://www.theguardian.com/australia-news/2020/sep/06/recipe-for-extinction-why-australias-rush-to-change-environment-laws-is-sparking-widespread-concern
    https://www.abc.net.au/news/2020-09-06/wwf-koala-loss-report-finds-71pc-decline-after-fires

10 https://www.theguardian.com/environment/2018/oct/30/humanity-wiped-out-animals-since-1970-major-report-finds
    Wahlquist, C, 'UN environment warning: 10 key points and what Australia must do', *The Guardian*, 7 May 2019 – https://www.theguardian.com/environment/2019/may/07/un-environment-warning-10-key-points-and-what-australia-must-do

11 Wahlquist, ibid.

12 https://www.nytimes.com/2018/11/27/magazine/insect-apocalypse.html
    Wahlquist, ibid.

13 https://www.dpi.nsw.gov.au/hunting/volunteer-non-commercial-kangaroo-shooting
    www.dpi.nsw.gov.au/hunting

14   https://www.theland.com.au/story/6316654/fence-fix-for-roo-damage/

15   White, A, 'Half of kangaroos killed in Victorian cull turned to pet food', *Herald Sun*, 11 May 2016 – https://www.heraldsun.com.au/news/victoria/half-of-kangaroos-killed-in -victorian-cull-turned-to-pet-food/news-story/47cf313222e57d0451f56808ccc648c4 https://www.abc.net.au/news/2019-03-13/kangaroo-pet-food-trial-leaves-one-million-dead/10894082

16   'Kangaroo Pet Food Trial Evaluation', an internal report by the Department of Environment, Land, Water and Planning, Victoria State Government, undated (accessed 2019)

17   Carey, A, 'Farmers win as government decides not to can kangaroo pet food trial', *The Age*, 29 March 2019 – https://www.theage.com.au/politics/victoria/farmers-win-as-government-decides-not-to-can-kangaroo-pet-food-trial-20190328-p518nx.html https://www.standard.net.au/story/6414726/kangaroos-to-be-shot-for-pet-food-across-region/

18   'Victoria scrapes bottom of barrel on wildlife management', *The District Bulletin*, 4 October 2019 – https://districtbulletin.com.au/victoria-scrapes-bottom-of-the-barrel -on-wildlife-management/

Hylands P, 'Australian Native Birds die in thousands to please rice growers and hunters', *The District Bulletin*, 18 December 2019 – https://districtbulletin.com.au/ australian-native-birds-die-in-thousands-to-please-rice-growers-and-hunters/

19   https://thenewdaily.com.au/news/national/2019/08/01/wombats-killing-crown-casino/

20   https://www.theage.com.au/national/victoria/welcome-to-victoria-the-most-wombat-unfriendly-state-20190806-p52eax.html

21   https://www.theage.com.au/link/follow-20170101-10n8iv

Additional Reading

https://www.smh.com.au/politics/federal/australia-s-climbs-the-list-of-wildlife-extinction-hotspots-20210303-p577dy.html

NSW land clearing June 2020 – https://www.smh.com.au/environment/sustainability/nsw-farmers-accelerate-land-clearing-rates-doubling-previous-decade-20200701-p5581j.html

Private property conflict between carer and neighbour – https://www.bombalatimes.com.au/ story/6390255/deans-a-wildlife-carer-his-neighbours-want-to-cull-kangaroos/

Outcome of official narratives – bad behaviour –

https://www.theguardian.com/environment/2019/aug/29/wedge-tailed-eagles-among-120-native-birds-found-dead-in-victoria-after-suspected-poisoning

https://7news.com.au/news/animals/man-laughs-as-he-crosses-onto-opposite-lane-of-regional-road-to-hit-kangaroo-c-309934

CHAPTER TWO: RED KANGAROO , THE HOUR IS LATE, BUT ...

1   Hutchinson L, 'Kangaroos: from icon to asset', *Barrier Daily Truth*, p1, 24 July 2002

2   Brenchley F, 'Boycotts threat could put kangaroo meat off the menu', *The Australian Financial Review*, 12 September 1997 – https://www.afr.com/politics/boycotts-threat -could-put-kangaroo-meat-off-menu-19970912-k7nl4

3   Frith H J, *Kangaroos*, ACF newsletter, 3 April 1968

4   Correspondence in AWPC archive
5   https://www.abc.net.au/news/2019-11-05/harvest-cancelled-while-millions-of-kangaroos-starve-in-drought/11669190

CHAPTER THREE: DATELINE 1788: PRIVATE PROPERTY TAKEOVER

1   Lines W J, *Taming the Great South Land, A history of the conquest of nature in Australia*, Allen and Unwin, North Sydney NSW, 1992, p112
2   https://www.australiangeographic.com.au/topics/wildlife/2017/03/the-plight-of-the-dingo/
3   Horne D, *Money Made Us*, Penguin, Ringwood Vic, 1976, p24ff
4   Ibid., p26
5   Flood J, *The Original Australians: Story of the Aboriginal People*, Allen and Unwin, Sydney, 2006
6   Rose D, 'The dead, the missing, the lost, and the voiceless: some thoughts on extinction from a dingo perspective', conference paper, *The relationships between humans and animals*, 2004
7   Ibid.
8   O'Connor M R, *Wayfinding: The Science and Mystery of How Humans Navigate the World*, Affirm Press, 2019
9   Ibid., p172
10   Ibid., pp127, 129, 149
11   Pascoe B, *Dark Emu, Aboriginal Australia and the birth of agriculture*, Magabala Books, Broome WA, 2014
     Gammage B, *The Biggest Estate on Earth, how Aborigines made Australia*, Allen and Unwin, Sydney, 2011
12   Pascoe B, *Dark Emu*, ibid., pp99–102, quoting Sturt, *Narrative of an expedition into central Australia*, T and W Boone, 1849
13   Ibid., p100
14   Moorehead A, *The Fatal Impact*, Penguin, London, 1966, p169
15   Bottoms T, *Conspiracy of Silence*, Allen and Unwin, Sydney, 2013
16   Bates D, *Passing of the Aborigines*, 1939; 1947 John Murray London; Benediction Classics. 2009
17   Redmond A, 'Tracks and shadows: Some social effects of the 1938 Frobenius Expedition to the north-west Kimberley' – http://press-files.anu.edu.au/downloads/press/n2618/html/ch16.xhtml
18   Stanner W.E.H, *White Man Got No Dreaming: Essays 1938–1973*, 1979
19   https://www.abc.net.au/news/2020-07-13/stan-grant-black-lives-matter-four-corners/12429206?nw=0
20   Pascoe, ibid., p112, quoting Mitchell, T.L *Three Expeditions into the Interior of Eastern Australia*, vol 1 and 2, T and W Boone, London 1839
21   Linklater A, *Owning the Earth, the transforming history of land ownership*, 2014, Bloomsbury, London
22   Ibid., p211

23 Arneil B, *John Locke and America: The Defence of English Colonialism*, 1996, Oxford University Press

24 Clark M, *A Short History of Australia*, Penguin, 1986 edition, p41

25 Ibid., p23

26 Ibid., p15

27 Massy C, *Call of the Reed Warbler, a new agriculture, a new earth*, UQP, Brisbane, 2017, p31

28 Horne D, *Money Made Us*, ibid., p34

29 Ibid., p35

30 Pascoe B, 'Australia Temper and Bias', *Meanjin*, Spring 2018 – https://meanjin.com.au/essays/11312/

31 Hughes-D'Aeth. T, http://theconversation.com/friday-essay-dark-emu-and-the-blindness-of-australian-agriculture-97444

32 Taylor M, *Global Warming and Climate Change: What Australia Knew and Buried … Then Framed a New Reality for the Public*, ANU Press, 2014, p82

33 White L, 'The historical roots of our ecological crisis', *Science*, 1967

34 Massy C, *Call of the Reed Warbler*, ibid., p39

35 Dunbar-Ortiz R, 'The Colonial Roots of Gun Culture', *In These Times*, April 2018; excerpt from her book *Loaded: A Disarming History of the Second Amendment*

36 Lines W J, Ibid., p65

37 Ibid., p82

38 Andreasson S, 'Stand and Deliver: private property and the politics of global dispossession', *Political Studies*, Vol 54, 2006, pp3–22

39 Babie P, 'Private property suffuses life', *Sydney Law Review* 2017 39:135, pp135–46

40 Ibid.

41 Clark A, 'The great Australian silence 50 years on', *The Conversation*, 3 August 2018 – https://theconversation.com/friday-essay-the-great-australian-silence-50-years-on-100737

42 McKenna M, *From the Edge, Australia's lost histories*, The Miegunyah Press, Melbourne, 2016, p126

43 Ibid., p142

44 Ibid., p139

45 Slezak M, 'Scorched country: the destruction of Australia's native landscape', *The Guardian*, 7 March 2018 – https://www.theguardian.com/environment/2018/mar/07/scorched-country-the-destruction-of-australias-native-landscape

46 Graham N, 'Land clearing laws bring out worrying libertarian streak', *The Conversation*, 4 August 2014

47 Maron M, et al, 'Queensland land clearing is undermining Australia's environmental progress', *The Conversation*, 22 February 2016 – https://theconversation.com/queensland-land-clearing-is-undermining-australias-environmental-progress-54882

48 https://www.theguardian.com/australia-news/2018/aug/04/clearing-of-native-vegetation-in-nsw-jumps-800-in-three-years

49 http://www.environment.nsw.gov.au/resources/nativeveg/09751NVActReview.pdf

50   https://theconversation.com/the-nsw-government-is-choosing-to-undermine-native-vegetation-and-biodiversity-59066
51   http://districtbulletin.com.au/conservation-group-exposes-clearing-threat-koalawildlife-habitat/
52   Taylor M, *Global Warming and Climate Change,* ibid.
53   Lines W J, *Taming the Great South Land,* ibid., p251
54   Lunn H, *Joh: The Life and Political Adventures of Sir Johannes Bjelke-Petersen* (2nd ed.), UQP, Brisbane, 1987, p349
55   Taylor, M, 'Destruction of the Leard and threat to the Pilliga concerns everyone', *The District Bulletin*, March 2016
56   Horne D, *Money Made Us,* ibid., pp30–31
57   http://www.abc.net.au/news/2019-07-19/most-severe-recorded-drought-across-the-murray-darling/11325216
Quiggan J, https://www.theguardian.com/commentisfree/2019/jan/22/the-darling-river-fish-kill-is-what-comes-from-ignoring-decades-of-science
58   Sheldon F, 'The Darling River is simply not supposed to dry out even in drought', *The Conversation*, 16 Jan 2019 – https://theconversation.com/the-darling-river-is-simply-not-supposed-to-dry-out-even-in-drought-109880
https://www.abc.net.au/news/2020-11-17/murray-darling-missing-water-in-floodplains/12887342?utm_source=abc_news_web&utm_medium=content_shared&utm_content=mail&utm_campaign=abc_news_web
59   Vivian H, 'Cry me a river: Mismanagement and corruption have left the Darling dry', *Sydney Morning Herald*, 9 March 2018.
60   Ibid.
61   https://www.abc.net.au/news/rural/2019-08-02/cubbie-staion-sells-down-foreign-investment-stake/11377774#:~:text=Cubbie%20Station%20is%20located%20500,the%20Foreign%20Investment%20Review%20Board
62   https://www.theguardian.com/australia-news/2019/feb/04/rex-patrick-to-push-for-cotton-export-ban-to-raise-plight-of-murray-darling
63   Ibid.
64   https://www.theguardian.com/australia-news/2019/jan/22/murray-darling-river-aboriginal-culture-dry-elders-despair-walgett
65   Green D and Connors L, *The European Explorers and Settlers* https://core.ac.uk/download/pdf/11038269.pdf

Additional reading

https://districtbulletin.com.au/they-are-still-destroying-the-darling-river-ecology/ 19 February 2021
https://www.theguardian.com/australia-news/2017/aug/04/nsw-minister-gives-himself-power-to-approve-illegal-water-works-in-murray-darling-basin?CMP=share_btn_link
http://www.abc.net.au/news/2019-02-03/murray-darling-basin-a-crisis-of-water-and-climate-law/10769722 (SA Commission report)

https://districtbulletin.com.au/national-party-hold-over-water-land-and-wildlife/ Jan 2019
https://www.smh.com.au/national/the-modern-bushranger-feudal-overlord-of-a-dying-river-20190124-p50ti3.html

CHAPTER FOUR: CARING, MEET THE MACROPODS

1   Tyndale-Biscoe H, 'Kangaroos and sheep: the unequal contest', *Australasian Science*, July 2005, 26, 6 p29
2   Ibid.
3   Dawson T J, *Kangaroos*, (2nd ed.), CSIRO Publishing, Collingwood, 2014, p8
4   Croft D, 'Kangaroos maligned' in *Kangaroos Myths and Realities*, in Wilson M and Croft DB (eds) Australian Wildlife Protection Council, Melbourne, (3rd edition) 2005, p19
5   Dawson T J, *Kangaroos*, ibid., p11
6   Dawson media release
7   Croft D, *Kangaroos Myths and Realities*, ibid., p31
8   'The Role of Biodiversity in Climate Change Adaptation – a report to the ACT Commissioner for the Environment', Canberra Environment and Sustainability Resource Centre, 2009;
9   Dawson T J, *Kangaroos*, ibid., p156
10 Coulson G, Alviano P, Ramp D, Way S, McLean N, Yazgin V, 'The kangaroos of Yan Yean', *Nature Conservation in Production Environment*, 2000, pp146–156
11 Taylor M, 'Survival in Queanbeyan, a good news story', *The District Bulletin*, July 2013
12 Nicholls D, 'The Kangaroo – Falsely Maligned by Tradition' in Wilson M and Croft D B (eds), *Kangaroos Myths and Realities*, Australian Wildlife Protection Council (3rd ed) 2005, p40
13 Garlick S and Austen R, 'Post-traumatic stress disorders in kangaroos', Australian Wildlife Rehabilitation Conference, Hobart, Tasmania May 2014;
Garlick S and Austen R, 'Learning about the emotional lives of kangaroos, cognitive justice and environmental sustainability', *Relations: Beyond Anthropocentrism*, Vol 2, June 2014
14 https://theconversation.com/hugs-drugs-and-choices-helping-traumatised-animals-80962

CHAPTER FIVE: EDEN LOST: WHAT THE EARLY EXPLORERS SAW

1   Ryan D G, Ryan J E, and Starr BJ, 'The Australian Landscape – observations of explorers and early settlers', *Murrumbidgee Catchment Management Committee*, NSW Government Printing Service, undated
2   Auty J, 'Red Plague, Grey Plague' in *Kangaroos Myths and Realities*, 2005, p57
3   Barrow G, *'Magnificent' Lake George: the biography*, Dagraja Press, Canberra, 2012
4   https://www.kangaroosatrisk.net/6-kangaroo-myths--legends.html
5   Lines W J, *Taming the Great South Land: A history of the conquest of nature in Australia*, ibid., p105
6   Mulvaney D J and Kamminga J, *Prehistory of Australia*, Allen and Unwin, 1999, p81
7   'Rain Forests', *Parks and Wildlife*, Vol 2, No 1, 1977, p3

8   Ibid., p7
9   Williams M, 1997, 'Imperialism and Deforestation', in Griffiths T and Robin L (eds) *Ecology and Empire: environmental history of settler societies*, University of Washington Press, Seattle, 1997, p175
10   Lines W J, *Taming the Great South Land*, ibid., p71
11   Ibid., p72; and Clements N, 'The truth about John Batman', *The Conversation*, 13 May 2011
12   Massy C, *Call of the Reed Warbler*, p241
13   Lines W J, *Taming the Great South Land*, p96, quoting from Hancock W K, *Discovering Monaro*, Cambridge University Press, 1972, p107
14   Lines, ibid., p82

CHAPTER SIX: FUR AND FEATHERS: AN EXPOSE

1   Sherratt T, 'The many battles of Jock Marshall', *Australasian Science*, 1966, Vol 17, p64, reprinted in Australian Science Archives Project; details also Australian Dictionary of Biography – http://adb.anu.edu.au/biography/marshall-alan-john-jock-11060
2   Ibid.
3   Marshall A J (ed), *The Great Extermination, A guide to Anglo-Australian cupidity, wickedness and waste*, William Heineman, London, 1966
4   Ibid., p13, quoting Charles Darwin's *Diary of the voyage of H.M.S Beagle*, Cambridge, 1934
5   Lines W J, *Taming the Great South Land*, p29–37
6   Marshall, ibid., quoting Cunningham P, *Two years in New South Wales* (2nd ed), Cambridge, 1827
7   Reordon, M, 'Corner Country, where outback QLD, NSW and SA meet', *Australian Geographic* Vol 25, 1995
8   Ibid.
9   Ibid.
10   Reed P, 'An historical perspective on: Conserving What? – The basis for nature conservation reserves in New South Wales 1967–1989', *Australian Zoologist*, Vol 26 No 2, June 1990, pp85–91
11   Ibid., p85
12   Turner J S, 'The Decline of the Plants', p148, in Marshall A J (ed), *The Great Extermination*, ibid
13   Marshall, ibid., quoting Gould, J, *The Mammals of Australia*, London, 1863
14   Ibid., p19–20
15   Brimsmead H F, 'Requiem for a Sunburnt Country', *Walkabout*, June 1973
16   Frith H J and Calaby J H, *Kangaroos*, FW Cheshire, Melbourne, 1969
17   Marshall, ibid., p24
18   Gelder K and Weaver R, 'Friday Essay; the art of the colonial kangaroo hunt', *The Conversation*, 31 August 2018
19   Ibid.

20   Ibid., (Lithograph: Troedel C, *The Melbourne Album*)

21   Ibid.

22   Marshall, ibid., p26 quoting Troughton E, *Furred Animals of Australia*, Sydney, 1941

23   Lunney D and Leary T, 'The impact on native mammals of land-use changes and exotic species in the Bega district, NSW since settlement', *Australian Journal of Ecology*, Vol 13, pp67–92, 1988

24   Marshall, ibid., quoting Troughton E

25   Marshall, ibid., p27

26   Marshall, ibid., quoting Fleay, D, *Talking of Animals*

27   Australian Koala Foundation

28   http://www.abc.net.au/news/2018-08-28/koala-rescued-from-road-sign-at-gold-coast-intersection/10172810;
Kinsella E, 'Fears for the future of Gold Coast koalas as report reveals significant decline', *ABC Gold Coast*, 30 August 2018 — www.abc.net.au/news/2018-08-30/gold-coast-koala -population.../10180020

29   Kirkpatrick and Amos cited in Boom, K, Ben-Ami, D, Croft, D B., Cushing, N, Ramp, D; and Boronyak, L, 'Pest' and Resource: A Legal History of Australia's Kangaroos, *Animal Studies Journal*, 1(1), 2012, 17-40. p23ff: fuller version available at http://ro.uow.edu.au/asj/vol1/iss1/3

30   Robertshaw and Harden, in Boom et al, ibid., quoting others as well

31   Croft D, in *Kangaroos Myths and Legends*, ibid., p 27

32   Short and Mikovits and Lunney quoted in Croft, ibid., and Boom et al

33   Boom et al, ibid.

34   Marshall, p35 quoting Jones, F. W, *The Mammals of South Australia*, Adelaide, 1923-1925

35   https://www.abc.net.au/news/rural/2019-01-11/pastoralists-call-for-cull-of-southern-hairy-nosed-wombats/10708550

36   Marshall, ibid., p37

37   Ibid., p57ff

38   Ibid., p 57 quoting Bennett G *Gatherings of a Naturalist in Australia*, London, 1860

39   Marshall, ibid.

40   Marshall, ibid., p58

41   Ibid., p59

42   Marshall, ibid., citing Chisholm A H, *The Romance of the Lyrebird*, Angus and Robertson, 1960

43   Marshall, ibid., p66

44   Lines, *Taming the Great South Land*, p117

45   Commonwealth govt figures

46   http://www.abc.net.au/news/2019-01-24/captain-cook-1970-bicentenary/10743830

Additional reading

http://www.birdlife.org/datazone/species/index.html?action=SpcHTMDetails.asp&sid= 7&m=1

Wikipedia emu entry which has some interesting info on role in landscape and general ecology

CHAPTER SEVEN: VOICES FOR THE VOICELESS: 1970s–90s

1   Australian Wildlife Protection Council submission to the US Fish and Wildlife Service, 28 May 1983

2   Commonwealth Parliamentary Hansard on 1981 Royal Commission

3   Australian Wildlife Protection Council submission to US Fish and Wildlife Service, ibid

4   'Roo a fugitive in its own land', *The Herald*, 12 August 1985, p7

5   'SA man's private fight to save roos', *The Advertiser*, 6 February 1975, p8

6   *Sydney Morning Herald* obit

7   https://www.csmonitor.com/1987/1112/akang.html

8   Australian Wildlife Protection Council submission to the US Fish and Wildlife Service, 28 May 1983

9   Rawlinson P, 'Let's Fight for the Fighting Kangaroo', candidacy statement standing for ACF council, *ACF Newsletter*, November 1983

10   *La Trobe University Record*, July 1983, p13

11   Rawlinson P, 'The commercial killing of kangaroos in Australia', *ACF, ANZFAS*, 7 September 1988

12   Ibid.

13   Rawlinson P, 'The Australian Kangaroo Slaughter', *report*, February 1987

14   https://www.csmonitor.com/USA/2015/0903/California-Kangaroo-Why-Australia-is-lobbying-in-the-Golden-State

15   Anon, 'Killing a Kangaroo every 10 seconds: Is our national conscience extinct?' Editorial, *Habitat* (ACF magazine), Vol 11, No 3, June 1983

16   Horwitz T, 'The Killing Fields', *Good Weekend*, 3 October 1986, p22

17   Anon 'Australia, killing kangaroos for fun and profit' *Mainstream* Vol 22/1, Winter 1991

18   Hoser R, *Smuggled-2: Wildlife trafficking, crime and corruption in Australia*, Kotabi Publications, 1996, p82, p81

19   AWPC archive

20   Taylor M, 'New evidence of flawed science, wishful counting, as kangas die for pet food', *The District Bulletin*, June 2012, p1; access Bulletin print archive, top of home page, by month and year – www.districtbulletin.com.au

21   Ibid.

22   Reed R, 'A Beautiful Nightmare: Infamous for Its Brutally Honest Take on the Australian Outback, Restored Kotcheff Classic Shakes Us Awake', *Observer*, 10 February 2012 – http://observer.com/2012/10/rex-reed-ted-kotcheff-gary-bond-wake-in-fright/

23   www.themonthly.com.au/issue/2009/july/1342411267/kate-jennings/home-truths

24   Ibid.

25   http://www.abc.net.au/news/2019-09-11/an-astronomical-rise-in-violence-and-a-system-struggling-to-cope/11496718

26   Barnes J, *Working Class Boy*, Harper Collins, 2016

27   http://www.wildlifematters.org.au/Primary_Industry.htm

28   https://www.abc.net.au/news/2019-01-14/media-attacked-outside-court-as-kangaroo-torturer-jailed/10713918

29   Wilson M, speech to Animals Australia AGM, 15 October 2006

30   Pople, T and Grigg G, 'Commercial harvesting of Kangaroos in Australia', Department
     of Zoology, The University of Queensland for Environment Australia, Chapters 10,11,12
     and 13 and Appendix 1, Environment Australia, August 1999 – http://www.environment.
     gov.au/node/16679

CHAPTER EIGHT: WILDLIFE TRADE EXPOSED

1   Hoser R, *Smuggled: the underground trade in Australia's wildlife*, Apollo Publishing, Moss
     Vale, 1993; (2nd ed.) Kotabi Publishing, Doncaster, Victoria
     Hoser R, *Smuggled-2: Wildlife trafficking, crime and corruption in Australia*, Kotabi
     Publications,1996
2   O'Byrne T, 'VCAT clears snake handler Raymond Hoser to resume demonstrations to
     schoolchildren', *Manningham Leader*, 12 August 2015
3   Cumming F and Condon M, 'Murder, wildlife smuggling claim rock Parliament', *Sydney
     Morning Herald*, 21 June 1992, Sunday Extra, p1
4   Wockner C, 'Minced body claim probed', *Herald Sun*, 19 June 1992, p3
5   Ibid. and Cumming F, 'Who Killed the Kangaroo King?' *Sunday Herald Sun*, 6 June 1993,
     pp31-33
6   Hoser R, *Smuggled-2*, 1996, p70 ff
7   Cumming F, 'Who Killed the Kangaroo King?', ibid
8   Roberts G, 'Blind eyes turned, faces blown away', *The Bulletin*, January 18 1994, p23
9   Hoser R, ibid., 1996.

CHAPTER NINE: ENTER AUSTRALIAN APPLIED ECOLOGY

1   Grigg G, 'Conservation benefit from harvesting, kangaroos: status report at the start of a
     new millennium: A paper to stimulate discussion and research', Department of Zoology
     & Entomology, The University of Queensland, in Lunney D and Dickman C, *A Zoological
     Revolution: Using native fauna to assist in its own survival*, Royal Zoological Society of
     New South Wales and Australian Museum, Sydney, 2002
2   Lewis, D, 'Harvesting the top paddock', *Sydney Morning Herald*, 21 October 2005, p13
3   https://www.queenslandcountrylife.com.au/story/3368293/graziers-must-hop-into-
     roo-fight/
4   https://www.canberratimes.com.au/national/act/national-disgrace-research-argues-
     commercial-roo-harvesting-humane-20190130-p50uht.html
     https://www.queenslandcountrylife.com.au/story/5892603/a-big-struggle-push-for-
     radical-shift-to-spark-kangaroo-meat-industry/
     https://www.2gb.com/the-smell-of-death-the-horrific-reality-facing-our-national-
     animal/
5   Grigg G, Ibid.
6   Robin L, 'Ecology: a science of empire?', in Griffiths T and Robin L (eds), *Ecology and
     Empire, Environmental History of Settler Societies*, University of Washington Press, Seattle
     1997, p67
7   Dunlop T.R, *Ecology and Environmentalism in the Anglo settler colonies*, in Griffiths and
     Robin, ibid., p79 citing Ratcliffe F, *Flying fox and drifting sand*, Chatto and Windus,

London, 1938, p322

8 Robin L, ibid., p71, 73

9 Frith H J, *Kangaroos*, Australian Conservation Foundation (ACF) newsletter, 3 April 1968

10 Lorkin J, 'Why kangaroo culling divides Australia', BBC, 15 February 2017 – www.bbc.com/news/world-australia-38964535
http://www.independent.co.uk/news/world/australasia/australia-kangaroos-culling-killing-murder-deaths-a-year-a7583186.html

11 https://journals.plos.org/plosone/article?id=10.1371/journal.pone.0105966
http://www.anu.edu.au/news/all-news/kangaroos-eating-reptiles-out-of-house-and-home

12 https://www.theguardian.com/environment/2019/feb/10/plummeting-insect-numbers-threaten-collapse-of-nature

13 Sarkar S, Conservation biology in *The Stanford Encyclopedia of Philosophy*, Winter 2014 – http://plato.stanford.edu/archives/win2014/entries/conservation-biology/

14 Orman T, 'The Self-Poisoning of New Zealand by Name and by Nature', *Tasmanian Times*, 14 June 2015 – https://tasmaniantimes.com/2015/06/the-self-poisoning-of-new-zealand-by-name-and-by-nature/

15 Hahner H, '1080, the nasty poison', *The District Bulletin*, November 2012, p18 – https://districtbulletin.com.au/1080-nasty-poison-australians-use/

16 Animal Justice party fact sheet, 1080 poison
https://nsw.animaljusticeparty.org/the-myth-of-1080-why-does-australia-still-use-such-a-brutal-poison/

17 *Proceedings, Australian Vertebrate Pest Conference, 21–25 May 2001*, Department of Natural Resources and Environment, Victoria

18 https://www.smh.com.au/business/consumer-affairs/kangaroo-meat-puts-commercial-industry-and-animal-welfare-groups-into-conflict-20160721-

19 https://www.australiangeographic.com.au/topics/wildlife/2017/03/the-plight-of-the-dingo/

20 Recher H F, 'What Revolution?', in Lunney D and Dickman C, *A Zoological Revolution: Using native fauna to assist in its own survival*, Royal Zoological Society of New South Wales and Australian Museum, Sydney, 2002

Additional reading

McLeod S and Sharp T, 'Improving the humaneness of commercial kangaroo harvesting' Rural Industries Research and Development Corporation, 2014 – http://www.agrifutures.com.au/wp-content/uploads/publications/13-116.pdf

CHAPTER TEN: BURN THE HERETIC

1 Ramp D, quoted in 'The Role of Biodiversity in Climate Change Adaptation', a report to the ACT Commissioner for the Environment, 2009

2 KMP https://www.environment.act.gov.au/nature-conservation/conservator-of-flora-and-fauna/eastern-grey-kangaroo-controlled-native-species-management-plan 2017

3 Coulson G, Alviano P, Ramp D, & Way S, 'The kangaroos of Yan Yean; history of a

problem population' in *Proceedings of the Royal Society of Victoria* Vol 111, No 1, pp121–30, 1999

4   Olsen P and Low T, 'Update on Current State of Scientific Knowledge on Kangaroos in the Environment, Including Ecological and Economic Impact and Effect of Culling', to NSW Kangaroo Management Advisory Panel, 2006

5   Peacock T, LinkedIn profile

6   Violante V, 'Peer reviews discredit kangaroo cull findings', *Canberra Times*, 7 November 2009, p8

7   Taylor M, 'A curious case: science, new ideas and the kangaroo', *District Bulletin*, July 2010, p4, print issue archive

8   http://www.abc.net.au/news/2016-06-11/government-probably-used-illegal-weapons-during-kangaroo-cull/7502206

9   'ACT parks reopen after 2592 kangaroos culled', *Canberra Times*, 8 July 2017, p 9

10   http://districtbulletin.com.au/survival-in-queanbeyan-the-good-news-story-continues/

11   https://the-riotact.com/million-dollar-contract-locks-in-kangaroo-cull-for-next-five-years/386363
     https://www.parliament.vic.gov.au/images/stories/committees/enrc/Invasive_Animals_on_Crown_land/205._2016.09.09__Strathbogie_Wildlife_Redacted.pdf

12   https://districtbulletin.com.au/goodbye-big-fella/
     https://districtbulletin.com.au/taxpayers-urged-to-look-away-as-injustice-and-death-dealt-to-kangaroos/

13   Eastern Grey kangaroo controlled native species management plan 2017, ibid.

14   Ibid.

15   'Living with Eastern Grey Kangaroos in the ACT – public land', 3rd report, ACT Kangaroo Advisory Committee, October 1997

16   'ACT Kangaroo Management Plan', Territory and Municipal Services, Canberra, 2010 – https://www.environment.act.gov.au/__data/assets/pdf_file/0020/902423/Kangaroo_Management_Plan_complete_for_web.pdf

17   Ibid., p37–38

18   Walker B, in: 'Living with Eastern Grey Kangaroos in the ACT – public land', 3rd report, ACT Kangaroo Advisory Committee, October 1997

19   https://www.environment.act.gov.au/nature-conservation/conservator-of-flora-and-fauna/eastern-grey-kangaroo-controlled-native-species-management-plan 2017

20   Vivian L and Godfree R, 'Relationship between vegetation condition and kangaroo density in lowland grassy ecosystems of the northern Australian Capital Territory', CSIRO report to the ACT Environment and Sustainable Development Directorate, 2014

21   Taylor, M, 'CSIRO independent analysis: no support for kangaroo research assumptions', *District Bulletin*, 18 October 2017 – https://districtbulletin.com.au/csiro-independent-analysis-no-support-kangaroo-research-assumptions-2/

22   'Environment, Planning and Sustainable Development Directorate', *Eastern Grey Conservation Culling Advice 2018*, ACT Government, March 2018

CHAPTER ELEVEN: COUNTING VIRTUAL KANGAROOS

1   Question by AJP Upper House member Mark Pearson, NSW Hansard Vol 16 No 58, 20 June 2018

2   Olsen P and Low T, 'Update on Current State of Scientific Knowledge on Kangaroos in the Environment, Including Ecological and Economic Impact and Effect of Culling', 2006, p11

3   https://www.theguardian.com/australia-news/2019/mar/22/mining-sector-met-nsw-ministers-almost-every-week-over-four-years

4   https://www.theland.com.au/story/5481672/ministers-challenge-ill-drive-you-out-to-see-how-bad-roo-plague-is/?cs=4941
https://www.theland.com.au/story/5574700/new-kangaroo-culling-rules-start-today/

5   http://www.abc.net.au/news/2018-06-13/nsw-budget-package-for-drought-assistance/9863166

6   Kelly J, 'Long time between drinks for NSW station owners', *The Weekly Times*, July 19 2018 – http://www.weeklytimesnow.com.au/news/national/news-story/473c4765b9f18bc78be7c18949040513

7   https://m.facebook.com/story.php?story_fbid=28472966420602568&id=421038011352810&anchor_composer=false

8   Olsen P and Low T, ibid., p17

9   Ibid., p47

10 Taylor M, 'New evidence of flawed science, wishful counting, as kangas die for pet food', *The District Bulletin*, June 2012, p1, Bulletin archive www.districtbulletin.com.au

11 www.kangaroosatrisk.net

12 http://www.environment.nsw.gov.au/research-and-publications/publications-search/2017-quota-report-nsw-commercial-kangaroo-harvest-management-plan-2017-21

13 https://www.qld.gov.au/environment/assets/documents/plants-animals/macropods/annual-report-2017.pdf Map Fig1, p12

14 https://www.kangaroosatrisk.org/biology.html

15 http://www.australiansocietyforkangaroos.com/documents/decimation_of_an_icon.pdf p10 ff

16 http://www.environment.gov.au/biodiversity/wildlife-trade/natives#a3

17 Ibid.

18 Ibid.

19 http://www.environment.nsw.gov.au/research-and-publications/publications-search/2017-quota-report-nsw-commercial-kangaroo-harvest-management-plan-2017-21 p10

20 https://www.qld.gov.au/__data/assets/pdf_file/0032/67757/annual-report-2017.pdf

21 Personal communication of statistics from NSW NPWS Landcare forum

22 'Kangaroo Pet Food Trial Evaluation', an internal report by the Department of Environment, Land, Water and Planning, Victoria State Government, 2019

23 https://www.theaustralian.com.au/national-affairs/kangaroo-cull-documentary-has--industry-hopping-mad/news-story/e7ae41211dfc27aa702f1c9329185af5

24 Gunn I, *The Kangaroo Betrayed, World's Largest Wildlife Slaughter*, Australian Wildlife Protection Council Inc, 1999, p39

Additional reading

Mjadwesch R, chapter introductory comment. about Australia's effort to reintroduce kangaroo skin exports to California, *Sacramento Bee,* 2015
  http://www.sacbee.com/opinion/california-forum/article24811063.html

Bilton A and Croft D, 'Lifetime Reproductive Success in a Population of Female Red Kangaroos Macropus Rufus in the Sheep Rangelands of Western New South Wales: Environmental Effects and Population Dynamics', *Australian Mammalogy,* Vol 26, pp45–6

Cairns S, et al, 'Kangaroo Monitoring: Hunter and Central Tablelands Commercial Harvest Zones Design and Analysis of Helicopter Survey', *A report to the New South Wales Department of Environment and Climate Change* (2009)

Pople A R and McLeod S R, 'Kangaroo Management and the sustainable use of rangelands', *conference paper* for 'Management for ecological sustainability', University of Queensland, September 1998

CHAPTER TWELVE: MYSTERY DISEASE PANDEMIC: NO ANSWERS, LESS INTEREST

1   https://www.abc.net.au/news/2020-07-28/3-billion-animals-killed-displaced-in-fires-wwf-study/12497976

CHAPTER THIRTEEN: END GAME: US AND THEM

1   http://www.abc.net.au/news/2018-04-21/lamb-boom-could-be-outback-community-savior/9677882

2   www.abc.net.au/news/rural/2017-01-17/premier-lauds-wild-dog-fencing.../8188806.

3   https://www.wool.com/globalassets/start/on-farm-research-and-development/sheep-health-welfare-and-productivity/pest-animals/wild-dogs-foxes-and-pigs/kondinin-exclusionfencing-jan2016.pdf

4   https://www.abc.net.au/news/rural/2019-03-07/replacing-parts-of-the-outback-dingo-fence/10876468

5   Letnic M; Crowther MS; Dickman CR; Ritchie EG, 2011, 'Demonising the dingo: How much wild dogma is enough?', *Current Zoology,* vol. 57, pp668–670
  https://www.ecosystem.unsw.edu.au/files/Letnic%20et%20al.%202018_Strength%20of%20a%20Trophic%20Cascade.pdf

6   Dawson T J, *Kangaroos,* (2nd ed.), CSIRO Publishing, Collingwood, 2014, p1457

7   http://www.dailymail.co.uk/news/article-3248511/Professional-kangaroo-culler-slams-inhumane-killing-30-animals-killed-just-fun.html
  Bradfield E, 'Kangaroos 'cruelly' killed with the help of Government-funded fencing, shooters say', *ABC news online,* 24 September 2017 – https://www.abc.net.au/news/2017-09-24/fences-control-wild-dogs-kill-native-wildlife-kangaroo-shooter/8941444

8   Ibid.

9   Cummins J, face-to-face with roos and wild dogs, *The Western Star,* 27 Jan 2018

10 https://www.queenslandcountrylife.com.au/story/6474143/roo-harvest-suspension-monumentally-foolish/

CHAPTER FOURTEEN: WHISTLEBLOWERS, BUSHMEAT, AND INTERNATIONAL PUSHBACK

1   http://www.agriculture.gov.au/export/controlled-goods/kangaroo
2   *The Kangaroo Betrayed: World's Largest Wildlife Slaughter*, 1992, 1999
    Kangaroos Myths and Realities, Australian Wildlife Protection Council Inc, 2005
3   Nicholls D, 'The kangaroo falsely maligned by tradition', *Kangaroos Myths and Reality*, ibid p33–41
4   McLeod S and Sharp T, 'Improving the humaneness of commercial kangaroos harvesting', Rural Industries Research and Development Corporation, 2014
    Ben-Ami D, Boom K, Boronyak L, Croft D, Ramp D, Townend C, 'The ends and means of the commercial kangaroo industry: an ecological, legal and comparative analysis', THINKK, The Think Tank for Kangaroos, University of Technology Sydney, 2011
5   Taylor M, 'Mark Pearson gets the evidence and changes minds', *The District Bulletin*, p7, 2 February 2016, Bulletin archive www.districtbulletin.com.au
6   http://thinkkangaroos.uts.edu.au/issues/hygiene.html
7   'Kangaroo industry stakeholders respond to the latest ban placed on the kangaroo meat trade to Russia', ABC News Online – https://www.abc.net.au/news/rural/2014-08-18/kangaroo-meat-ban/5678216?nw=0 18 August, 2014
8   Ben-Ami D, 'A shot in the dark', 2009 – https://www.researchgate.net/publication/2746 36824_A_Shot_in_the_Dark
9   Ibid., p46–7
10 ABC Rural, *Russia bans kangaroo meat due to unacceptable levels of E.coli*, 18 August 2014
11 Letter to shooters, Macro Investments (Macro Meats) May, 2012 – http://www.kangaroosatrisk.org/uploads/1/0/8/3/10831721/20120819_macroletter_aceticacid.png
12 http://www.smh.com.au/nsw/nsw-kangaroo-meat-fails-basic-hygiene-tests-20150306-13uyft.html
13 Ben-Ami, D 'A shot in the dark', ibid.; THINKK UTS fact sheet on kangaroo disease, hygiene issues in meat trade – http://thinkkangaroos.uts.edu.au/issues/hygiene.html
14 Ben-Ami D, 'A shot in the dark', ibid., 2009, p48
15 http://www.eurogroupforanimals.org/eu-act-responsibly-import-cruel-contaminated-kangaroo-meat
16 https://www.dailyadvertiser.com.au/story/5314033/ending-capitalism-an-industry-at-a-time/
17 https://www.csmonitor.com/1987/1112/akang.html
18 Ibid.
19 https://www.csmonitor.com/USA/2015/0903/California-Kangaroo-Why-Australia-is-lobbying-in-the-Golden-State
20 Ibid.
21 https://www.theguardian.com/us-news/2015/sep/14/california-set-to-ban-kangaroo-imports-despite-lobbying-efforts-by-australia
22 http://www.sacbee.com/opinion/opn-columns-blogs/dan-morain/article125056924.
    http://www.sacbee.com/news/politics-government/capitol-alert/article33192168.html

23   'California recognises the "swampy" world of kangaroo politics – species at risk', media release, Lee Rhiannon, 11 January 2017
24   https://www.kangaroosatrisk.org
25   http://www.kangaroosarenotshoes.org/

Additional reading
Petfood recall 2020
    https://www.fda.gov/safety/recalls-market-withdrawals-safety-alerts/real-pet-food-company-phoenix-az-voluntarily-recalls-one-lot-billymargot-wild-kangaroo-and

CHAPTER FIFTEEN: SHARING
1   Tyndale-Biscoe H, 'Kangaroos and sheep: the unequal contest', *Australasian Science*, July 2005, 26, 6 p29
2   Dunlap T, 'Ecology and Environmentalism in the Anglo settler colonies', in Griffiths T and Robin L (eds.), *Ecology and Empire, Environmental History of Settler Societies*, University of Washington Press, 1997, p79
3   Marshall A J, (ed), *The Great Extermination, A guide to Anglo-Australian cupidity, wickedness and waste*, William Heineman, London, 1966, p24
4   http://www.abc.net.au/news/2019-01-10/tourist-pledge-to-keep-distance-from-wombats-on-maria-island/10701674
5   Massy C, *Call of the Reed Warbler, a new agriculture, a new earth*, UQP, Brisbane, 2017, p504
6   Ibid., pp505–506
7   Ibid., p73ff

Additonal reading
Olle E, 'Emus overrun West Australian town of Nannup', *7 News*, 18 January 2020 – https://7news.com.au/entertainment/viral-weird/emus-overrun-west-australian-town-of-nannup-c-652382
https://www.smh.com.au/environment/conservation/forget-worms-and-gophers-lyrebirds-are-the-world-s-best-soil-shifter-20200901-p55rel.html
Dig this: a tiny echidna moves 8 trailer-loads of soil a year, helping tackle climate change – https://theconversation.com/dig-this-a-tiny-echidna-moves-8-trailer-loads-of-soil-a-year-helping-tackle-climate-change-155947?utm_medium=email&utm_campaign=Latest%20from%20The%20Conversation%20for%20March%205%202021%20-%201880218345&utm_content=Latest%20from%20The%20Conversation%20for%20March%205%202021%20-%201880218345+CID_25c5a8412dd3dc0239f6862dc3833b57&utm_source=campaign_monitor&utm_term=Dig%20this%20a%20tiny%20echidna%20moves%208%20trailer-loads%20of%20soil%20a%20year%20helping%20tackle%20climate%20change

SELECT BIBLIOGRAPHY

2019 open letter from scientists and organisations about the kangaroo trade: https://www.kangaroomatters.org/

Andreasson S, 'Stand and Deliver: private property and the politics of global dispossession', *Political Studies*, Vol 54, 2006, pp3–22

Animal Justice party fact sheet, 1080 poison

https://nsw.animaljusticeparty.org/the-myth-of-1080-why-does-australia-still-use-such-a-brutal-poison/

Anon, 'Killing a Kangaroo every 10 seconds: Is our national conscience extinct?' Editorial, *Habitat* (ACF magazine) Vol 11, 3 June 1983

Anon, 'Killing Kangaroos for fun and profit', *Mainstream*, Animal Protection Institute of America, Vol 22,1, Winter, 1991, p13

Arneil B, *John Locke and America: The defence of English colonialism*, 1996, Oxford University press

Australian Government kangaroo and wallaby population, quota and harvest statistics http://www.environment.gov.au/biodiversity/wildlife-trade/natives#a3

Australian Government National Code of Practice for the Humane Shooting of Kangaroos and Wallabies for Commercial Purposes [and for Non-Commercial Purposes] Ibid.

Auty J, 'Red plague grey plague: The kangaroo myths and legends', *Australian Mammalogy*, Vol 26, 2004, pp33–6

Babie P, 'Private property suffuses life', *Sydney Law Review* 2017 39:135, pp135–46

Bates D, *Passing of the Aborigines*, 1939; 1947 John Murray London; Benediction Classics. 2009

Beeby R, 'The truth about Kangaroos', *The Canberra Times*, 10 October 2005, p4

Ben-Ami D, 'A shot in the dark', 2009 https://www.researchgate.net/publication/274636824_A_Shot_in_the_Dark

Blumenfeld L, 'Boing, Boing, Boing … BANG', *The Washington Post*, Sunday Style, 18 December 1994

Bottoms T, *Conspiracy of Silence*, Allen and Unwin, Sydney, 2013

Bradfield E, 'Kangaroos "cruelly" killed with the help of Government-funded fencing, shooters say', *ABC news online*, 24 September 2017 – https://www.abc.net.au/news/2017-09-24/fences-control-wild-dogs-kill-native-wildlife-kangaroo-shooter/8941444

Burdon A, Outcast, the plight of the dingo, *Australian Geographic*, 20 March 2017 https://www.australiangeographic.com.au/topics/wildlife/2017/03/the-plight-of-the-dingo/

Carrington D, 'Fifth of countries at risk of ecosystem collapse, analysis finds', *The Guardian*, 12 October 2020 – https://www.theguardian.com/environment/2020/oct/12/fifth-of-nations-at-risk-of-ecosystem-collapse-analysis-finds

Chatwin B, *The Songlines*, Vintage, 1998

Clark M, *A Short History of Australia*, Penguin, 1963

Cooke K, *Wake in Fright*, Michael Joseph, London 1961

Cruttenden S, 'Poisoned pills showered on burned parks and reserves, NSW', Australian Wildlife Protection Council, 9 April – https://awpc.org.au/poisoned-pills-showered-on-burned-parks-and-reserves-nsw/

Dawson T J, *Kangaroos*, (2nd ed.), CSIRO Publishing, Collingwood, 2012

Dunbar-Ortiz R, 'The Colonial Roots of Gun Culture, In These Times', April 2018, p17, excerpt from *Loaded: A Disarming History of the Second Amendment*

Flood J, *The Original Australians: Story of the Aboriginal People*, Allen and Unwin, Sydney, 2006

Frith H J, 'Kangaroos', *Australian Conservation Council newsletter*, 3 April 1968

Gammage B, *The Biggest Estate on Earth, how Aborigines made Australia*, Allen and Unwin, Sydney, 2011

Greenpeace Australia Ltd, *Kangaroos Under Fire*, brochure, 1989

Griffiths T and Robin L (eds), *Ecology and Empire, Environmental History of Settler Societies*, University of Washington Press, 1997

Hannam P, 'NSW koalas on course to be extinct in the wild before 2050, inquiry finds', *Sydney Morning Herald*, 30 June 2020 – https://www.smh.com.au/environment/conservation/nsw-koalas-on-course-to-be-extinct-in-the-wild-by-2050-inquiry-finds-20200630-p557j2.html

Horwitz T, 'The killing fields', *Good Weekend*, 3 October 1986, p22

Horne D, *Money Made Us*, Penguin, Ringwood Vic, 1976

Hoser R, *Smuggled: the underground trade in Australia's wildlife*, Apollo Publishing, Moss Vale, (2nd ed) Kotabi Publishing, Doncaster, Victoria 1993

Hoser R, *Smuggled-2: Wildlife trafficking, crime and corruption in Australia*, Kotabi Publications, 1996

Hutchinson L, 'Kangaroos: from icon to asset', *Barrier Daily Truth*, 24 July 2002, p1

Hylands P, essay on kangaroos and emus, treatment in Australia http://www.creativecowboyfilms.com/blog_posts/kangaroo

Lewis D, 'Harvesting the top paddock', *Sydney Morning Herald*, 21 October 2005, p13

Lines W J, *Taming the Great South Land, A history of the conquest of nature in Australia*, Allen and Unwin, North Sydney NSW, 1992

Linklater A, *Owning the Earth, the transforming history of land ownership*, 2014, Bloomsbury, London

Management Plan for the Commercial Harvest and Export of Brushtail Possums in Tasmania – https://www.environment.gov.au/system/files/resources/98744979-0ea9-4d19-b35a-be3421f0c559/files/tas-brushtail-possums-management-plan-2015-2020.pdf

Manigian S, 'Tasmanian possum meat trade', *Habitat Australia*, ACF, August 1996

Marshall A J, (ed), *The Great Extermination, A guide to Anglo-Australian cupidity, wickedness and waste*, William Heineman, London, 1966

Massy C, *Call of the Reed Warbler, a new agriculture, a new earth*, UQP, Brisbane, 2017

Mayes C, 'Cultivating a nation: why the mythos of the Australian farmer is problematic', 11 January 2019 – https://theconversation.com/cultivating-a-nation-why-the-mythos-of-the-australian-farmer-is-problematic-106517

McLeod S R, and Hacker R B, 'Balancing stakeholder interests in kangaroo management – historical perspectives and future prospects' *The Rangeland Journal* Vol 41, No 6, 24 March 2020, pp567-579 – https://doi.org/10.1071/RJ19055

McKenna M, *From the Edge, Australia's lost histories*, The Miegunyah Press, Melbourne, 2016

Moorehead A, *The Fatal Impact*, Penguin, London UK, 1966

Mulvaney D J and Kamminga J, *Prehistory of Australia*, Allen and Unwin, 1999

Olsen P, and Low T, *Update on the current state of scientific knowledge on kangaroos in the environment, including ecological and economic impact and effect of culling*, report to NSW Kangaroo Management Advisory Panel, March 2006

Parkhurst J, *The Butchulla First Nations People of Fraser Island (K'Gari) and their dingos*, Australian Wildlife Protection Council, 2015 http://www.fraserislandfootprints.com/?page_id=694

Pascoe B, *Dark Emu, Aboriginal Australia and the birth of agriculture*, Magabala Books, Broome WA, 2014

Pascoe B, 'Australia Temper and Bias', *Meanjin*, Spring 2018 – https://meanjin.com.au/essays/11312/

Ramp D and Rogers E, 'Our 'common' wildlife may be the next 'sleeping' threatened species, in AWPC submission to ACT inquiry on ecotourism potential: 2012 https://www.parliament.act.gov.au/__data/assets/pdf_file/0005/409388/05._Australian_Wildlife_Protection_Council.pdf

Rawlinson P A, 'Kangaroo conservation and kangaroo intrinsic value versus instrumental value of wildlife', *Australian Zoologist*, 24(3), 29 August 1988 (proceedings of a Royal Zoological Society (NSW) conference, May 14, 1988

Rawlinson P A, 'Kangaroo killing: Macropods as protected wildlife', *Animal Liberation*, January–March 1987, p8

Reilly D, 'The Growing Culture of Institutionalised Wildlife Exploitation in South Australia', in conference proceedings 'Self-regulation in the Kangaroo Industry is the Code of Practice an Appropriate Mechanism?', Canberra ACT, Australian Wildlife Protection Council, 1 September 1996

RSPCA Australia, 'A Survey of the Extent of Compliance with the Requirements of the Code of Practice for the Humane Shooting of Kangaroos', 2002

Rose D B, 'The dead, the missing, the lost, and the voiceless: some thoughts on extinction from a dingo perspective', from conference paper 'The relationships between humans and animals', 2004 conference paper

Rose D B, *Dingo makes us human, life and land in Australian Aboriginal culture*, Cambridge University Press, 2000

Ryan D G, Ryan J E, and Starr BJ, 'The Australian Landscape – observations of explorers and early settlers', *Murrumbidgee Catchment Management Committee*, NSW Government Printing Service, undated

Slezak M, *Scorched country: the destruction of Australia's native landscape*, The Guardian, (online) 7 March 2018 https://www.theguardian.com/environment/2018/mar/07/scorched-country-the-destruction-of-australias-native-landscape

Sheldon F, 'The Darling River is simply not supposed to dry out even in drought', *The Conversation*, 16 January 2019 – https://theconversation.com/the-darling-river-is-simply-not-supposed-to-dry-out-even-in-drought-109880

Stewart K, 'Genocide: A Great Australian Tradition? Queensland's Culls Makes you Wonder', online discussion paper – http://www.omplace.com/articles/Kangaroo_Cull.html

Taylor M, *Global warming and climate change: what Australia knew and buried ... then framed a new reality for the public*, ANU Press, 2014

Taylor M, environment/kangaroo archive – wildlife articles, *The District Bulletin*, 2010-2020 www.districtbulletin.com.au

Treves A, et al, 'Working constructively toward an improved North American approach to wildlife management', 10 December 2018 – https://www.researchgate.net/publication/328054693

THINKK UTS fact sheet on kangaroo disease, hygiene issues in meat trade http://thinkkangaroos.uts.edu.au/issues/hygiene.html. Other THINKK research papers

Tyndale-Biscoe H, 'Kangaroos and sheep the unequal contest', *Australasian Science*, 26,6. July 2005, p29

White L, 'The historical roots of our ecological crisis', *Science* 1967

Williams J, Talking about drought-proofing, simplistic solutions that will destroy Australia, need to stop fighting nature of Australia, *The Guardian*, 25 September 2019

Williams M, 'Imperialism and Deforestation', in *Ecology and Empire: environmental history of settler societies*, University of Washington Press, Seattle, 1997

Wilson M and Croft D B (eds), *Kangaroos Myths and Realities*, Australian Wildlife Protection Council (3rd ed) 2005

Wilson M (ed.), *The Kangaroo Betrayed, world's largest wildlife slaughter*, Hill of Content Pty Ltd (AWPC publication), 1999

Woinarski J.C, Burbidge A, Harrison P, 'Ongoing unraveling of a continental fauna: Decline and extinction of Australian mammals since European settlement', *PNAS*, Vol 112, No 15, 14 April 2015, pp4531–40 – https://www.pnas.org/content/112/15/4531

ACKNOWLEDGEMENTS

A tale of historical injustice emerged from years of reporting, aided by research and investigation. I am greatly indebted to, and thank, all those who helped and informed this work. Many of those who spoke to me, or whose work furthered my understanding, appear in these pages.

I also thank my terrific collaborators on the publication and distribution side, starting with Ann Wilson and her great professional team at Independent Ink. Finalising this book also greatly benefited from the expert work and support of Sam Cooney, Sue Van Homrigh, Charlie Vincent, Ian McDonald, Kelda Murray, Michael Garmarroongoo Huddleston as well as on image hunt Eloise Ribeny and library support at the State Library of NSW. Family and friends offered invaluable advice and encouragement. Thank you all.

Above all, thanks to my partner and wise counsel Bill Taylor who unstintingly supported me through the process, not least by diving into the daunting waters of rough drafts and diplomatically tendering some observations on surfacing.

I know that those who have supported me through this investigation and writing did so also because they care about exposing and righting the lethal injustices aimed at our most defenceless fellow inhabitants of this unique continent – before it becomes too late. The voiceless who don't vote and employ no lobbyists will thank them.

Maria Taylor is an investigative journalist and author and a former award-winning documentary film-maker analysing environmental conflicts. She has travelled widely in Australia, observing government decision-making and the rural sector, also editing a national magazine reporting agricultural science. In the past decade she has focused on regional news and wildlife/environmental investigations while publishing *The District Bulletin* in southern NSW near the national capital.

Taylor's previous book of documentary journalism and cultural history is *Global warming and climate change: what Australia knew and buried, then framed a new reality for the public*. 2014, ANU Press.

This is a crucially important book. It is exceptionally well researched and thoughtfully written. It should be essential reading for everyone if we are to understand the debate on climate change in Australia. It tells us clearly and analytically how public understanding was reframed in Australia by conservative think tanks, politicians, the business community and the media, by exploiting beliefs and values held by our society.

— THE HON JOHN KERIN, FORMER MINISTER IN
THE HAWKE AND KEATING GOVERNMENTS

mariataylor.com.au
maria@mariataylor.com.au

www.ingramcontent.com/pod-product-compliance
Lightning Source LLC
Chambersburg PA
CBHW060020030426
42334CB00019B/2111